Gretchen Braun.

CASE STORIES FOR ELEMENTARY METHODS

MEETING THE INTASC STANDARDS

Sheila G. Dunn

D'Youville College

Allyn & Bacon
Boston   New York   San Francisco
Mexico City   Montreal   Toronto   London   Madrid   Munich Paris
Hong Kong   Singapore   Tokyo   Cape Town   Sydney

Editor in Chief: Paul Smith
Acquisitions Editor: Kelly Villella-Canton
Editorial Assistant: Annalea Manalili
Director of Marketing: Quinn Perkson
Senior Marketing Manager: Darcy Betts
Prybella
Project Manager: Renata Butera
Operations Specialist: Renata Butera
Art Director: Jayne Conte

Cover Designer: Bruce Kenselaar
Cover Art: Getty Images, Inc.
Media Director: Kevin Davis
Full-Service Project Management: Mohinder
Singh/Aptara®, Inc.
Composition: Aptara®, Inc.
Printer/Binder: Bind-Rite
Cover Printer: Bind-Rite
Text Font: Palatino

Credits and acknowledgments borrowed from other sources and reproduced, with permission, in this textbook appear on appropriate page within the text.

Copyright © 2010 Pearson Education, Inc., publishing as Allyn & Bacon, 501 Boylston Street, Suite 900, Boston, MA 02116. All rights reserved. Manufactured in the United States of America. This publication is protected by Copyright, and permission should be obtained from the publisher prior to any prohibited reproduction, storage in a retrieval system, or transmission in any form or by any means, electronic, mechanical, photocopying, recording, or likewise. To obtain permission(s) to use material from this work, please submit a written request to Pearson Education, Inc., Permissions Department, 501 Boylston Street, Suite 900, Boston, MA 02116 or fax your request to 617-671-2290.

Many of the designations by manufacturers and seller to distinguish their products are claimed as trademarks. Where those designations appear in this book, and the publisher was aware of a trademark claim, the designations have been printed in initial caps or all caps.

Library of Congress Cataloging-in-Publication Data
Dunn, Sheila G.
   Case stories for elementary methods: meeting the INTASC standards/Sheila G. Dunn.
     p. cm.
   Includes bibliographical references and index.
   ISBN-13: 978-0-13-179125-1 (alk. paper)
   ISBN-10: 0-13-179125-7 (alk. paper)
   1. Case method—United States. 2. Elementary school teaching—Standards—United States.
   3. Interstate New Teacher Assessment and Support Consortium.   I. Title.
   LB1029.C37D86 2010
   372.139—dc22

               2009002806

Allyn & Bacon
is an imprint of

www.pearsonhighered.com

10 9 8 7 6 5 4 3 2 1
ISBN 13: 978-0-13-179125-1
ISBN-10:   0-13-179125-7

BRIEF CONTENTS

CONTENTS

PREFACE

ORGANIZATION OF THIS BOOK

Case Stories for Elementary Methods: Meeting the INTASC Standards consists of ten chapters with two case stories in each chapter, twenty cases in all. Each chapter focuses on one of the standards developed by the Interstate New Teacher Assessment and Support Consortium (INTASC). Essentially, these are model standards for licensing, assessment, and development of beginning teachers. Key indicators for each standard are examined in individual case stories.

The text is intended as a supplement in K–6 methods courses or curriculum planning courses. It is also suitable for any other courses in which course goals reflect standards-based concerns. As such, the text provides case stories related to real-life problems, issues, and concerns, teachers are likely to encounter during their careers. Situations are often complicated by the human element—that is, teaching in real life is not as simple as figuring out what lesson to teach or which rule or policy to follow. Teachers and students are unique individuals who experience all the complexities of life. This may be as mundane as the need to work extra hours to pay bills or as complex as having to care for members of the family who are ill. These cases tend to include more dialogue or to be slightly longer than usual in a deliberate effort to have the personalities of the characters shine through to emphasize this human element of teaching. Analysis and reflection on each case allow readers to consider not only the facts of the case but also the interactions of people involved in each case.

UNIQUE FEATURES OF THE BOOK

- First and foremost, the text consists of cases for discussion, interpretation, analysis, and problem solving. Cases are open ended and sufficiently complex to allow for multiple plausible solutions.
- The book begins with an introduction that includes a brief history of case-based instruction, responsibilities of students in preparing for discussion, and guidelines for analyzing cases. A helpful mnemonic strategy (DEEPS) guides students in analysis of and reflection on the issues in each case. Students are also directed to consider content, pedagogy, and the impact of decisions on student learning. An example of a completed case analysis is given at the end of this book.
- Each chapter focuses on a specific INTASC standard and the unexpected issues, problems, and concerns a teacher or prospective teacher might face when attempting to meet the standard. The case is related to one or more key indicators for the specific standard.
- Each case story is followed by a section entitled *What the Research Says*, which provides current research related to the issues discussed in the case story and a

useful base of knowledge so that students better understand the complexity of issues involved in each case.

- Topics for discussion follow each case to provide an opportunity for students to interact with each other, share insights and values, and begin to build their identity and worldview as teachers.
- *Exploring the Issues* affords an opportunity to broaden understanding related to the case. In this section, students may be asked to participate in activities as diverse as writing a lesson plan related to the case, observing in a classroom, visiting a virtual classroom, or reviewing related research.
- A matrix of all of the cases is provided. Although each chapter is related specifically to one of the INTASC standards and related key indicators, this matrix illustrates cases that overlap with topics in other chapters. The intent is to make it easy for instructors and students to use the book in the order that best fits their class schedule.
- In keeping with good case story design, cases are purposely kept to three to six pages to allow ample time for reading, analysis, and discussion.

ACKNOWLEDGMENTS

Sincere thanks to the many teachers and colleagues who over the years have shared their stories and reflections on teaching. It was a pleasure to retrieve the main ideas from the pages of old notebooks. Thanks also to David Gorlewski, Julie Gorlewski, Catherine Lalonde, and Hilary Lochte, who shared their own experiences firsthand by writing some of the case stories contained in this book. David Gorlewski, a former school administrator and currently a professor of education, is the author of three case stories: Cases 10, 15, and 17. Julie Gorlewski, a respected high school teacher and recent Ph.D. recipient, is the author of six case stories: Cases 7, 9, 13, 14, 18, and 19. Catherine Lalonde reflected on her experiences teaching courses in cultural diversity and critical issues in education to write Case 12. Hilary Lochte drew on her experience as a professor of social foundations to write Case 16. Thanks go, of course, to all the people at Pearson Education who helped with this book, especially Annalea Manalili, Aurora Martinez, Annette Joseph, and Kelly Villella-Canton. Very special thanks to Heath Lynn Silberfeld for her outstanding work copy editing this book and for her many helpful editing suggestions that appeared magically through midnight e-mails. Thanks also to Mohinder Singh for his careful and detailed review of each chapter. I am also grateful to the following reviewers: Sue Abegglen, *Culver-Stockton College*; Lisa Coval, *Metropolitan State College of Denver*; Laura Davis, *Texas State University*; Joyce Frazier, *University of North Carolina–Charlotte*; Margaret Ferrara, *University of Nevada–Reno*; Lee Freeman, *University of Alabama*; Randa A. Gick, *Arizona State University*; Helen Harrington, *University of Michigan*; Honor Keirans, *Chestnut Hill College*; Honor Keirans, *Chestnut Hill College*; Carol Rasowsky, *The College of St. Rose*; Carol M. Shepherd, *National University*; and Michele Wilson Kamens, *Rider University*.

INTRODUCTION

THE TEACHING EXPERIENCE

As much as we would like it to be so, effective teaching does not happen by chance. From a pedagogical standpoint, effective teaching requires a considerable amount of understanding of all of the following: social and philosophical foundations of education, curriculum planning and instruction, learning and motivational theory, principles of fair assessment, ethical wisdom, and the needs of learners in a diverse society. From a knowledge standpoint, effective teaching requires a thorough grounding in the liberal arts and sciences, a grounding that should result in a high level of verbal ability and a broad understanding of content. Pedagogical and content knowledge is acquired largely from coursework in various disciplines, coupled with other courses in methodology and extensive experience related to education and schooling. Knowledge develops slowly, in other words, and wisdom even more slowly. What is often missing in teacher preparation coursework, however, is real-life experiences. Students learn what they should know to be effective teachers but lack practical experience with real-life situations related to teaching. Case-based teaching and learning provide one way to narrow the gap between knowledge and experience.

A SHORT HISTORY OF CASE METHOD

The use of cases in education began as far back as 1870 in Harvard Law School. There, an innovative Dean put together a representative set of court decisions and created the first legal case book. The Harvard Business School followed approximately 50 years later. The Dean of the Harvard Business School in 1920 happened to have been a graduate of the law school. He championed the use of case story as a means of providing authentic learning experiences. Next came Harvard Medical School but not until the mid-1980s. Case stories of individual patients were used in practice to provide authentic and active learning for students. Case teaching has only recently made its way into schools of education but has quickly gained in popularity. In education, case teaching is used primarily as a whole class or small group discussion method, most often with the purpose of providing problem-based learning opportunities involving the use of authentic problems and concerns.

DEFINITION OF CASES AND THEIR USE IN EDUCATION

Cases are frequently described as descriptive research documents, "often presented in narrative form [and] based on a real-life situation or event" (Merseth, 1996, p. 722). Well-written cases reflect current research and provide opportunities for users to conduct an analysis that results in multiple plausible "solutions" to the case. As Merseth states, an emphasis on "reality-based cases is important for teacher education because it enables students of teaching to explore, analyze, and examine representations of actual classrooms" (p. 722).

Clyde Herreid, a distinguished teaching professor and frequent writer on case study teaching, describes the key characteristics of a good case. Although he is writing particularly about the characteristics found in business and science cases, his descriptions are applicable to education as well. According to Herreid, among other characteristics good cases

- are short enough to be covered in a single class period; some excellent cases, however, can conceivably extend for several weeks or even an entire semester.
- provide controversy.
- have dialogue; this characteristic serves the purpose of making the cases appear more authentic to the reader.
- are relevant to the student; that is, good cases focus on real-life problems that the student is likely to encounter.
- have a dilemma to be solved; this forces the student to be involved in the outcomes of the discussion.
- have learning objectives and lessons that can be generalized to other situations. (Adapted from Herreid, 2005)

The cases in this text share these characteristics. They also are open-ended cases that, as Merseth suggests they should, allow for the possibility of several plausible solutions. The value of open-ended cases for educators is that they require higher-order thinking skills. Analysis, synthesis, and evaluation of facts, options, and consequences of decisions are all required with open-ended cases.

Of great importance when using case method in the classroom is the incorporation of course content into discussion. Ideally, students should connect case material to course concepts to make connections between current learning and past understandings. What makes case method both challenging and engaging for educators is, in fact, that it allows them to "practice analysis, the assimilation of differing perspectives, and contemplation of action" (Merseth, 1996, p. 722). Cases also allow educators to practice decision making through the analysis of day-to-day problems that occur in schools. Simply put, using case method with preservice teacher candidates and/or novice teachers forces them to "think like a teacher" (Wassermann, 1994).

SOME NOTES ON THE PORTRAYAL OF CHARACTERS IN THIS TEXT

Case stories in this text address issues, problems, and concerns that teachers might encounter in the schools where they are employed. Each case relates the experiences of individuals similar to ourselves who, as classroom teachers, are confronted with controversies, competition, ethical dilemmas, uncomfortable interpersonal relationships, and, in the face of all this, determining which methods to use to meet individual student needs and improve learning outcomes.

Teachers, in other words, are described not just as dedicated and knowledgeable individuals, but also as human beings who are confronted with all the problems of daily life, including family relationships, illness, lifestyle decisions, and employment satisfaction and dissatisfaction. It is difficult, of course, to amend our childhood image of the teacher as a superhuman being who is all knowing and all capable and in any crisis or any circumstance never fails to make the right decisions. The reality, however, is that teachers and administrators, like all human beings, have good and bad days, subjects they love and subjects they try to avoid, students who reaffirm their commitment to teaching and others who tempt them daily to give up teaching once and for all. They have families, distant relatives, friends, and even pets who influence their moods both positively and negatively. What sets teachers apart from other human beings is that teaching is the career they chose, largely because of their own love of lifelong learning and a desire to provide young learners with schooling experiences that help to create the kind of scholars and citizens that will make the world a better place. On their best days, no amount of praise is sufficient to acknowledge their work; on their worse days, understanding, forgiveness, and then a renewal of effort are expected and needed. When children ourselves, it probably never occurred to us that our teachers had any other concerns than our penmanship, homework, and general understanding of the lessons for the day. As adults, however, we are all too aware that even the best teacher can wake up to a leaking roof, a car that won't start, or a child who is ill. What do the best teachers do in these circumstances? Call the plumber, quickly find other transportation, and call that neighbor they can always count on and ask her to watch their child for the day. Then they go off to school worrying all the while how all these matters are being resolved. The case stories in this text attempt to portray teachers, administrators, and even preservice teacher candidates as unique human beings who have all the complexities and dreams that are part of life on earth. Readers of this text are urged to read and analyze case stories, not only with an eye to finding educational solutions but also with a keen awareness of how the strengths and weaknesses, likes and dislikes, and lingering concerns of each character affect daily performance. When looking for solutions, it should be remembered that an individual's own upbringing, experiences, beliefs, and disbeliefs all have an impact on the classroom environment and on the outcomes in any case.

THE INTASC STANDARDS

The establishment of standards in teacher education programs has a long history. This history begins as far back as 1927 when the American Association of Teachers was established to develop standards for teacher preparation programs and to ensure that teachers were competent in the disciplines in which they taught. In 1954 the National Council for the Accreditation of Teachers (NCATE) was established. The mission then, as it is now, was to ensure rigorous standards for teacher education and to determine whether or not teacher preparation programs lived up to these standards (Kraft, 2001). Recent reform and restructuring documents, such as the 1983 *A Nation at Risk, Goals 2000* and the *No Child Left Behind Act* of 2001 have given the standards movement high visibility.

In 1987, the Interstate New Teacher Assessment and Support Consortium (INTASC) was sponsored and formed by the Council of Chief State School Officers, a nonprofit organization of public officials who head departments of elementary and secondary education throughout the United States. The INTASC standards reflect the knowledge, skills, and attitudes beginning teachers are expected to have as a starting point for their career. INTASC standards are not mandates. They represent a consensus of the best thinking of educational practitioners and researchers regarding sound educational beliefs related to what P–12 teachers should know and be able to do to help all students succeed. INTASC's role, in other words, has been one of consensus building among the states, not one of decision making. The INTASC standards are viewed as models and intended to be a resource that all states can use in developing their own standards (http://www.ccsso.org/projects).

REFLECTIVE PRACTICE

As with any standards for teaching, however, some caveats must be kept in mind. The INTASC standards are organized around 10 principles that reflect the core knowledge, skills, and dispositions beginning teachers should possess. Each standard is accompanied by key indicators that link performance to specific teacher practices as, for example, understanding central concepts of the discipline to be taught or linking the curriculum to students' prior experiences. On the surface this seems to be an effective way to ensure well-trained teachers who are accountable for what happens in the classroom. On a deeper level, however, some concerns arise. On one hand, schools of education hope to produce teachers who are autonomous, reflective practitioners. On the other, established standards have the possibility of reducing individual teachers to mere technicians. This view of teaching in which teachers are seen primarily as artful and skilled technicians with the task of achieving set ends is rejected by any number of well-informed educators (Hostetler, 2002).

Although these concerns are certainly worthy of serious consideration, they do not negate the value of INTASC standards. Such concerns, nonetheless, do remind us to pay attention to what the early Greeks termed *phronesis* or "practical wisdom." For Aristotle, *phronesis* referred to "intelligence and soundness of judgment, especially in practical contexts" (Honderich, 1995, p. 679).

INTASC standards, or any standards for that matter, do not have value outside of the individuals who employ them or the practical contexts in which they are used. While standards may serve as practical guidelines, it is individuals who are accountable for carrying out ethically good actions. Not only are ends important, but how they are achieved is equally important. Ethical means and practical ends must be integrated, and doing so demands that teachers reflect on their actions and outcomes on a daily basis. Employing established standards as guidelines for our actions requires us to ask questions such as *What knowledge is important? Who benefits by our teaching this knowledge? What aspects of a child's experience are important? What kind of professional growth is needed for technical practice? What kind of professional growth is needed for ethical practice or practical wisdom?* Answering any of these questions, of course, requires experience, and this experience is by its very nature limited when it comes to beginning teachers. The case stories in this text provide one means of obtaining a head start in acquiring much needed experience and decision-making skills for teaching.

CASE ANALYSIS AND REFLECTION

Case method has the potential to fail if discussion and analysis of the case are too superficial. This can happen for any number of reasons, including failure on the part of students to have read the case thoroughly prior to discussion, lack of tools for analysis, and simple fear of speaking in front of the class. Kenneth Davis, from the University of Stanford in California, cautions his students that the maximum benefits when studying under case method are likely to be achieved only when students recognize that

- all students must participate actively in class discussions about the case.
- effective classroom case discussion and analysis can be realized only if each participant has the "facts" of each case before beginning discussion. It is essential for students to read each case thoroughly *prior to* class discussion.
- decisions often have to be made without all the data one would desire. This reflects the conditions we face as educators. Students must be willing to contribute assumptions and inferences—and equally willing to put them aside if they turn out not to contribute sufficiently to analysis of the case.
- there may be several acceptable solutions to a problem in a case. It is important to be open to exploring options.
- students must accept a critical atmosphere and be open to debating their own conclusions with others. (Adapted from Davis, 1972)

ANALYZING CASES

Following each case story, readers must reflect on what they believe is the primary issue, problem, or concern in the case and then to consider what additional content knowledge and pedagogical knowledge/skills the protagonist must possess in order to ensure a positive outcome for the issue under consideration. Students are also asked to consider the impact of decisions on teaching and learning. During this reflection, students are cautioned to consider that the source of the issue may not be as obvious as one would think with just a cursory glance at the case. It is important to carefully consider the personalities, life events, and actions of all involved. Ultimately, case solutions in education should lead to improved teaching and learning.

Once students have completed this preliminary analysis of the case, they are asked to analyze the case more deeply. The DEEPS Method of problem solving was devised (by this author) for this purpose. It is a five-step method that prepares students for in-depth discussion of the case. Each letter represents a step students should take to prepare thoroughly for discussion with peers. (A completed case analysis is included at the end of this book.)

Determine the primary issue, problem, or concern in this case.

Enumerate the facts that support your belief regarding the primary issue, problem, or concern in this case.

Evaluate the case to find all the possible solutions for resolving the issue, problem, or concern.

Problem solve by critically thinking about each possible solution and accepting or rejecting the solution based on its value in ensuring the professional growth of the teacher in relation to the INTASC standard on which the case is centered.

Summarize your conclusion/solutions and be prepared to present the best possible solution and your rationale to your professor and colleagues.

CONCLUSION

Case method teaching and learning provides opportunities for preservice teachers to vicariously experience real-life situations they are likely to encounter in their careers. At the same time, alignment of cases with INTASC standards presents an early insight into the impact of standards-based movements on our school systems. Students are encouraged to approach cases with an open mind and a high degree of curiosity and creativity. Their ultimate goal should be, as suggested, to develop the habit of good decision making and, in the process, learn to "think like a teacher."

REFERENCES

Davis, K. (1972). Note on the case method of instruction. Adapted in part from *Marketing Management* (New York: Ronald Press, 1972). Retrieved January 3, 2009, from http://www.stanford.edu/class/engr145/materials/case_davis.htm

Herreid, C. F. (2005, Winter). Because wisdom can't: Using case studies to teach science. *Peer Review, 7*(2), 30–31.

Honderich, T. (ed.). (1995). *The Oxford Companion to Philosophy.*, New York: Oxford University Press.

Hostetler, K. (2002, Summer). Responding to the technicist challenge to practical wisdom in teaching: The case of INTASC standards. *Educational Foundations*, 45–64.

Interstate New Teacher Assessment and Support Consortium. Washington, DC: Council of Chief State School Officers. Retrieved May 4, 2006, from http://www.ccsso.org/projects.

Kraft, N. (2001). Standards in teacher education: A critical analysis of NCATE, INTASC, and NBPTS. Paper presented at the Annual Meeting of the American Research Association, Seattle, WA, April 10–14, 2001. ED 462378

Merseth, K. (1996). Cases and case methods in teacher education. In J. Sikula (Ed.), *Handbook of Research in Teacher Education* (pp. 722–744). New York: Macmillan.

Wassermann, S. (1994, April). Using cases to study teaching, *Phi Delta Kappan, 75*(8), 602–609.

1

INTASC Standard 1: Content Pedagogy

Description of INTASC Standard 1: *The teacher understands the central concepts, tools of inquiry, and structures of the discipline he or she teaches and can create learning experiences that make these aspects of subject matter meaningful for students.*

KEY INDICATORS FOR STANDARD 1

The Teacher

- demonstrates an understanding of the central concepts of his or her discipline.
- uses explanations and representations that link curriculum to prior learning.
- evaluates resources and curriculum materials for appropriateness to the curriculum and instructional delivery.
- engages students in interpreting ideas from a variety of perspectives.
- uses interdisciplinary approaches to teaching and learning.
- uses methods of inquiry that are central to the discipline.

CASE 1: CURRICULUM AND INSTRUCTIONAL DELIVERY

Thinking Ahead

As you read this case, reflect on the following:

- Are both teachers in this case equally effective in spite of the different methods they use to convey content?
- What criteria are important when choosing an instructional approach?
- What is the relationship between personal experiences as a student and the instructional approaches one later employs as a teacher?

Tom, Susan, and their student teacher, Maria, sat across from each other waiting for someone to arrive and take their orders. Maria had spent the first 6 weeks of her student teaching placement in Tom's fourth-grade class and the remaining 6 weeks in Susan's second grade. She liked both teachers and felt that she had benefited immensely from their expertise. Now, on her last day of student teaching, Tom and Susan had invited her to dinner. She was flattered by their attention and was looking forward to the opportunity this informal setting provided for her to talk with them about her student teaching experiences. Just as their entrées arrived Tom switched the discussion from the light conversation they had been having to one about teaching.

"Susan and I really enjoyed having you as our student teacher," Tom began. "I hope you enjoyed the experience, too."

"I did," Maria said with a sincere smile. "I really learned a lot." She grinned at both of them and added, "Yesterday my mother asked me about the job and I actually said, 'I have to find a way to bridge my experience as a student teacher with having my own class.'"

Tom and Susan laughed out loud at this, but Susan quickly added, "So, you've noticed the difference in Tom's and my teaching styles, I see. Do you favor one style over the other?"

Maria hesitated, not wanting to offend either of them. "You both seemed to me to have great classes," she answered diplomatically. "I don't think I favor one over the other."

"Oh no," Tom laughed. "You have to take a stance. Come on. Tell us what works for you and what doesn't."

Maria glanced over at Susan to make sure she was open to this conversation. "It's okay," Susan said quickly, seeing Maria's distress. "Tom's right. You have to know what works for you and what doesn't."

"Okay . . . well I think you have a more direct teaching style than Tom," Maria replied to Susan. "That's more the way I was taught, too, so it made a lot of sense to me." Maria thought for a moment and then added, "Although . . . our classes in my teacher ed program tend to be more like Tom's style. My professors are big on constructivist practices, and they pretty much model them in their teaching. It can be confusing at times. I'm not always sure what they want me to learn."

"But we still get lots of paper-and-pencil tests," she added quickly, "and I hate them. I really prefer the lengthy discussions we have in class " They all laughed at this addition.

"I think students have to be able to make sense of what they're doing," Tom interjected. "If I just tell them what they should know, they will never take ownership of it."

"Yeah, but the problem with all this constructivist stuff for me is that it wastes a lot of time and never really gets to the point," Susan said vehemently.

"Sure we get to the point," Tom responded with an equal amount of vehemence. "Don't we, Maria?" he said, turning to her for confirmation.

Maria decided to jump headlong into the discussion. "I'm not sure we *always* do," she said. "There's always some kids who just don't get it, I think. But it does seem like the kids that do get it are really able to talk about what they know in interesting ways."

"Who doesn't get it?" Tom asked with mock surprise. Susan simultaneously nodded her head in affirmation of Maria's comments. "Duh! Maybe like most of the class," she said with a broad grin.

Maria laughed, too. "No, that's not what I meant," she said. "But look at kids like Jimmy Pearson. He's so far behind, and no matter what we tried he didn't seem to really understand much of it. And I bet there are lots of kids who would be happy if we just told them what they needed to know and let them ask questions and get some feedback and practice with the material."

"Could have benefited from some direct instruction," Susan quipped.

Maria laughed appreciatively at the exchanges between Tom and Susan. "I'm still learning," she said, "so I don't really know what I think yet. I must have a couple of years of teaching experience before I can be much of a contributor to these conversations. But I learned a lot in both of your classes."

"I'm willing to concede a little bit," Tom said. "I've spent some time in Susan's class, and I think one of the things I've really learned from her is to present goals clearly and to finish up by reviewing the main points—"

"But?" Susan said impishly.

"Okay," Tom answered, taking the bait. "*But*, the problem I have with teacher-centered approaches like yours is that the whole focus is on what *you* do and not on what the student will do." "Don't get me wrong," he added, "everyone knows you do a great job in your classroom. But, like Maria says, you tell the kids what they need to learn, and they learn exactly that and that's it."

"Fair enough," Susan replied. "But the problem I have with your student-centered approach is that the kids have no idea at all what they should be learning. What does it mean anyway when you say they 'construct meaning'? How many meanings can there be?"

Just then Tom glanced over at Maria who seemed eager to be involved in the conversation. "Let's let our new colleague answer some of this," Tom said. "Come on, Maria, you've spent a good amount of time in both of our classes. What do you think about all of this?"

Maria was delighted to be brought fully into the conversation. "Well, the first part," she offered, "the part Susan was just talking about—well, we just talked about that in our student teacher seminar."

"And?" they both asked at once.

Maria smiled. She really enjoyed the friendship and bantering between Tom and Susan. "My professor was saying last week that the idea is not for students to construct just any old meaning. The teacher has to use probing questions to get students to arrive at *best* meanings. And there should be some consensus in class that it really is a good meaning. Maybe *understanding*. I think *understanding* is the word my professor used."

"And just how is Tom with those probing questions?" Susan asked. "Does he actually ask any, or will anything the students say and do be fine with him?"

Maria and Susan both laughed at Tom's comic reaction to this. "No, he really does ask good questions," Maria said honestly.

"Okay, so give us some examples," Susan said, pretending to take notes as Maria talked.

"Oh no, now I'm really stuck," Maria said, "but let me think a second. . . . Okay, here's an example. Last week during Science a student said he didn't understand how chlorophyll worked in plants. Rather than just telling him, Tom asked him what he did know about chlorophyll."

"Unfortunately, he didn't know much," Tom said with a grimace.

"Yeah, but when you asked him about grass and why it's greener in summer, he had some good ideas about it," Maria added.

"Ah! Now that's my point!" Susan said dramatically. "This is *science!* It's not like any good idea will do. They have to know facts!" Seeing the laughter her dramatic response caused she added, "Maria, I tried so hard to save you from this man!"

"Yes, but this is my point," Tom said, "I could have this student just recite a bunch of facts for me, but if I connect learning with something he already knows he will really get it. His mind will make a connection."

"A bridge!" Maria said, laughing.

"Yes, exactly," Tom said appreciatively. "As teachers we need to form a bridge between what kids already know and the new stuff we want to teach them."

"You've got to explain that to me," Susan said. "How do you do that?"

"I think ideas develop from practical experience," Tom replied without hesitation. "It's the connections kids make between this new experience and their prior knowledge and experiences that lead to higher learning."

"I sort of agree," Maria said. "We talk about that a lot in our classes at my college. But sometimes I think Susan's method has more advantages. And she does connect one lesson to another, so that doesn't seem like it's really an issue. She always knows what individual kids already know and what they need to know."

"Please continue," Susan said with mock haughtiness. "At last I am vindicated."

"The kids know exactly what's expected of them in your class," Maria explained. "If kids think they can get away without doing any work, they will. But in your class you hold them responsible for the content and they know that. You go over it with them and they have to know it. And the other thing is that I'm kind of like those kids myself. I hate taking tests, for example, but if I have to take them, I study for them. Otherwise, I probably wouldn't study at all." She paused for a second. "And one test builds on another," she added. "I can see the connections as we go along."

"I rest my case," Susan said smugly.

"Okay, now wait a minute. Don't I get to defend my side?" Tom asked. "Okay, here goes," he said without waiting for a reply.

"Learning has to be relevant," he began. "This means it has to begin with what the child already knows. To use Maria's example, I can't explain the function of chlorophyll in a plant if the child doesn't have any experience with plants, can I?"

Maria and Susan encouraged Tom to continue.

"I mean what happened with Kevin today in class is a perfect example. He really got it. As soon as we started talking about how grass got darker in summer, we moved right on to pigments. And he figured out that chlorophyll must be the darkest pigment. So we didn't get to chlorophyll A and B and chloroplasts and all that yet, but now he has a reference point to think about all of this. I think that's pretty neat."

"Oh, okay. It *is* pretty neat," Susan said with a smile. "Especially for Kevin. I remember the way he struggled through some concepts, so if you found a way to get him thinking, it really is pretty neat."

"But wouldn't he learn just as much if you just told him what he needed to know?" Maria asked. "At least he would know *some* answers when he takes those standardized tests in a couple of weeks. And it would be quicker to just tell him. Kids like Kevin don't have forever to catch up."

Tom and Susan looked at each other. "We've created a monster," Tom said with a smile.

CASE 1: ISSUES FOR ANALYSIS AND REFLECTION

1. Case 1 is related to the INTASC Standard for Content Pedagogy and to the following three key indicators for this standard: The teacher (a) demonstrates an understanding of the central concepts of his or her discipline, (b) uses explanations and representations that link curriculum to prior learning, and (c) uses methods of inquiry that are central to the discipline. Once you have identified the primary issue, problem, or concern in this case, determine what other content knowledge is needed to ensure positive outcomes.
2. What pedagogical knowledge and skills are needed?
3. What needs to be done to ensure that desired student learning outcomes are obtained?

Use the DEEPS Method to analyze this case. As you work through this case, remember to keep in mind the INTASC Standard for Content Pedagogy and the three key indicators listed in item 1.

Determine the primary issue, problem, or concern in this case.

Enumerate the facts that support your belief regarding the primary issue, problem, or concern in the case.

Evaluate the case in order to find all the possible solutions for resolving the issue, problem, or concern.

Problem solve by thinking critically about each possible solution and accepting or rejecting the solution based on its value in ensuring the professional growth of the teacher in relation to the INTASC Standard for Content Pedagogy.

Summarize your conclusion/solutions and be prepared to present the best possible solution and your rationale to your professor and colleagues.

CASE 1: WHAT THE RESEARCH SAYS

One of the key indicators for the INTASC standard on content pedagogy states "teachers use explanations and representations that link curriculum to prior learning" (INTASC Standards, n.d.). The concept of linking current learning to prior knowledge and experience is derived from various interpretations of schema theory. *Schema* are defined as high levels of complex structures used to interpret and organize experience. They form the foundation for the way in which learners interpret new information. That is, already formed schema enable the learner to integrate new experience with what is already known (Myhill & Brackley, 2004). Piaget, the twentieth-century theorist, describes this process as *assimilation*, or "the process of incorporating a new object or event into an existing schema or mental framework" (Piaget, 1970, p. 63). In other words, when the mind takes in new information, it tries to make sense of it. If this new information is consistent with prior understandings, it is assimilated into existing schema. Sometimes, however, new information might be in conflict with what the individual already understands. In this case, existing schema must change to *accommodate* the new information (Dunn, 2005, p. 235).

Lev Vygotsky, a contemporary of Piaget, did not agree completely with this concept. For Vygotsky, more than just the child's readiness to take in new information is important. Vygotsky believed that language is one of the most important tools of learning. The ability to communicate thoughts and ideas in a social environment is, according to Vygotsky, what distinguishes human beings from all other animals and is also what directs future learning. For Vygotsky, concepts are conveyed through words and the child must be able to receive them and interpret them. It is the social interaction in the environment that permits this to happen (Vygotsky, 1978). According to Vygotsky, the social context of learning is of supreme importance. A classroom that provides multiple and rich opportunities for interaction among students and between teacher and students is far more likely to accomplish learning goals than one that does not.

The work of Piaget and Vygotsky on how children learn sets the stage for a discussion of how the teacher helps to connect prior knowledge to current learning. The first INTASC standard incorporates an assumption that the teacher who is an expert in content pedagogy also is someone who will assist students in making connections between what is already known and new material being taught. Some researchers, however, believe explanations of how teachers do this are too grandiose. According to these researchers, we cannot really understand the constructions of another's mind because schema are constantly changing (for both teacher and student) as a result of social interaction. In practice, therefore, it is far more likely that the only way the teacher can truly connect new learning to the students' prior knowledge is by reviewing previous lessons or by listening to students' explanations of what they already know about various topics (Myhill & Brackley, 2004; Mercer, 2000).

Other researchers contend that students learn best with direct guidance and are less likely to be successful academically if the teacher relies on constructivist approaches when trying to help the student to make connections to prior learning. Kirschner, Sweller, and Clark (2006) refer to constructivist approaches such as discovery learning or project learning as *minimally guided* instructional approaches. They claim that instructional approaches in which the students are expected to discover or construct meaning are effective only when "learners have sufficiently high prior knowledge to provide 'internal' guidance" (p. 75). The problem, these researchers state, is that minimally guided instructional approaches fail to take into account working memory, long-term memory, or the intricate relations between them. With direct instruction the teacher fully explains concepts and procedures and, if appropriate, learning strategies necessary to grasp major concepts in the discipline. Kirschner et al. claim that giving students a full explanation of what is to be learned, rather than leaving students to construct meanings on their own, will result in a greater possibility that learners will construct mental representations or schemas that lead to further learning. These researchers conclude that there is no empirical evidence to support minimally guided instructional approaches. On the contrary, when empirical evidence has been analyzed, it overwhelmingly supports the central role of the teacher in providing instructional guidance for the student (p. 85).

There does seem to be full agreement that some form of scaffolding or deliberate assistance is needed to help the student make connections. *Scaffolding* refers to whatever help is given to the learner to ensure desired learning outcomes. Scaffolding may consist of hints, prompting, visual representations, conversation, or whatever else meets the needs of the individual. In the preceding case story, Tom used scaffolding with Kevin to get him to recall what he already knew about pigments in plants. Of great importance, however, is that the help given to Tom took place in a social context and that the rapport between Tom and his student coupled with a supportive classroom climate contributed to a positive outcome. As Vygotsky stated, "whatever language and logical structures children use in their thinking, they first learned through social interactions" (as cited in Shephard, 2005, p. 63). Geelan adds support to this belief when he suggests that "teaching, learning, and research in education should be re-imagined as 'collaborative social learning' in which students, teachers, and researchers recognize in one another human beings with whom they can play, think, and learn. In the process, the learners teach and the teachers learn as new knowledge is generated through rich social interactions" (Geelan, 1997, p. 28).

As teachers, therefore, we must pay a great deal of attention to the classroom climate we create and the opportunities provided for meaningful social interaction. For new learning to be relevant to a diverse population of learners, instruction must take into account enough shared experiences so that joint understandings can be developed (Mercer, 2000, p. 26). For this to occur, social interaction is required. All scaffolding and all social interactions, however, are not equal. Research by Shephard, for example, indicates that scaffolding is most effective when it focuses on the features of a task. Students are more likely to achieve desired learning outcomes when the teacher temporarily ignores inconsequential errors and focuses on what was done correctly, what still needs to be done, and how it might be done (Shephard, 2005). When this strategy is combined with positive social interaction, cognitive connections are more easily made by students. According to Shephard, one strategy teachers can use to help students make cognitive connections to new learning is to ask meaningful questions. Examples of such questions might include "What do we already know about fractions that can help us to understand decimals?" or "How is learning about ratios and proportions the same—and different from—learning about fractions?" (Shephard, 2005, n.p.). Such questions guide the student to explore connections within subject matter and across disciplines. How these same students construct their understandings, however, is something we cannot know (Shepard, 2005).

As teachers, it is important that we reflect honestly on what we *can* do in the classroom. A child's internalized understanding of the connections that link curriculum to prior learning cannot be easily measured, as suggested by the research. It is of value, however, to reconceptualize the concept of prior knowledge and take into account how it has an impact on student learning. This requires us to extend the concept of prior knowledge to helping the child to make cognitive connections that can be evaluated for their effectiveness by the teacher and even by the student (Myhill & Brackley, 2004, p. 271). There is value, in other words, to judicious review of what the student already knows and what has been taught. This information can be connected to new learning so that the teacher begins and carries out instruction with clear knowledge of the student's strengths and weaknesses when it comes to tackling new learning.

Summary of Research

Schema theory forms the foundation for discussions of what it means to link prior knowledge to current learning. Although it is not possible to know exactly how the child forms understandings, to aid the child in making cognitive connections to current learning it is of value to review what the child already knows and what has been taught previously. Vygotsky emphasizes the importance of the social environment in which learning takes place. As teachers we must pay a great deal of attention to the classroom climate we create and to the opportunities it provides for meaningful social interaction. What the teacher can do, therefore, is create rich, social environments in which instruction is relevant to the learner. Some effective methods for working within this environment include making the child aware of what was done correctly, what still needs to be done, and how it might be done. Teachers also must be skilled at asking questions that aid the child in making connections between past and present learning.

CASE 1: TOPICS FOR DISCUSSION

- An effective teacher is one who thoroughly understands the central concepts of his or her discipline and can create learning experiences that make this content meaningful to students. The teachers who simply stay a chapter or two ahead of the students may be good classroom managers but are not effective teachers.
- The only way a teacher can truly connect new learning to students' prior knowledge is by reviewing previous lessons or by listening to students' explanation of what they already know about previous topics.
- Giving students a full explanation of what is to be learned, rather than leaving students to construct meanings on their own, will result in a greater likelihood that students will construct mental representations and schema that lead to further learning.
- Students are more likely to achieve desired learning outcomes when the teacher ignores inconsequential errors and focuses on what was done correctly, what needs to be done, and how it might be done.

CASE 1: EXPLORING THE ISSUES

1. In the preceding case story, two teachers share similar goals for learning but use different instructional approaches to arrive at these goals. To gain further insight into using student ideas and contributions to help them make connections to subject matter, open your preferred Web browser and type in http://www.prenhall.com/teacherprep. This will take you to Merrill Education's Teacher Prep Web site. Once you are logged in, select the *Video Classroom* tab on the left navigation bar; a list of choices will drop down. Select *General Methods* by clicking on it. Then select *Module 1: The Effective Teacher.* Click on *Video 1: Using Student Ideas and Contributions.* After watching the video, open a discussion with your peers about the effectiveness of the methods used by the teacher in the video.
2. Read the following article: Aubrecht, G. J. (2005). Grounding inquiry-based teaching and learning methods in physics experiences for prospective elementary teachers. AIP Conference Proceedings, *790*(1), 89–92. In this article, Gordon

Aubrecht describes the success and ongoing concern regarding inquiry-based teaching and how preservice teachers plan to incorporate inquiry-based teaching into their own classrooms. After reading the article, reread the case story and discuss how Tom and Maria, the two teachers in the story, might adopt some of the author's techniques into their own teaching.

3. Following Aubrecht's guidelines, write a science lesson of your own that meets National Science Teachers Standards and that is appropriate for middle-school children (Grades 4 to 6).

4. In the preceding case story, one of the teachers is trying to help one of his students understand photosynthesis, chlorophyll, and chloroplasts. Write a one- to two-page imaginary dialogue you might have as a middle school teacher with one of your students. In your dialogue, use inquiry-based teaching to help the student understand major concepts related to photosynthesis.

5. Work with a small group of students and have one member of the group teach one of the science lessons that were written (issue 3). At the end of the lesson, each student in the group should fill out a card stating three to five major concepts they learned as a result of the lesson. They should also state their perception as to whether the lesson was inquiry based or didactic. Finally, state how the lesson might have been improved. Collect all the cards and compare them for areas of agreement and disagreement.

CASE 2: CARMEN'S INTERDISCIPLINARY UNIT

Thinking Ahead

As you read this case, reflect on the following:

- What criteria add up to making a lesson "good" or "bad"? Can this criteria be applied to interdisciplinary lesson plans as well?
- For a profession as old as teaching, why is there still widespread disagreement as to whether or not interdisciplinary units are an effective approach to instruction? Other professions such as law and medicine have been quicker to agree on what is a good approach.
- When is it best to use an interdisciplinary approach, and when is it best to use a single-subject approach to instruction?

Carmen leaned back in her chair in the teachers' lounge and smiled at the piece of paper she was holding. "It's my first *real* interdisciplinary lesson plan," she said to anyone willing to listen. Her friend, Alicia, took the bait. "So what's the lesson?" she asked pleasantly.

"I've integrated my language arts and science lessons for this week," Carmen answered, her excitement showing in her voice. "I'm really proud of it! We're reading one of *The Magic Tree House* books, and it really lends itself to talking about science."

"Which one are you reading?" Alicia asked. "I have them in my fourth-grade class, too, but I haven't used any of them in a lesson."

"The one about dinosaurs," came the quick reply. "It's perfect. And it's a good way for me to talk about plants and animals and evolution and mutations and—"

"There's not much research that really supports this," came a voice from the far corner of the room.

Carmen and Alicia looked over to see Sharon, a veteran teacher, sitting there writing. "A lot of new teachers like to try out these thematic, integrated units," she continued, "but you always end up going back to traditional lessons. You know why?"

"Okay, why?" Alicia asked dryly.

"Because it's hard to follow a sequence in subjects like science. You're always just making it fit. You lose out on meaningful concepts, too, because you're trying to make connections that don't really exist."

Alicia shifted her position and, after a glance at her friend Carmen, said, "Well, that's kind of discouraging, Sharon. But, I think Carmen should try it out and see what works and what doesn't work." Then, seeing Sharon's hurt expression, she added a little more kindly, "Really, it's worth trying, don't you think?"

"Of course it is," Sharon answered. "Sorry if I seemed too snappy about it. Maybe I'm just jealous. I've never had any success with interdisciplinary approaches."

"Don't let Sharon get you down," Alicia said, once Sharon had gathered up her books and left the lounge. "I think she means well. She's probably just a little burned out."

"That would be the good news," Carmen replied with a laugh. "The bad news would be if she's right."

"If who's right?" Constance asked, striding into the room. "And how come you guys are still here?" she added. "Didn't I see you thirty minutes ago?"

Carmen and Alicia laughed. "We have a double period," they answered. "Our kids are in art, and from there they go to gym. This good fortune only happens on Tuesdays."

"So I've written my first real interdisciplinary lesson—unit, really," Carmen announced. "I think it's pretty good. I think I'm getting the hang of this stuff."

"Well, you go, girl!" Constance replied. "Those plans take a lot more time to write, but they're worth it in the end."

Alicia smiled appreciatively. "Do you think so?" Carmen asked. "I saw Sharon earlier, and she wasn't quite so supportive."

"Hey, new girl," Constance said, "you can't expect all of us to think the same way." Constance plopped herself down in the chair next to Carmen and reached for the lesson plan she was still holding. Carmen and Alicia watched intently as Constance's face changed expressions as she skimmed down the pages. Occasionally Constance uttered a "Hmmmmm" or smiled slightly as she read. Finally she looked up and said, "It's a good lesson, Carm. Wanna come and teach it in my class, too?"

Carmen beamed. "Thank you so much," she said sincerely. "I really worked hard on it. I want to be able to do this well."

Constance laughed. "Okay, now do you want a little advice?" she asked.

"Of course. Anything, " Carmen replied.

"Just take it easy," Constance said. "With any kind of lesson plan there's some things to make sure you get in there. Like central concepts," she said. "Make sure you know what you want students to know."

Carmen nodded her head. "And assessment methods, too," Constance added. "How will you know the kids know what you want them to know? Assessment is always a big part of it."

"Are those two things missing from Carm's lesson plan?" Alicia asked.

"No, not completely. I would just emphasize them more. Make sure you don't skip over them, Carm. And make sure your assessment methods really focus on whether or not your objectives were met, okay?"

"Okay," Carmen answered. "Thank you again. This really means a lot."

"Well, hey, it really is good. I think your kids will enjoy it, too," Constance said. Just as she was going out the door, she turned around and said, "I have an 8-year-old and a 9-year-old at home, by the way. They love those books!" Carmen and Alicia smiled happily.

"Remember that methods class we had together?" Alicia said on their way back to their classrooms. "The prof had us writing one integrated unit after another."

Carmen and Alicia both laughed at the memory of their class. "But now I'm a little worried," Carmen said. "I just remembered the part about emphasizing relationships among concepts. I just list them in my unit." She hesitated for a second and then added, "Maybe that's what Constance was alluding to."

"Don't start second-guessing yourself on everything," Alicia warned. "You do that all the time. If you start thinking about the relationships between concepts and about flexible schedules, and flexible student groupings and interlocking themes that match methods and objectives and all those other things Professor Hicks used to harp on, you'll never try anything."

Carmen stopped and stared at her friend. "I think I forgot about *all* those things, Alicia. No kidding. I'm just having my class read the book and then I'm talking about the obvious science parts in it."

Alicia started to respond but then broke into a wide grin. "I think we'd better get together this weekend and go over our notes from Professor Hicks's class last year," she said. "Do you want to come over Saturday? We can work on this for a while so you'll be ready to teach your unit next week."

"Yeah," Carmen said, now smiling herself. "We really are the new kids on the block, aren't we? Now I'm thinking I don't really know much about science either. What if I don't even get the science connections right?"

CASE 2: ISSUES FOR ANALYSIS AND REFLECTION

1. Case 2 is related to the INTASC Standard for Content Pedagogy and to the following three key indicators for this standard: The teacher (a) evaluates resources and curriculum materials for appropriateness of the curriculum and instructional delivery; (b) engages students in interpreting ideas from a variety of perspectives; and (c) uses interdisciplinary approaches to teaching and learning. Once you have identified the primary issue, problem, or concern in this case, determine what content knowledge is needed by the teacher or teacher(s) to resolve the issue.
2. What pedagogical knowledge and skills are needed?
3. How can the teacher or teachers in this case ensure that instruction leads to desired student learning outcomes?

Use the DEEPS Method to analyze this case. As you work through this case, remember to keep in mind the INTASC Standard for Content Pedagogy and the three key indicators listed in item 1.

Determine the primary issue, problem, or concern in this case.

Enumerate the facts that support your belief regarding the primary issue, problem, or concern in the case.

Evaluate the case in order to find all the possible solutions for resolving the issue, problem, or concern.

Problem solve by thinking critically about each possible solution and accepting or rejecting the solution based on its value in ensuring the professional growth of the teacher in relation to the INTASC Standard for Content Pedagogy.

Summarize your conclusion/solutions and be prepared to present the best possible solution and your rationale to your professor and colleagues.

CASE 2: WHAT THE RESEARCH SAYS

Interdisciplinary approaches to instructional planning are generally known under a variety of headings, including integrated curriculum, curriculum integration, or thematic teaching. This is not a new concept. Basic definitions were offered by Jacobs and Shoemaker over fifteen years ago. Jacobs defines interdisciplinary approaches as "a knowledge view and curriculum approach that consciously applies methodology and language from more than one discipline to examine a central theme, issue, program, or experience" (Jacobs, 1989, p. 8). Put more simply, interdisciplinary approaches consist of instructional components that are "organized in such a way that they cut across subject-matter lines, bringing together various aspects of the curriculum into meaningful association" (Shoemaker, 1989, p. 5).

It is worth recounting some of the history of interdisciplinary planning. The utilization of this approach grew in popularity as a consequence of standards-based movements and the increased demands to cover vast amounts of knowledge. A related concern was that the curriculum was too fragmented and connections between disciplines were not made obvious. Jacobs points as well to the frustration of teachers trying to "get it all in" in a school day that simply didn't seem long enough (Jacobs, 1989). Earlier educational thinkers and researchers, such as Dewey, Kilpatrick, Bruner, and Piaget, saw interdisciplinary approaches as supporting a move away from isolated figures and facts. They favored a more holistic approach in which concepts across a variety of subjects are connected so that education became more relevant and meaningful. Interdisciplinary approaches were viewed by these educators as a more natural method of teaching and learning (Dunn, 2005). This makes sense to curriculum experts such as Shoemaker, who reasons that the brain processes many things at the same time. It stands to reason, therefore, that holistic experiences would be processed more readily. According to Shoemaker, "the human brain actively seeks patterns and searches for meaning through these patterns" (Shoemaker, 1989). Kovalik and Olsen, contemporaries of Shoemaker, elaborate on this when they explain that, rather than artificially dividing knowledge into separate subjects and using textbooks to present this knowledge logically and sequentially, interdisciplinary approaches can be used to immerse students in a rich environment that mirrors the complexities of daily life. According to Kovalik and Olsen, interdisciplinary approaches provide a context for learning that leads to a great ability to make and remember connections and to solve problems (Kovalik & Olsen, 1994).

Some of the earlier research related to interdisciplinary approaches, however, points to concerns with this approach. As suggested by the character of Sharon in this case story, for example, without careful planning interdisciplinary approaches may not address logical sequences within subject areas such as math or science. It will require some skill and retraining of teachers, in fact, to move from the logical sequence of thought and activity we have become accustomed to in textbooks to incorporating broad concepts that have to be linked together when designing integrated or thematic units. Doing so requires a firm knowledge base in the disciplines being taught. Flexible schedules may also be necessary to allow ample time to fully explore topics (Lake, 1994). This last concern is echoed by Danielson (1996, pp. 26–28), who states that any curriculum process, whether a single subject approach or a thematic unit, has to take into account six components: (a) demonstrate knowledge of content and pedagogy; (b) demonstrate knowledge of students; (c) select suitable instructional goals; (d) demonstrate knowledge of resources; (e) design instruction; and (f) assess student learning and components of planning and preparation tasks required of beginning teachers. It is insufficient, therefore, to develop interdisciplinary units simply because it is expected or because it seems like a good idea. As Gibson and Mitchell (2005) tell us, regardless of the population of students, educators must employ instructional planning processes and curriculum models that best incorporate all the components of effective teaching (p. 164). Pappas (2006) gives an excellent example of the need for careful planning in science, the subject of this case story. Pappas argues that science books must be chosen very carefully and with attention paid to the language of the book. "Because science is a particular discipline," Pappas writes, "—a specific way of thinking and knowing—its concepts and ideas are realized in a distinctive social language or genre: learning science is also learning its linguistic registers" (p. 246). In other words, learning the language of science improves the learning of language itself. Pappas often favors information books for young children over storybooks because "it is critical to emphasize that children cannot *truly* learn science unless they also learn the distinctive language of science, and using *only* stories of hybrid books will not accomplish such a goal" (p. 246). Although we don't know for sure from the facts of this case, there is no indication that Carmen, the teacher planning the lesson, gave any consideration to the value of the book in terms of how well it uses scientific language and how well it conveys scientific concepts.

More recently, there has been renewed interest in interdisciplinary approaches to instruction, along with research-based suggestions to guide planning. Reform movements such as No Child Life Behind (NCLB) have also added an element of accountability when it comes to covering content. One researcher, for example, writes that all teaching begins with knowing student learning needs and creating multiple opportunities for students to learn in ways that compliment their needs, interests, and experiences. The teacher must be able to connect curriculum content not only to other subject areas but also to the lives of the students (Virtue, 2007, p. 243). The ability to do this reinforces the need for teachers to be content experts in the disciplines in which they teach. One researcher writes that there tends to be a disconnect between content and pedagogical practice when it comes to preservice teachers. Inexperienced teachers tend to favor the affective side of teaching and put less emphasis on content, but both are important for learning to be meaningful (Koeppen, 2003). According to Koeppen, "the better the teachers' understandings, the more likely they will be able to present complex concepts using age/grade appropriate vocabulary and strategies" (p. 262).

Because interdisciplinary units are frequently team taught, there is also a concern that the differences between each teacher's knowledge of content and pedagogical preferences can contribute to uneven instructional delivery. According to Shibley (2006), the effects of uneven content and pedagogical knowledge between teachers can be far reaching. Areas of potential conflict might include inequality of content delivered to students, ineffective assessment, and insufficient time devoted to planning. Shibley goes on to say that this can be avoided by ensuring that sufficient collaboration takes place *prior to* instructional planning. This time spent in collaboration will ensure that each teacher understands the other's level of content knowledge and pedagogical viewpoint (p. 273). One strategy that has proven useful when team teaching an interdisciplinary unit has been to begin with taxonomies such as that of Bloom. Bloom's taxonomy categorizes the level of abstraction of questions that might occur in school settings. It begins with types of questions that require lower level cognitive skills (knowledge, comprehension, application) and progresses to questions that require higher order thinking (analysis, synthesis, evaluation). According to Ferguson (2002), differences in content knowledge between teachers collaborating on an interdisciplinary unit are minimized when the teachers work together to develop the appropriate sequence of study in each discipline. Using a taxonomy such as that provided by Bloom provides a common language in which to write objectives and plan assessment.

Planning an interdisciplinary unit that has desired student learning outcomes is, in the final analysis, like planning any lesson or unit. Essential components are objectives, methods of delivery, and assessment—and, of course, teacher reflection in order to make any adjustments necessary both during instruction and after instruction. Kellough (2007) offers some specific guidelines for planning any interdisciplinary unit. He states that good planning begins with agreeing on the nature or source of the unit—in other words, agreeing on what students are expected to learn from the unit. Secondly, individuals planning the unit should agree on subject-specific standards, goals, and objectives, as well as curriculum guidelines, textbooks, and materials already in place. At this point, topics or themes can be chosen, time lines can be put in place, and the unit can be field tested. This sequence should end with all parties involved evaluating the successes and failures of the unit and making any modifications necessary to the unit. Kellough points out, however, that these are only guidelines and, depending upon the knowledge and experience of teachers involved in planning the interdisciplinary unit, a variety of approaches may be used (pp. 201–203).

Summary of Research

The INTASC standards point to the ability to apply interdisciplinary approaches to teaching and learning as an essential teacher characteristic. On the positive side, some researchers and curriculum planners view interdisciplinary approaches as a more holistic and natural approach to learning since it is human nature to think about and study more than one subject at a time. By connecting concepts across disciplines, students are more likely to retain and be able to apply new learning. On the negative side, other researchers see interdisciplinary units as creating the possibility that none of the subject areas will be covered thoroughly or in logical sequence. Concern has also been voiced over possible inequality in content and pedagogical knowledge between teachers or across subject areas. Both sides in this long-standing debate believe that interdisciplinary approaches require sufficient time for careful planning. Learning objectives, methodology, and assessment practices must align and must be clearly articulated *prior to* delivery of the lesson.

CASE 2: TOPICS FOR DISCUSSION

- Rather than artificially dividing knowledge into separate subjects and using textbooks to present this knowledge logically and sequentially, interdisciplinary approaches can be used to immerse students in a rich environment that mirrors the complexities of daily life. This same possibility does not exist with single-subject approaches.
- There tends to be a disconnect between content and pedagogical practice when it comes to preservice teachers. Inexperienced teachers tend to favor the affective side of teaching and put less emphasis on content.
- The number-one problem facing new teachers is not their level of content pedagogy or their knowledge of state learning standards but the lack of practical, ongoing support in the classroom.
- Each state should have state-level assessments to measure student progress toward meeting state learning standards. This ensures student learning and teacher accountability.

CASE 2: EXPLORING THE ISSUES

1. Open your preferred Web browser and type in http://www.prenhall.com/ teacherprep. This will take you to Merrill Education's Teacher Prep Web site. Once you are logged in, select the *Video Classroom* tab on the left navigation bar; a list of choices will drop down. Click on *Language Arts Methods,* and when this screen opens, click on *Video 1: Pre-writing in 6th Grade.* In this video, the teacher conducts an interactive writing lesson with primary-level children. The teacher explains how she structures writing in her class. She also follows a logical sequence of activities. After watching the video, make some judgments about writing in this classroom and about how effective the teacher's strategies are. Was this an interdisciplinary lesson or a single-subject lesson? What were the objectives of the lesson? What kinds of formative assessments can you make as you watch this lesson? How would you carry out a summative assessment?

2. Collaborate with a classmate to write an interdisciplinary lesson plan that combines interactive writing and science. Make sure your lesson meets State learning standards and that objectives cover both interactive writing skills and science knowledge and skills.

3. Visit an elementary school. Before your visit, obtain a copy of the curriculum for a specific grade level in your state. After reviewing the curriculum and observing several lessons, engage in a discussion as to which has the greatest influence on learning: the curriculum or instructional delivery.

4. In education, we often talk about the importance of creating productive teaching–learning environments. What do these words mean? Write a one- or two-page, double-spaced paper describing components of a *productive teaching–learning environment.*

5. INTASC Standard 1 is related to content pedagogy and states that the candidate "understands the central concepts, tools of inquiry, and structures of the discipline he or she teaches and can create learning experiences that make these aspects of subject matter meaningful for students." As well, the press and policy makers have recently emphasized the importance of teachers' content knowledge in order for effective student learning to occur. Review the No Child Left Behind (NCLB) document at http://www.whitehouse.gov/news/reports/no-child-left-behind.html#1. After reading the Foreword by former President George W. Bush, click on the link for the Executive Summary of this document. Given the diversity of to-day's schools, as well as issues such as funding, a mobile population, and a shortage of qualified teachers, how realistic are each of these proposals?

References

Aubrecht, G. J. (2005). Grounding inquiry-based teaching and learning methods in physics experiences for elementary teachers. *AIP Conference Proceedings, 790*(1), 89–92. Retrieved July 2, 2007, from ebscohost.com.

Danielson, C. (1996). Enhancing professional practice: A framework for teaching. Alexandria, VA: Association for Supervision and Curriculum Development.

Dunn, S. G. (2005). *Philosophical Foundations of Education.* Upper Saddle River, NJ: Pearson/Prentice Hall.

Ferguson, C. (2002, Autumn). Using the revised taxonomy to plan and deliver team-taught, integrated, thematic units. *Theory Into Practice, 41*(4), 239–244.

Geelan, D. R. (1997, August). Prior knowledge, prior conceptions, prior constructs: What do constructivists really mean and are they practicing what they preach? *Australian Science Teachers, 43*(3), 26–28.

Gibson, K. L., & Mitchell, L. M. (2005). Critical curriculum components in programs for young gifted learners. *International Educational Journal, 6*(2), 164–169.

INTASC Standards. (n.d.). Retrieved December 29, 2008, from http://www.wresa.org/Pbl/The%20INTASC%20Standards%20overheads.htm.

Jacobs, H. H. (1989). *Interdisciplinary curriculum: Design and implementation.* Alexandria, VA: Association for Supervision and Curriculum Development.

Kellough, R. D. (2007). *A resource guide for K–12 teachers.* Upper Saddle River, NJ: Merrill/Prentice Hall.

Kirschner, P. A., Sweller, J., & Clark, R. E. (2006). Why minimal guidance does not work: An analysis of the failure of constructivist, discover, problem-based, and inquiry-based teaching. *Educational Psychologist, 42*(2), 75–86.

Koeppen, 2003. Convincing elementary preservice teachers to value content as they do kids. *International Social Studies Forum, 3*(1), 261–263.

Kovalik, S., & Olsen, K. (1994). *ITI: The Model. Integrated Thematic Instruction.* Kent, England: Books for Educators, Covington Square.

Lake, K. (1994). *Close-up #16: Integrated curriculum.* Northwest Regional Educational Laboratory. Retrieved February 26, 2006, from http://www.nwrel.org/scpd/sirs/8/c016.html.

Mercer, N. (2000). *Words and Minds.* London: Routledge.

Myhill, D., & Brackley, M. (2004, September). Teachers' use of children's prior knowledge in whole class discourse. *British Journal of Educational Studies,* 52(3), 263–275.

Pappas, C. (2006, April–June). The information book genre: Its role in integrated science literacy research and practice. *Reading Research Quarterly,* 41(2), 226–250.

Piaget, J. (1970). *Structuralism.* New York: Harper & Row.

Shephard, L. A. (2005, November). Linking formative assessment to scaffolding [Electronic version]. *Educational Leadership,* 63(3).

Retrieved February 10, 2006, from http://search.ebscohost.com.

Shibley, Jr., I. A. (2006, Summer). Interdisciplinary team teaching. *College Teaching,* 54(3), 271–274.

Shoemaker, B. J. E. (1989). Integrative education: A curriculum for the twenty-first century. *Oregon School Study Council,* 33(2). Eugene, OR: University of Oregon, ED 311602.

Virtue, D. C. (2007, May). Teaching and learning in the middle years. [Electronic version]. *Clearing House.* 80(5), 271–274. Retrieved August 1, 2007, from ebscohost.com.

Vygotsky, L. (1978). Tool and symbol in child development. In M. Cole, V. John-Steiner, S. Scribner, & E. Souberman (Eds.), *Mind in society: The development of higher psychological processes.* Cambridge, MA: Harvard University Press.

2

INTASC Standard 2: Student Development

Description of INTASC Standard 2: *The teacher understands how children learn and develop, and can provide learning opportunities that support a child's intellectual, social, and personal development.*

KEY INDICATORS FOR STANDARD 2

The Teacher

- evaluates student performance to design instruction appropriate for social, cognitive, and emotional development.
- creates relevance for students by linking with their prior experiences.
- provides opportunities for students to assume responsibility for and be actively engaged in their learning.
- encourages student reflection on prior knowledge and its connection to new information.
- assesses student thinking as a basis for instructional activities through group/individual interaction and written work (listening, encouraging discussion, eliciting examples of student thinking orally and in writing).

CASE 3: EXPLORING CHILD DEVELOPMENT: GIFTED OR UNDERACHIEVER?

Thinking Ahead

As you read this case, reflect on the following:

- What accounts for uneven development among the cognitive, social, and emotional domains?
- What prior learning for both the child and the teacher in this case contribute to their present behavior?
- How could the teacher in this case make his student, Lydia, more responsible for her own learning?
- Based on the limited amount of knowledge you have about Lydia's parents and your own knowledge base about giftedness, what factors contribute to Lydia's parents not being sure if she is gifted or not?

Lydia could hear her parents talking in the other room. "She doesn't even participate in class," her mother said softly. "And Mr. Saren said she doesn't know the vocabulary for reading and is not completing her workbook pages. He's thinking about placing her in a lower group for a while."

"Let's just pull her out. Send her to a private school," her father replied, the frustration showing in his voice. "Not that we can afford a private school. But, come on, Saundra. She's been reading since before kindergarten. They should put that teacher in a remedial group."

Lydia put her hand over her mouth and giggled at hearing her father's comment. She could easily imagine Mr. Saren's bewilderment at being told he was being sent for remediation. Her parents shot each other a knowing glance upon hearing their daughter's muffled laughter.

"Hey, are you hiding back there and listening to us old folks talk?" her father called to her. "Come in here, you rascal." Lydia came into the adjoining room and flashed her father a smile that warmed his heart. "What's all this about you and school?" he asked, lifting her into his lap. "It's only October, you know, and your teacher and mom and I are worried about you."

"I don't really like second grade," Lydia replied. "I wish I could stay in first grade with Mrs. O'Flannery."

"Well, that's not going to happen, Lydie, so suppose you tell us what's going on," her father retorted.

"I know you loved Mrs. O'Flannery," Lydia's mother interjected. "But Mr. Saren seems nice, too."

"He is nice," Lydia answered, sliding down her father's lap and circling around the table to take a sip of her mother's coffee. Lydia took a drink of the coffee, looked up, and made a face, then added. "He doesn't think I'm smart though. I don't want him to, so I tricked him."

"Well, what kind of a trick did you play, young lady"" her mother asked, feigning indignation. Lydia giggled and moved closer to her mother.

"Well," she said, imitating her mother's tone, "when he asks me a question, I look down and say, 'Ummm—I don't know.'"

"You don't!" her father said. "And what other tricks do you have?" he asked, also copying the tone of mock indignation.

"I don't finish my work, and I pretend I can't read—well, I pretend I can read *a little* but not very well." Lydia gave her parents a happy look that made it clear that she was very pleased with herself. Her parents looked at each other quizzically and then burst into wide grins.

"Come over here, Lydie," her father said. "We need to talk about something important."

"Do you know that Mommy and I expect you to do well in school and learn all you can?" her father asked as Lydia walked back around the table to him.

"Of course," she said. "I do learn a lot. I know all the continents, and I know about holidays and rivers and oceans and all sorts of things, and I read all the books in the back of the class, and I play with the maps my teacher has."

"But Mr. Saren doesn't know you know all those things," her father said. "Why is that?"

"Because I don't want him to know, so I tricked him," Lydia replied with a smile.

"Lydia," her mother said, "Mr. Saren needs to know that you know what he's teaching. He needs to know what all the kids know so he can plan his lessons."

Lydia looked concerned when her mother switched to this harsher tone. "But nobody will like me," she said softly.

"What do you mean nobody will like you?" Lydia's mother's asked.

Lydia thought for a moment before answering her mother's questions. "That's what Sammy told me," she said. "He said I shouldn't be a show-off in second grade like I was in first grade."

"Oh, honey," her mother said. "You can't base what you do on what your friend Sammy says."

"But Doris and Winnie said it, too!" Lydia said in protest. "They said I'm always talking about stupid stuff, and no one wants to play with me."

"What kind of stupid stuff?" her father asked gently, noticing that his daughter was now on the verge of tears.

"Monday we were talking about hurricanes, and I told the class about a book I read that talks about weather patterns. Then in art class Doris and Winnie said it was stupid stuff and no one wanted to hear me talking about stupid stuff anymore."

Lydia's father put his arm around her. "So I see your trick now," he said. "If you pretend you can't read or do the class work, then all the kids will like you."

"Right, Daddy," Lydia said, smiling again. "But I do a little bit of work because I don't want Mr. Saren to think I can't do anything at all. I do whatever Doris does."

"Well, you're a clever little girl," her father said. "But we've got to talk about this some more."

"We sure do," her mother said with a long sigh. "But for now we both agree you played a clever trick."

"Thanks, Mommy," Lydia said happily. "I'm going to go out back and see if Sammy is outside, okay?"

"Okay," both parents replied. "See you in a little while."

After Lydia left, her parents sat silently for a few seconds. "I did that, you know," her mother said, suddenly interrupting the silence.

"Did what?" Lydia's father asked. "Pretended you didn't know anything?"

"Exactly," came the quick reply. Lydia's mother grinned. "Not in second grade but in high school. I really liked this boy in my chemistry class, and I didn't want him to think I was smarter than he was."

"So you failed chemistry because you liked this boy?" Lydia's father laughed.

"No, not fail. But I did let myself get only a C+, and the boy I liked got a B. He was pretty pleased with himself. He thought he was just so cool and smart. He even offered to help me do better in chemistry."

"Did it pay off?" her husband asked. "Did you go out with him?"

"Yup," she replied. "Went out with him and later married him." Lydia's father laughed out loud at the realization his wife was talking about him.

"You know," Lydia's mother said after they had stopped laughing at her high school story, "maybe we should get Lydia tested. Mr. Saren doesn't have any information to go on except what he sees in class." She paused for a second. "And we don't really have much information either. Lydie was an early reader, and she's curious about all kinds of things, but that doesn't necessarily make her gifted." Then she added with a laugh, "It does make her interesting, though."

"And challenging!" Lydia's father laughed. "I think you're right. Let's find out who does this kind of testing and schedule an appointment for Lydia."

"Maybe we should give Mr. Saren a call and relate the conversation we had with Lydie, too. He might have some techniques for getting her more involved if he knows she's purposely holding back."

A week later Mr. Saren was feeling a bit overwhelmed by the task before him. His school district took part in statewide achievement testing at the end of October, so that was one burden off his shoulders. Second grade was one of the targeted grade levels, and results of the standardized achievement tests would let him know how Lydia compared to her peers in terms of achievement. Other than getting these test results, however, he didn't have too many ideas about how to figure out if Lydia really was above average or, as he suspected, a slower-than-average learner. "She doesn't do anything to show she's above average," he thought to himself. "So where does this all come from?" Then he answered his own question. "Just one more family trying to shift the blame from the child to the teacher. And no matter what these kids do in school, the parents always think *their* child is gifted."

Mr. Saren knew how to write tests related to the cognitive domain, and he knew how to arrange tasks according to the level of complexity. Instructional time was planned to be developmentally appropriate for his 7-year-old Grade-2 students, and Mr. Saren always followed a logical sequence that started with major concepts to be learned and worked downward through each component. But now Lydia's parents were telling him that their daughter was purposely doing poorly in his class. "How can that be possible?" he mused. "I make it a point to pay attention to individual students, and lately I've been paying a lot of attention to Lydia. Yet now I'm supposed to meet with the primary school coordinator to talk about this child."

"You really have to think about adding performance assessments." Alice Cornbeth, the coordinator told him. Mr. Saren looked bewildered.

"I guess I'm lost," he said. "I don't know much about performance assessment. I pretty much rely on different classroom tests at the end of units. It doesn't seem like that's what you're talking about now."

"No, it's not," Ms. Cornbeth replied. "The written unit tests give you some helpful information. But you can learn a lot from performance assessments because they simulate real-world activities." Ms. Cornbeth waited for a response from Mr. Saren, but when he remained silent she continued with her explanation. "You can observe and rate learners pretty easily if you plan ahead. And you will get a good idea of how well a child is doing in comparison to other kids in the class, too. You have to remember that all kids won't do equally well on all tasks."

"I really am totally lost," Mr. Saren said again. "Can you give me some examples?"

"Sure," Ms. Cornbeth replied. "Try things like observing your kids solving problems or making decisions or cooperating with others—all the things we do in everyday life."

Mr. Saren looked visibly discouraged. In an attempt to encourage him, Ms. Cornbeth added, "You also might find that other students in your class have unique talents. Paper-and-pencil tests do give a lot of important information, but they can't tell you much about social and emotional development." Instead of encouraging Mr. Saren, however, this last remark had the effect of creating some hostility.

"Whoa!" Mr. Saren said. "You mean you want me to use these performance assessments to measure social skills? What's the point of that?"

"It can be very valid," Ms. Cornbeth answered a little defensively. "If you plan ahead, there's no reason you can't design rubrics to measure things like self-direction and even interaction with peers and attitudes toward instruction."

"How much time do these parents think we have?" Mr. Saren said, now thoroughly annoyed with this discussion and the new expectations for assessment. "I can barely get in my daily lessons. Now you want me to develop rubrics for so-called 'special' kids." He fumed to himself for a second and then added, "In my book, if one of my kids takes a test and fails it, that means they don't know the stuff. Sure they can just have a bad day, but over time there's a record of either understanding the content and passing or not understanding content and failing. And this is what happens with Lydia," he added after a short pause. "She fails them all. Every single time. So now she's gifted?"

It was clear to Ms. Cornbeth that changing Mr. Saren's attitude toward assessing student development was not going to be easy. She fought back her own annoyance in order to give a helpful response. "It looks like there are a few tasks we should discuss further," she said. "If we want to be more sure of Lydia's social and emotional development along with cognition, maybe we can work together to determine assessment goals and then design some tasks to see where she stands in relation to the goals."

"You mean like develop some rubrics for some real-life assignment?" Mr. Saren retorted, the annoyance still showing in his tone. "Great," he said without waiting for a response. "Then I can take up some more time going over the rubrics with her parents. What's next? Then I change my whole instructional style just to accommodate this one child?"

Ms. Cornbeth knew she was not going to accomplish anything at this first meeting. "Maybe I could visit your class," she offered. "I could do an observation, and we could go from there."

"Why not?" Mr. Saren said. "Sure. Why not?"

CASE 3: ISSUES FOR ANALYSIS AND REFLECTION

1. Case 3 is related to the INTASC Standard for Student Development. It addresses two key indicators for this standard. The teacher (a) evaluates student performance to design instructions appropriate for social, cognitive, and emotional development and (b) accesses student thinking as a basis for instructional activities through group/individual interaction and written work (listening, encouraging discussion, eliciting examples of student thinking orally and in writing. Once you have identified the primary issue, problem, or concern in this case, determine what other content knowledge about child development is needed by the parents or teacher(s) to ensure positive outcomes for the child in this case.
2. What pedagogical knowledge and skills are needed?
3. What must be done to ensure that desired student learning outcomes are obtained? What must be done to ensure that the teacher(s) in this case has a positive effect on student learning?

Use the DEEPS Method to analyze this case. As you work through this case, remember to keep in mind the INTASC Standard for Student Development and the three key indicators listed in item 1.

Determine the primary issue, problem, or concern in this case.

Enumerate the facts that support your belief regarding the primary issue, problem, or concern in the case.

Evaluate the case in order to find all the possible solutions for resolving the issue, problem, or concern.

Problem solve by thinking critically about each possible solution and accepting or rejecting the solution based on its value in ensuring the professional growth of the teacher in relation to the INTASC Standard for Student Development.

Summarize your conclusion/solutions and be prepared to present the best possible solution and your rationale to your professor and colleagues.

CASE 3: WHAT THE RESEARCH SAYS

Leta Hollingworth, a forerunner in research on gifted children, had this to say about the uniqueness of gifted children: "To have the intelligence of an adult and emotions of a child combined in a childish body is to encounter certain difficulties" (Hollingworth, 1942, as cited in Klein, 2000, n.p.). In this case story, we encounter two such difficulties. The first is Lydia's advanced intellectual development but typical emotional development. The second is the lack of experience her current teacher has in working with young, gifted children.

It is not unusual for gifted youngsters to enter school having already mastered much of the curriculum for their particular grade level. By the same token, their emotional need to fit in with their classmates may result in behavior similar to that of Lydia in the case story. These children learn quickly that making their abilities known may result in harmful teasing. It is not uncommon for a very bright child, for example, to have the experience of a teacher asking a difficult question and then, when the question goes unanswered, having the teacher retort with a remark such as "Ha! If you were really so smart, you would know the answer!" (Rotigel, 2003, p. 209). Gifted children quickly learn that the best way to avoid such hurtful remarks from adults and peers is to pretend to know far less than they actually do. This should not necessarily be mistaken, however, for immaturity on the child's part. Lydia's behavior in this case could be explained just as easily in terms of her language competence. According to Hoh (2005), a gifted child might be motivated to exert control over a situation that causes discomfort or unhappiness. In Lydia's case, language is a tool that she can use to conceal the amount of knowledge she has in various subject areas.

Other research indicates that discomfort in school settings for gifted children—and particularly the highly gifted—may begin as early as kindergarten and continue through the school years. Some of this discomfort can be due to the overemphasis on academic achievement for these children at the expense of social and emotional developmental needs (Peterson, 2006). Although research has shown that high ability and gifted students are as well adjusted as students from any population (Reis & Renzulli,

2004), it is important to note that any child repeatedly put in situations that cause discomfort may encounter risks to their social and emotional development if needs are not met (Reis & Renzulli, p. 121). In this regard, the need for teachers to know and understand the implications of young children's developmental stages cannot be underestimated. A report from the National Council for the Accreditation of Teacher Education (NCATE), in fact, states that teacher training programs are somewhat at fault for paying so much attention to content in their courses that they fail to devote sufficient time to developing understandings about child development, and particularly about how knowledge of child development can be applied in the general classroom. The NCATE report states that some methods for improving this area are to lengthen teacher preparation programs, require longer student teaching practica and/or require an internship period, make research related to child development more accessible to preservice teachers, and perhaps to even increase the number of credits required for earning a degree and certification in teaching (Honawar, 2007).

An added concern relates to engaging high ability children in learning activities. The current emphasis on testing, some researchers fear, has left less time in the school day for authentic activities that engage students' interests and abilities. This focus on cognitive aspects of the curriculum also takes away time from social and emotional aspects (Renzulli, Gentry, & Reis, 2004). These researchers do not deny the worth of improved test scores as a reliable measure of what students have learned and what schools must do to improve learning opportunities. Authentic learning opportunities, however, allow for the application of knowledge to real-life situations (Renzulli et al.) and are the kinds of activities that lead to lifelong learning. Part of the reluctance of teachers, such as Mr. Saren in this case story, to incorporate more authentic learning opportunities may be that this requires a role reversal for the teacher. Rather than the teacher being the focus of classroom learning, much of the responsibility for learning shifts to the students and the teacher is more of a facilitator. For some teachers, this is not an easy shift.

In the preceding case story, it also can be inferred that Mr. Saren resents what he views as the intrusion of the child's parents in his classroom. This is not an uncommon feeling. Some teachers are highly effective in the classroom but lack important skills when it comes to involving the family in the child's education. Research points to this being another area of training that is often neglected in teacher preparation programs. Baum and McMurray-Schwarz (2004), for example, suggest that more can be done to prepare preservice teachers to work collaboratively with parents, particularly in the early years of schooling. It is also important for preservice teachers to develop a sensitivity to and an understanding of children's daily lives, including the impact of mobility, poverty, and caretaking arrangements on school learning. Rather than devoting an entire teacher preparation class just to this subject, these same researchers suggest that learning might be more effective if training related to parent involvement permeated the entire curriculum. For example, activities such as role playing, conflict resolution, parent–teacher meetings, and simulations of simple communication between the teacher and the family could easily be incorporated into existing classes (Baum & McMurray-Schwarz). In short, one aim of teacher preparation programs should be to provide authentic opportunities for preservice teachers to increase their comfort level with families prior to being fully employed as classroom teachers.

Along these same lines, a key concern in any discussion of gifted education is the readiness of teachers to provide an appropriate education for these learners. There may well be a need for better teacher preparation for working with high-ability children. As suggested, this may require a restructuring of teacher preparation programs. As it now stands, "teachers may lack specific information that would assist them in meeting the [gifted] child's educational needs, and they be uninformed regarding the social and emotional factors that must be considered in planning for the child" (Rotigel, 2003, p. 211).

The research on the need for teacher preparation programs and schools themselves to better address the developmental needs of high achieving youngsters is extensive and spans decades. One researcher (Bynoe, 1998), for example, expresses a concern that all teachers bring their own beliefs and values with them to the classroom and that these "personal histories and experiences guide their beliefs about teaching as well as their attitudes and intentions for the children they will teach" (p. 38). This problem is particularly acute when working with children who are gifted but linguistically, culturally, and/or economically different from the teacher. It can, in fact, be quite difficult for teachers—often from middle-class backgrounds—to see potential in a child who is strikingly different from themselves in terms of dress, attitude, speech pattern, or cultural norms. According to Bynoe, however, certain changes can be implemented in teacher preparation programs to sensitize preservice teacher candidates to the needs of culturally and linguistically diverse student bodies. Bynoe suggests that schools of education take the following three steps:

1. Reduce the mismatch between the student and teacher population through innovative strategies to recruit, retain, graduate in a timely fashion, certify, and induct a culturally and linguistically diverse pool of teachers.
2. Align teacher thinking and teacher practices with the conditions and needs of students by establishing protocols that promote self-reflection and that engage the quality and content of intent and effort necessary to be effective teachers who guide students to viable career choices.
3. Measurably affect teacher thinking to accommodate the changing demographics of schoolchildren through approaches that (a) immerse preservice teachers into schools within communities that approximate their intended teaching job and (b) provide broad scope and depth of experiences that facilitate a realistic understanding of real school conditions (p. 38).

This perceived need for the restructuring of teacher preparation programs also received early support from other researchers. Begoray and Solvinsky (1997) suggest that more attention must be paid to teaching preservice teachers about alternative forms of assessment. These researchers found that early identification of gifted children is more likely to occur as a result of systematic observation of performance assessments such as nonverbal demonstrations of talent (for example, drawing and acting), independence in action, unusual and advanced choices of independent reading materials, and the ability to wrestle with abstract ideas and concepts (Begoray & Solvinsky). Because paper-and-pencil tests are not the only means, or always the best means, of identifying gifted children, the teacher must also create authentic situations in which to make observations. Ideally, authentic tasks require students to display behaviors exactly as they would be displayed in the "real world."

Summary of Research

Gifted children may exhibit an uneven pattern of development. Although one area of development may be far in advance of same-age peers, other areas may be only typical for the child's age. Identifying giftedness may also present unique problems in some children. Problems with identification of gifted children may be complicated when the child does not share the same cultural or linguistic background as the teacher. Teachers may misinterpret behaviors for which they lack familiarity.

One way to sensitize future teachers to working with diverse populations of students, including high-ability students, is to restructure teacher preparation programs so more attention is paid to training teachers to be knowledgeable regarding the developmental needs of all students, to be able to communicate effectively with parents of students and involve them fully in the education of their children, and to be able to effectively incorporate both traditional and alternative forms of assessment into instruction.

CASE 3: TOPICS FOR DISCUSSION

- It is not only high-ability children who may show uneven patterns of development. Because of a concern about emotional maturity, educators increasingly suggest that parents delay the entry of boys into kindergarten, especially boys born in the autumn months, which may make them some of the youngest children in a kindergarten class. Other educators suggest that delaying kindergarten entry will result in boredom by the time the child is in first or second grade.
- Teacher preparation programs must do much more to prepare preservice teachers to work with diverse populations of students, including paying more attention to the impact of cultural and linguistic differences on teaching and learning, teaching alternative assessment techniques, and teaching preservice teachers how to involve parents in their children's education.
- Paper-and-pencil tests are an ineffective method of learning anything about an individual student's abilities.
- Developing the ability to analyze, evaluate, and synthesize content requires extension beyond the regular classroom—not just more class work. Yet the usual approach for gifted children is pullout programs and/or additional classroom work. Teachers are not well prepared to extend curriculum content to challenge the most able students.

CASE 3: EXPLORING THE ISSUES

1. Go to http://www.funderstanding.com/content/piaget to very quickly refresh your memory and understanding of Piaget's developmental stages. After you have read this overview, discuss the impact of developmental stages on classroom learning.
2. Go to http://www.funderstanding.com/content/vygotsky-and-social-cognition to refresh your memory and understanding of social cognition theory and Vygotsky's beliefs about the importance of language in learning. After you have read this overview, discuss the impact of the social cognition model on classroom learning.

3. To gain further insight into the impact of child development on learning open your preferred Web browser to http://www.prenhall.com/teacherprep. This will take you to Merrill Education's Teacher Prep Web site. Once you are logged in, select the *Video Classroom* tab on the left navigation bar; a list of choices will drop down. Select *Child Development* by clicking on it. Then select *Module 4: Cognitive Development: Piaget and Vygotsky*. Click on *Video 2: Cognitive Development, Part 2*. After watching the video, open a discussion about the two youngsters in the video. What is the role of experience in being able to answer the questions regarding proverbs and the story that was told to them? Is there any validity to the claim that culture—including family culture—is the primary determinant of individual development? Is intelligence a birth gift, or is it an attribute that develops through being nurtured in the environment? The two children in this video are typical children who any of us might have in our classrooms. How does knowledge of developmental stages influence teaching?

4. Imagine in your third-grade classroom you have two or three children who are above average intellectually and perhaps gifted. Imagine also that you have two or three children who are performing below average and appear to be of average or below-average ability. Design a lesson plan on the rotation of planets around the sun that not only meets the needs of all students in your classroom but also engages them in the content.

5. Open your preferred Web browser to http://www.prenhall.com/teacherprep. This will take you back to Merrill Education's Teacher Prep Web site. Once you are logged in, select the *Articles and Readings* tab on the left navigation bar; a list of choices will drop down. Click on *Assessment.* When this window opens click on *Article 1: Classroom Assessment: Minute by Minute, Day by Day.* Read the article by Leahy et al. on formative assessment strategies. After reading, check your understanding by answering the six questions that follow. Then go back to the case story about Lydia and open a discussion about what strategies Mr. Saren might use in his own teaching to improve learning opportunities, not just for Lydia but for all his students.

CASE 4: HELPING LEARNERS TO ASSUME RESPONSIBILITY

Thinking Ahead

As you read each case, reflect on the following:

• Is Rory an individual who will eventually become an effective teacher or is she someone who is not likely to make the effort needed to be effective?

• What prior experience is Rory lacking that might have helped her with this lesson?

• When a cooperating teacher is assigned a student teacher who does not seem to be making progress, should the cooperating teacher fail that student or let him or her continue and complete the student teaching practicum with a satisfactory grade?

"And if it says 'How much is left?' what does that tell us we have to do?" Rory asked, simultaneously writing the words across the chalkboard. She turned to face her class of sixth-grade students. Some students looked up at her expectantly. Others kept their heads down and stared at their workbooks. A few seemed totally disinterested. Rory took a deep breath. "Let's read the problem again," she suggested. Rory read the problem again and then began outlining it on the board.

"Okay," she began. "So Susan spent a dollar thirty-seven. Thomas spent two dollars and forty cents. And Allen spent five dollars." Rory added this together on the chalkboard. "Together they spent eight dollars and seventy-seven cents. So how much is left over from ten dollars?" she asked. The class continued to look at her with expressions of either boredom or expectancy. Rory turned back to the chalkboard and began writing out the subtraction problem.

"We began with ten dollars," she said. "And the three children spent eight dollars and seventy-seven cents. That leaves one dollar and twenty-three cents," she said, circling the answer in yellow chalk. "Does everyone understand how we got this answer?" The class nodded in agreement. Just then a bell rang and the children hurriedly put their workbooks away and lined up for lunch.

After the class filed out for lunch, Mrs. Collins, Rory's cooperating teacher, asked her how she thought the lesson had gone. "I'm so frustrated by it," Rory replied almost instantly. "I did all the work for the kids. They just sat there. And I don't know if they understood it or not. This is so much harder than I thought it would be!"

"Don't be so hard on yourself," Mrs. Collins said kindly. "Suppose you tell me what you thought went well and what you would like to improve?"

Rory thought for a few seconds and then replied that she would like the students to be more autonomous and think about how to solve problems for themselves. "We talked about this all the time in my methods classes," she said. "My professors really emphasized encouraging students to reflect on their own work and develop learning strategies they could use in a lot of different situations." Rory paused for a second to gain control of her emotions. "I know I'm not doing well," she blurted out. "I'm doing all the work for them and just asking them if they understand. And they don't seem at all interested either."

Mrs. Collins remained quiet to give Rory a chance to vent her feelings.

"What am I doing wrong?" Rory asked. "They don't even try to answer. They just sit there waiting for me to tell them!"

Mrs. Collins smiled. "Let's start with what you're doing right," she said. "You are doing some good things, you know." Rory brightened at this remark. She didn't expect to hear any compliments after her lesson.

"For one thing," Mrs. Collins began, "when you talk through the problems the way you did in this lesson, you're helping the class to understand how to solve a problem."

"Really?" Rory asked. "How does that help?"

"It's a way of modeling," Mrs. Collins said. "Thinking aloud is one of the best ways I know to model the process of problem solving. The students hear how someone experienced solves the same problem. You'll be surprised. In a few weeks, a lot of students will be mimicking this." Rory beamed. For the first time, she was beginning to feel more confident in her ability to get through student teaching.

"Are there other things I should be doing?" she asked, newfound pleasure showing in her voice.

"Let's go back to your goal of wanting the students to be more reflective," Mrs. Collins said. "Did your professors ever talk to you about math journals?"

Rory blushed. "They did," she replied honestly, "but I don't think I was paying much attention."

Mrs. Collins went to her desk and pulled out a folder. "I'm going to show you some lesson plans from previous years," she said as she sorted through the folder. "Having the children keep math journals," she continued, "is a good way to get them to really think about how they do math." She pulled a page out of the folder and placed it in front of Rory.

"This is the review lesson you were doing today," Mrs. Collins explained. "And this is a page from a student's math journal from last year." Rory skimmed through the open-ended questions Mrs. Collins had written for the student to answer. *What did you do to solve this problem?* was the first question. Directly underneath this two additional questions were written: *What made this problem easy to solve? What made it difficult to solve?*

Rory looked at the student's carefully written answers. *I know when it says, "How much is left?" that I have to subtract something,* the student wrote. *I don't know what to do with the decimal points when I add money,* the student wrote in response to the next question.

Rory looked up from the paper. "Those are the kinds of answers I wanted today!" she said excitedly.

Mrs. Collins laughed out loud. "Don't get too excited," she cautioned, "because you won't always get a response that is this good." She pulled out another paper and showed it to Rory. In response to all of the questions, the student had written *I don't know.* Now it was Rory's turn to laugh.

Mrs. Collins went on to explain that it was very important to create a problem-solving atmosphere in the class so that students were not afraid to ask questions or say they did not know something. "Eventually, even this student starts to think about strategies to solve math problems," she explained. "When other students read their responses out loud, everyone gains new insights."

"But there must be as many different responses as there are students," Rory said. "Or do they all use just one strategy for problem solving?"

"No, that's another concern," Mrs. Collins said, smiling again. "The kids will have lots of different perspectives on how to solve problems. But that's good because ultimately we want them to be able to generalize strategies to solve other kinds of problems." Mrs. Collins looked at Rory to see if she was taking all of this in. Rory looked a little overwhelmed.

"I know I'm really simplifying this explanation," Mrs. Collins said. "But maybe after school today we can work together to develop a lesson using some of these strategies. What do you think?"

"Wow," Rory said, "a few minutes ago I was feeling like I would never get through student teaching successfully. Now I'm really excited to be here." She paused for a second and then added hesitantly, "But I can't stay tonight. I have to be at my job at four o'clock. Can we meet another time?"

Mrs. Collins tried not to let her temporary feelings of annoyance show in her voice. "What about tomorrow?" she asked. "How will you conduct the math lesson tomorrow?"

"I know it would be better if I could go over this for tomorrow," Rory answered apologetically. "I really am excited to learn something new. Can we just wait a couple of days? I'll have more time on the weekend, and then maybe I can be ready for Monday."

There was more than a hint of exasperation in her voice when Mrs. Collins replied, "Okay. We'll wait till Monday."

"Thanks," Rory managed to respond before turning away to fight back the tears she could feel welling up in her eyes. She knew she could not afford to quit her job, but she could not afford to do poorly in student teaching either.

CASE 4: ISSUES FOR ANALYSIS AND REFLECTION

1. Case 4 is related to the INTASC Standard for Student Development. It addresses three key indicators for this standard: The teacher (a) creates relevance for students by linking with their prior experience; (b) provides opportunities for students to assume responsibility for and be actively engaged in learning; and (c) encourages student reflection on prior knowledge and its connection to new information. Once you have identified the primary issue, problem, or concern in this case, determine what content knowledge related to the key indicators for INTASC Standard 3 the teacher and/or student teacher in this case needed to ensure effective instruction.
2. What pedagogical knowledge and skills are needed?
3. What must be done to ensure that new learning is linked with prior experience and that students take responsibility for their own learning and reflect on those experiences?

Use the DEEPS Method to analyze this case. As you work through this case, remember to keep in mind the INTASC Standard for Student Development and the three key indicators listed in item 1.

Determine the primary issue, problem, or concern in this case.

Enumerate the facts that support your belief regarding the primary issue, problem, or concern in the case.

Evaluate the case in order to find all the possible solutions for resolving the issue, problem, or concern.

Problem solve by thinking critically about each possible solution and accepting or rejecting the solution based on its value in ensuring the professional growth of the teacher in relation to issues related to diversity.

Summarize your conclusion/solutions and be prepared to present the best possible solution and your rationale to your professor and colleagues.

CASE 4: WHAT THE RESEARCH SAYS

When we think about how we as educators might support a child's intellectual, social, and personal development, we have to consider student autonomy. Oddly, classroom practice both encourages and discourages self-directed learning and reflection. On the one hand, some teachers assume all the responsibility for student learning and thinking activities. The student teacher in this case story, for example, led the students step by step through problem-solving activities and even reached conclusions for them. At the other end of the spectrum, students perform learning and thinking activities relatively independently of any direct instruction. The teacher's role is that of a facilitator who provides assistance only when it is needed to reach the next step in problem solving (Birenbaum, 2002). Assistance might take many different forms, including asking appropriate and probing questions to serve as catalyst for student thinking, or it might take the form of providing resources in the form of text or graphic illustrators. Mrs. Collins, the cooperating teacher in this case story, tried to provide this form of assistance to her student teacher, Rory.

Research supports the need for developing self-directed learners. A report released by Northwest Regional Laboratories (NWREL, 2004) stated that "helping students become self-directed learners who took responsibility for their own academic performance" was ranked as exceedingly important by 75% of teachers in the survey. These same teachers stated that self-directed learning was especially important for teachers in schools ranked as "low performing" because it is perceived to be a strategy that helps to narrow the gap between students from high and low socioeconomic status. Activities such as exploring one's own thinking in math journals, as described in the case story, provides one example of how to engage students in self-directed learning. Math journals can help students to begin to demonstrate their mathematical thinking and understanding (Koirala, 2007). One teacher-researcher who used math journals with children as young as kindergarten age credits them with helping children to "think and use various symbols to represent their thoughts; keep them actively involved in reasoning, comparing, counting, and other mathematical concepts; and [it] encourages them to explore the many uses of language" (Fuqua, 1997/1998, p. 1). In another case, MacMillan and Wilhelm (2007), the authors discuss the disconnect students have when reading numerous natural descriptions and metaphors in literature. These authors contend that many students have had only limited experience with natural phenomena and are perplexed when it comes to understanding some descriptions and metaphors (e.g., waning or waxing moon). Such disconnects between the written word and personal experiences hinder comprehension. The authors, one an English/language arts teacher and the other a science teacher, provided each of their students with a field journal. Students were told to keep a journal of their observations of nature. They were also directed to keep a list of nature-oriented language found in their literature readings. Once a week, time was set aside to share journals in both small group and whole class discussions. According to MacMillan and Wilhelm, the result of this journal project was raised literacy levels and increased interest in both science and literature.

According to another researcher on problem-solving and self-directed learning activities, students using this process come to recognize strengths and deficiencies in their skill sets and can direct their learning toward overall improvement (Hmelo-Silver, 2004). This same researcher states that all approaches that encourage student autonomy also recognize the need for students to actively construct knowledge. In this process, students engage in inquiry, reflection, and critical thinking. Teachers serve as facilitators for these activities and not solely as a repository of knowledge to be handed out to students at various times during the day.

It is important for teachers to develop skills and strategies themselves in order to be able to encourage autonomy in their students. It can be as much a learning task for the teacher as it is for the elementary schoolchild. Students and teachers alike may initially approach self-directed learning activities with the same hesitancy as the student teacher in the case story. Sometimes it is less stressful—though not necessarily more effective—to stick with what is already comfortable and familiar. And the demands on teachers to learn new strategies to encourage student autonomy can be challenging. Teachers are expected to "bring to the pupil's attention the learning strategies that they are employing, to discuss them with the pupils, and ask for their motives and intentions." They are also expected to "encourage the learner to inquire about the world around him or her. To look for what is relevant, and to integrate the information in order to achieve, cognitive, social, and emotional well-being" (Birenbaum, 2002, p. 122).

Teachers must also recognize the significant role student motivation plays in learning. As one researcher stated, "motivation drives the decision to participate" (Abdullah, 2001, n.p.). It is equally important for the teachers to realize that motivation fluctuates across subject areas. Most students find certain subjects interesting and other subjects difficult or irrelevant to their lives. The context in which learning takes place also influences motivation (Anderman, 2004).

Research points to several strategies that contribute to developing a sense of autonomy and responsibility in students. In one study, Lutz, Guthrie, and Davis (2006) found that reading comprehension was greatly improved when teachers used questions that required higher order thinking. This increased both interest and motivation. When reading outcomes were compared for primary-level children, it was found that teachers who asked their students to answer higher level questions outperformed those who did not (p. 4). In a fascinating review of the popular *Harry Potter* series, one researcher noted the emphasis placed on practical experience at Harry's school. Numerous examples are given of students studying and conducting research on their own and even conducting separate classes of their own. Harry and his peers may sometimes fall asleep in class, but they are highly motivated to learn the content of their various classes. According to this researcher, students at this school are highly motivated by the practical applications of their school curriculum. It is the practical application of knowledge—more than the quality of the instructors—that interests students, motivates them to continue learning outside the classroom, and makes being accountable for learning appealing to them (Dickinson, 2006).

A promising strategy for teacher preparation programs is making use of *critical incident* reports. Preservice teachers such as Rory in the case story would no doubt have benefited from this method. During initial field placements, preservice teachers are required to write a report regarding a critical incident, an event, activity, or occurrence in which they felt discomfort and/or an insufficient knowledge base to handle it effectively. These reports of critical incidents are later reviewed by instructors and discussed in class. Several preservice teachers who were part of an initial study using this strategy reported that it increased open-mindedness on their part. The class discussions about various critical incidents led them to consider problems from multiple perspectives. Others stated that they began their field placements by blaming external factors for problems (such as certain disruptive students, their family and employment commitments, lax school policy, etc.). Discussing critical incidents moved them to accept some or all of the responsibility for what occurred in their classrooms (Griffin, 2003).

Kuhn (2007) writes that the lack of student engagement and student responsibility for learning that accompanies disinterest stems from the fact that not much of what we do in schools has relevance for students. Kuhn states that schools need a curriculum in which relevance is immediately obvious to learners. In the math lesson for Mrs. Collins's sixth-grade students, for example, the relevance of the review lesson was not apparent to them. By the same token, Rory's financial need to have a job outside of her student teaching had far more relevance to her than did mastering a new teaching strategy. Kuhn argues for the utilization of teaching methods that require intellectual content—for example, methods that require inquiry and argument. The power of such intellectual tools are immediately obvious to learners of any age and serve as motivators to learn. By the same token, Kuhn states, schools have to do a better job of connecting learning to adult life. According to Kuhn, if the purpose and value of educational activities are apparent to the learner, there will be no difficulty in engaging students in learning and having students be accountable for their learning. The motivation to do so will be powerful.

Summary of Research

Encouraging student autonomy is an important educational goal. It may, in fact, be one way of narrowing the achievement gap between students of high and low socioeconomic status. Self-directed learning requires a shift from teacher-directed classrooms to those where students feel comfortable taking risks, asking questions, and constructing understandings that are relevant to their current levels of development.

Several strategies may aid students in developing a sense of responsibility for their own learning. These strategies include ensuring the relevance of the curriculum to the learner's level of development and using other techniques, such as critical incident reports and journaling.

CASE 4: TOPICS FOR DISCUSSION

- In this case story, the student teacher chooses going to her after-school job over learning new strategies to teach math. This seems to be because her job has more immediate relevance to her than does whether or not she can engage her students in learning.
- Regardless of other factors, if you know the socioeconomic status of a group of learners, you can pretty much predict their achievement with some accuracy (Borich, 2004).
- Student autonomy requires student choice.
- Encouraging student autonomy for academic tasks makes sense for most learners, but direct instruction is a better method for students with moderate to severe cognitive disabilities.

CASE 4: EXPLORING THE ISSUES

1. Open your preferred Web browser to http://www.prenhall.com/teacherprep. This will take you to Merrill Education's Teacher Prep Web site. Once you are logged in, select the *Video Classroom* tab on the left navigation bar; a list of choices will drop down. Select *Child Development* by clicking on it. Then select *Module 11: Development of Motivation and Self-Regulation.* When this opens, click on *Video 2: Intrinsic Motivation.* In this video four youngsters of different ages are interviewed to see what aspects of schooling they find motivational. As you listen to each child speak, think about the impact of their level of development on their ability to clearly articulate their viewpoints. What does this mean in terms of the content of classroom instruction?

2. Open your Web browser again to Merrill Education's Teacher Prep Web site. Then select the *Strategies and Lessons* option from the tab on the left navigation bar. Once this opens, select *Mathematics Methods.* Then click on *Module 6: Problem Solving* and click on *Developing Students' Word Problem-Solving Skills.* After reading the strategies that are given to improve problem solving in mathematics, reread Case 4. Then imagine that you are Mrs. Collins, the sixth-grade teacher and cooperating teacher for Rory. Write a dialogue between yourself and Rory in which you attempt to explain to her how to integrate one or more of these strategies into her word problem on adding and subtracting money.

3. Choose a subject area for the grade level in which you plan to teach. Write a mini research proposal related to ways in which students assume responsibility for their own learning. Your research proposal should consist of the following three parts: your research questions or hypotheses, the population that will participate in the study, and the methods you will use.

4. Morgan (1996) describes focus group methodology as "a research technique that collects data through group interactions on a topic determined by the researcher" (p. 130). Divide into small groups. After watching a video related to classroom instruction (perhaps one chosen from Merrill Education's Teacher Prep Web site or one provided by your instructor) meet with members of your focus group to answer the following questions: (a) Did the teacher in the video create relevance for students by linking with their prior experiences? (b) Did the teacher in the video provide opportunities for students to assume responsibility for and be actively engaged in learning? (c) Did the teacher in the video encourage student reflection on prior knowledge and its connection to new information? Continue your discussion until your focus group can come to agreement on what the teacher did and did not accomplish.

5. Critical incident reports can be powerful instruments in helping preservice teachers reflect on understanding and beliefs. A critical incident report can take many forms but generally contains the following eight components:
   - What occurred
   - Date and time when the incident occurred
   - Person(s) involved
   - Location where the incident occurred
   - Description of the incident
   - Thoughts and feelings about the incident

- Recommendations regarding this incident
- The rationale for recommendations

Sometimes these eight components are reduced to three simple questions: *What?* (What happened?), *So what?* (What do you think about what happened?), *Now what?* (What do your thoughts or feelings about this incident mean in the bigger picture of teaching and learning?).

Use either format and write a critical incident report related to an incident you observed in a K–6 school. Share your incident report with your peers.

References

Abdullah, M. H. (2001). *Self-directed learning* [ERIC digest No. 169]. Bloomington, IN: ERIC Clearinghouse on Reading, English, and Communication. (ERIC Document Reproduction Service No. ED459458).

Anderman, L. H. (2004). Student motivation across subject area domains. *Journal of Educational Research, 97*(6), 283–285.

Baum, A. C., & McMurray-Schwarz, P. (2004, August). Preservice teachers' beliefs about family involvement: Implications for teacher education. *Early Childhood Educational Journal, 32*(1), 57–61.

Begoray, D., & Solvinsky, K. (1997, September/October). Pearls in shells. Preparing teachers to accommodate gifted low income populations. *Roeper Review, 20*(1), 45–50. (ERIC Document Reproduction Service No. EJ555545).

Birenbaum, M. (2002). Assisting self-directed learning in primary schools. *Assessment in Education: Principles, Policy, and Practice, 90*(1), 119–138.

Borich, G. (2004). *Effective teaching methods.* Upper Saddle River, NJ: Merrill/Prentice Hall.

Bynoe, P. F. (1998, Spring). Retooling and rethinking teacher preparation to prevent perpetual failure of our children. *Journal of Special Education, 32*(1), 37–40.

Dickinson, R. (2006, July/August). *Harry Potter* pedagogy: What we learn about teaching and learning from J. K. Rowling. [Electronic version]. *Clearing House, 79*(6), 240–244. Retrieved August 1, 2007, from http://www.ebscohost.com.

Fuqua, B. (1997/1998, Winter). Exploring math journals. *Childhood Education, 74*(2), 73–77.

Griffin, M. (2003, June). Using critical incidents to promote and assess reflective thinking in preservice teachers. *Reflective Practice, 4*(2), 207–220.

Hmelo-Silver, C. E. (2004, September). Problem-based learning: What and how do students learn? *Educational Psychology Review, 16*(3), 235–266.

Hoh, P. (2005, Spring). The linguistic advantage of the intellectually gifted child: An empirical study of spontaneous speech. *Roeper Review, 27*(3), 178–185.

Honawar, V. (2007, May). Teacher colleges urged to pay attention to child development. *Education Week, 26*(35), 11.

Klein, A. G. (2000, December). Fitting the school to the child: The mission of Leta Stetler Hollingworth, founder of gifted education. Retrieved April 30, 2006, from http://www.ebscohost.com.

Koirala, H. P. (2007, July). Facilitating student learning through math journals. (ERIC Document Reproduction Service No. ED476099).

Kuhn, D. (2007, June). How to produce a high achieving child. *Phi Delta Kappan, 88*(10), 757–763.

Lutz, S., Guthrie, J. T., & Davis, M. H. (2006, September/October). Scaffolding for engagement in elementary school reading instruction. *Journal of Educational Research, 100*(1), 3–20.

MacMillan, S., & Wilhelm, J. (2007, February). Students' stories: Adolescents constructing multiple literacies through nature journaling. *Journal of Adolescent and Adult Literacy, 50*(5), 370–377.

Morgan, D. L. (1996). Focus groups. *Annual Review of Sociology, 22:*129–152.

Northwest Regional Educational Laboratories, Office of Planning and Service Coordination. (2004, December). Developing self-directed learners. Retrieved May 4, 2007, from www.nwrel.org/planning/reports/self-direct.

Peterson, J. S. (2006, October). Addressing counseling needs of gifted students. *Professional School Counseling, 10*(1), 43–51.

Reis, S., & Renzulli, J. (2004, January). Curriculum research on the social and emotional development of gifted and talented students: Good news and future possibilities. *Psychology in the Schools, 41*(1), 119–130.

Renzulli, J. S., Gentry, M., & Reis, S. (2004). A time and a place for authentic learning. *Educational Leadership, 62*(1), 73.

Rotigel, J. V. (2003, June). Understanding the young gifted child: Guidelines for parents, families, and educators. *Early Childhood Education Journal, 30*(4), 209–214.

3

INTASC Standard 3: Diverse Learners

Description of INTASC Standard 3: *The teacher understands how students differ in their approach to learning and creates instructional opportunities that are adapted to diverse learners.*

KEY INDICATORS FOR STANDARD 3

The Teacher

- designs instructional approaches to students' stages of development, learning styles, strengths, and needs.
- selects approaches that provide opportunities for different performance modes.
- accesses appropriate services or resources to meet exceptional learning needs when needed.
- adjusts instruction to accommodate the learning differences or needs of students (time and circumstances of work, tasks assigned, communication and response modes).
- uses knowledge of different cultural interactions within the community (socioeconomic, ethnic, cultural) to connect with the learner through types of interaction and assignments.
- creates a learning community that respects individual differences.

CASE 5: LANGUAGE DIFFICULTY OR DISABILITY?

Thinking Ahead

As you read this case, reflect on the following:

- Consider the attitudes, skills, and understandings Addie Taylor brings to teaching. How do they impact on Ena?
- What challenges does Ena pose for the teacher in this case?
- What changes does Addie Taylor have to make in her instructional approach with the whole class to accommodate the learning needs of students such as Ena? Does this improve or harm the learning environment?

Ena sat glumly at her desk and watched her classmates laughing and joking with each other. She was eager for the morning bell to ring so that this homeroom period would be over and class would start. It's not that she enjoyed class any more than she did during these brief periods of free time, but at least she didn't stand out as much when the teacher was in control of the class and the students were required to pay attention to her. Twelve-year-old Ena didn't have a lot of experience with schooling back home in Cambodia. Still, the principal of her new school in the United States had placed her in the sixth grade, a fact that made her mother very proud. Ena lived in dread of the disappointment her mother would experience when she discovered that her daughter couldn't do the work at all and, in fact, didn't even understand what was expected of her.

Her classmates scurried to their desks when the bell rang. "Good morning, boys and girls," Ms. Taylor said with a smile.

"Good morning, Ms. Taylor," the children chanted back, Ena along with them. This time Addie Taylor noticed Ena reciting the words "Good morning" and smiled at her. Ena beamed, happy to be recognized for this little bit of English she had mastered.

Addie, in fact, had been concerned about Ena's placement in her sixth-grade class. She had been in her class a little over a month now but didn't seem to be making much progress. She made plans to talk with the school counselor about Ena's lack of progress.

"I'm beginning to think the real problem might be that Ena has a learning disability," she told the counselor, Shelley Sheerwin. Shelley asked what she had observed that led her to this conclusion.

"She really just keeps to herself most of the time," Addie had answered. "I don't think she has many social skills really. Sometimes a couple of the girls will try to get her to join in, but she doesn't participate at all."

"Do you know anything about her background?" Shelley asked. "Did she experience any tragedy like separation from her family or even hunger or homelessness—anything that would make her feel more insecure than most kids her age?"

This was a new thought for Addie. "I don't know," she said. "I don't know much about Cambodia—only enough to say it's near Laos and Vietnam. But I don't think I could find any of those places on a map," she added with a nervous chuckle.

Shelley smiled. "There's time for that," she said. "How about other things? How does she do with class assignments?"

"Oh!" Addie exclaimed. "A disaster! Usually she just sits there looking at the paper. Sometimes I think she looks so sad staring at that paper and not knowing what to do. If it's a discussion, she doesn't participate at all. But then if I ask her if she understands, she always says 'Yes' and smiles."

"Do you think she understands what you're saying in class, even if she doesn't have the language to respond?" Shelley asked. As Addie answered, Shelley jotted down a few notes to remind herself about the details of this conversation.

"Sometimes," Addie replied thoughtfully. "And I know she can say things like 'good morning' and 'good-bye.'" Addie broke into a wide grin. "She knows a bit of slang, too. Earlier today I heard her say to one of the boys, 'Hey, I don't think so, buddy.'" Addie repeated it slowly, giving special emphasis to the consonant sounds in the phrase.

Shelley and Addie both laughed at this imitation of Ena. "It might be a good starting place to get her involved," Shelley said after a few seconds. Addie was intrigued.

"How do you mean," she asked? "Do you have an idea?"

"Well," Shelley began, "it's sounding like Ena might be doing a little better with mastering receptive language. And she's really hesitant to try out expressive language. But I guess when the boys were bothering her the context forced her to say something." Shelley paused for a second to mull this over. "Can you incorporate some kind of task into your instruction where she has to at least use the greetings she knows?" she asked.

"That's a great idea!" Addie said, already fully committed to this idea. "My kids are doing a little skit from one of the short stories in language arts. There's one character that doesn't have too many lines, but the lines are perfect for Ena." Addie's whole face brightened. "They're simple." she said, "Just *How are you today? What's wrong? I'm sorry*, and *Good-bye till tomorrow.* Shelley, thank you! This is such a good idea," Addie said with true enthusiasm.

"It'll get her interacting with the other kids, too," Shelley said. "Do you mind if I come in to see this skit performed? It would give me a better sense of her social skills, and I can also start to get a sense of her attention span, emotional balance, and so on."

"Of course. Please come," Addie said. Addie paused for a second and then said wistfully, "It would be interesting, wouldn't it, if everyone else in class had to speak Ena's language? *Khmer* I think it's called. When I think about it that way, I can see why Ena is having a hard time with English. Maybe I'm asking about referrals for special services way too early."

"Maybe," Shelley replied honestly. "But we can test Ena in her own language and get a better picture of her abilities. And don't forget she hasn't had much schooling. That can be a big factor in how ready she is to learn sixth-grade material."

"This is a lot of stuff I haven't thought about," Addie said. "Do you have any other suggestions that might get her involved with the other kids?"

"It sounds like you're doing pretty well on your own, Addie. It can take time to learn a new language, but I'm glad to hear the receptive language is coming along." Shelley paused for a second. "And we don't really know much about Ena other than she's twelve and a little shy," she said.

"Are you thinking she's just a second-language learner and doesn't have a disability? Am I way off track with my concerns?" Addie asked a little apologetically.

"Not at all," Shelley said. "In this case, we really don't know. Sounds like she has some behaviors typical of an LD kid: short attention span, incomplete work, poor social skills."

"All the things I worry about," Addie interjected, now wavering in her thoughts about Ena. "She's small for twelve, too. Maybe we don't even know her right age. Now that I think about it, she came in with her mother to get registered, and her mother doesn't speak any English either." Addie stood up and straightened her skirt before heading back to her classroom. "Shelley, I know you have to do testing and all that, but I really don't think Ena belongs in a regular sixth grade. She's just not developmentally ready for this kind of challenge." Addie read the displeasure in Shelley's eyes.

"Addie, come on. We can't just dump kids in special ed because they come here speaking another language," Shelley said.

"Not *dump* them," Addie replied, the same apologetic tone still in her voice. "But Ena is never going to be able to do sixth-grade work. She's just not ready." Shelley remained quiet so Addie continued. "She hardly speaks at all," she said. "And she's small and withdrawn and she looks so sad most of the time. Shelley, you know I think the district needs a special school for these immigrant children."

"Okay, I get it," Shelley said, putting up her hand to halt the conversation. "But let's just start at the beginning. You put Ena in that little skit, and I'll come and observe. Then we'll go from there."

"All right," Addie agreed. "That's good enough for now, I guess." As she opened the door to leave, she turned to Shelley and said, "I really appreciate your help, Shelley. Thanks."

"My pleasure," Shelley replied. "Keep me posted on what's going on. And don't forget to tell me when you're doing that little play for language arts." Shelley walked back to her desk, her head full of the number of immigrant children in her district receiving special education services.

CASE 5: ISSUES FOR ANALYSIS AND REFLECTION

1. Case 5 is related to the INTASC Standard on Diverse Learners. It addresses three key indicators for this standard: The teacher (a) designs instructional approaches appropriate to students' stages of development, learning styles, strengths, and needs; (b) selects opportunities that provide for different performance modes; and (c) accesses appropriate resources to meet exceptional learning needs. Once you have identified the primary issue, problem, or concern in this case, determine what other content knowledge is needed to ensure positive outcomes.
2. What pedagogical knowledge and skills are needed by the teacher(s) in this case?
3. What must be done to ensure that desired student learning outcomes are obtained?

Use the DEEPS Method to analyze this case. As you work through this case, remember to keep in mind the INTASC Standard for Diverse Learners and the three key indicators listed in item 1.

Determine the primary issue, problem, or concern in this case.

Enumerate the facts that support your belief regarding the primary issue, problem, or concern in the case.

Evaluate the case in order to find all the possible solutions for resolving the issue, problem, or concern.

Problem solve by thinking critically about each possible solution and accepting or rejecting the solution based on its value in ensuring the professional growth of the teacher in relation to the INTASC Standard for Content Pedagogy.

Summarize your conclusion/solutions and be prepared to present the best possible solution and your rationale to your professor and colleagues.

CASE 5: WHAT THE RESEARCH SAYS

The child who gets referred for special education services is supposedly a child who is perceived to be in need of special assistance because of cognitive, behavioral, or physical delays or disabilities. Historically, however, concerns have been raised about the overrepresentation of culturally and linguistically different children in special education. Addie Taylor's concerns about Ena's developmental readiness for sixth grade typifies the issues involved in referral of these children.

According to Garcia and Ortiz (2006), referral of children who are culturally and linguistically underrepresented in the mainstream often reflects a lack of knowledge about the characteristics of these learners and what constitutes normal and atypical behavior for specific populations. The primary concern with special education referral models, according to these researchers, is that too little focus is placed on distinguishing students with disabilities from "those whose academic or behavioral difficulties reflect other factors, including inappropriate or inadequate instruction" (p. 64). In the case story about Ena, the learning environment is shaped by dominant culture and "in cases where dominant cultural practices shape school culture, many culturally and linguistically diverse students and their families find it challenging to function and participate in school" (p. 64).

Other researchers suggest that the problem of disproportionate representation of culturally and linguistically different students in special education may be related to the culture and values some children bring with them to the classroom and the way these values are perceived by their teachers. According to Esposito and Favela (2003), "teachers' beliefs and attitudes are not apolitical; rather they are grounded in life experiences that deem immigrant students' language and culture as assets or deficits, depending on the teachers' world view" (p. 74). The attitudes and values teachers bring with them to the classroom can play an important role in decision making when it comes to referral to special education. Simply put, the way teachers perceive students' beliefs, values, and culture is often directly related to their own mainstream ideology. This sentiment is echoed by other researchers who find that "because children come to school socialized to language in culture-specific ways, the discourse structure and communication styles used by many children from culturally and linguistically diverse populations [are] incongruent with the teacher's style of interaction" (Lovelace & Wheeler, 2006, p. 303). This can impact negatively on academic achievement. Lovelace and Wheeler suggest that children from culturally and linguistically diverse populations have to develop new ways of interacting in order to be successful in navigating between the language and culture of the home and the language and culture of the school. All of the burden, however, should not be on the child. Teachers are ultimately responsible for quality instruction and, to ensure that instruction is adapted to meet the needs of all students, teachers must learn to engage "in practices that are reflective of the diversity rooted in the racial, cultural, and individual differences of students in their classrooms" (Lovelace & Wheeler, p. 304). Simply put, it is the teacher's responsibility to create a learning environment that establishes continuity between home and school.

In the case story, however, the issue is more complex. If a child does have a true disability but doesn't get referred for evaluation, the lack of early intervention may have long-term negative effects. With this in mind, Ena's teacher has some reason to at least question the possibility of a learning disability. Research suggests that students learning a second language and students with a learning disability may exhibit similarities when it comes to academic and social behavior. These behaviors may manifest themselves as poor academic performance, short attention span, distractibility, frustration, emotional fragility, and poor social skills (Salend & Salinas, 2003). One way of lessening the likelihood of inappropriately referring students who are linguistically and culturally different from mainstream students is to make available a range of general and specific support services to all children. It is important, however, that these support services be offered by competent teachers who have expertise related to linguistically and culturally diverse student populations. Without this in place, the possibility of inadequate instruction becomes an issue, and it may well be the teacher's inexperience working with diverse populations that plays the greatest role in low achievement (Garcia & Ortiz, 2006).

The provision of positive school experiences, including authentic forms of activity and assessment, is one way to assist children who are culturally and linguistically diverse. *Scaffolding* is an effective method of providing assistance and is used to provide assistance with tasks that the child is unable to complete independently but would be able to do so if given appropriate assistance (Dunn, 2005, p. 238). In this case story, for example, Ena is beginning to be able to use simple greetings on her own but is still dependent on prompts from her teacher. With continued appropriate assistance from her teacher and peers, she should quickly learn to generalize her present knowledge to other contexts and gradually expand on it.

Culturally and linguistically diverse children also benefit from alternative assessment techniques. These may include nonverbal instructional and assessment strategies, such as the use of materials that use pictures to express concepts. K-W-L charts can also be helpful with students who have limited but functional language proficiency. In a K-W-L chart, the K represents what the child already knows; the W represents what the child wants to learn; and, the L represents what was learned once the activity or task is completed. The value of K-W-L is that it provides an opportunity for the teacher to become more familiar with the child's background knowledge and interests. Other authentic activities might include role-playing, one-on-one assistance, storytelling, and dialogue journals. Dialogue journals are an excellent means of introducing written communication skills. Entries can begin very simply with nothing more than a simple greeting. Teacher responses can gradually extend the dialogue. The journal itself serves as a record of the student's progress (Tannenbaum, 1996). Harris-Murri, King, and Rostenberg (2006) also discuss the importance of the Response to Intervention (RTI) model in tracking the progress of linguistically and culturally diverse students. In this model, the child's progress is carefully monitored and, if an intervention does not result in improved performance, alternative interventions are considered. "As the child's needs increase, the amount of educational resources to support the child's needs simultaneously increases" (Fuchs, Mock, & Young, 2003, p. 163). This model has been found to be one of the most effective in preventing the inappropriate referral of students to special education (Fuchs et al. 2003; Harris-Murri et al., 2006).

According to Margolis (2006), a curious fact is that, as the population of students has become increasingly linguistically and culturally diverse, colleges of education have not exerted a concurrent effort to develop teacher knowledge, skills, and dispositions that will ensure culturally sensitive and effective teaching practices. In part, this may be because the effort to put more focus on diversity in teacher training programs is overshadowed by other pressing concerns, such as integrating technology into instruction, assessment of student learning outcomes, testing and accountability, and competency-based performance.

Yet a significant portion of the responsibility for preparing teachers for today's diverse schools belongs to colleges of education. In an article on precisely this topic, Smolen, Colville-Hall, Xin, and MacDonald (2006) draw attention to the work of a number of prominent researchers in education (Fuller, 1994; Cochran-Smith et al., 2004; Bennett, 1995; Gay & Howard, 2000) who state that U.S. teachers are predominantly white and predominantly middle class and, as a group, have little significant interaction with people different from themselves. Succinctly stated, Smolen et al. believe many teachers lack requisite knowledge and skills for teaching in a culturally diverse society (p. 46). A related problem, these researchers state, is that professors in colleges of education are expected to prepare preservice teachers for working with diverse populations of students. The folly of this expectation, however, is that the professors themselves may lack multicultural competence. An empirical study conducted by these same researchers indicates a correlation between the amount and time of interaction professors of education have with individuals from cultures different from their own and how much diversity is incorporated into course work, their level of comfort in discussing diversity, and their level of sensitivity toward racial and ethnic issues. Among recommendations Smolen et al. makes is that there is a "need to explore ways colleges of education can develop frameworks to promote diversity and prepare teacher candidates to effectively teach culturally diverse students" (p. 47).

Summary of Research

Concerns have been raised about the overrepresentation of culturally and linguistically diverse children in special education. It is important for teachers to acquire knowledge about what constitutes typical and atypical behavior for specific populations. It is equally important for school policies to reflect understanding of cultural and linguistic differences among children.

Several interventions have been proven effective in working with a diverse population of learners. These include providing a wide range of general and specific support services to all children, using authentic forms of assessment, applying research-validated models of intervention such as the RTI model, and putting more emphasis in teacher training programs on preparing teachers for working with diverse populations of learners.

CASE 5: TOPICS FOR DISCUSSION

- Referral to the special education committee of children who are culturally and linguistically underrepresented in the mainstream often reflects a lack of knowledge about the characteristics of these learners and what constitutes normal and atypical behavior for specific populations.
- Attitudes and values teachers bring with them to the classroom can play an important role in decision making when it comes to referral for special education services.

- One way of lessening the likelihood of inappropriate referral of students who differ from mainstream students is to make available, and have offered by culturally competent teachers, a wide range of specific and general support services.
- As the population of students has become increasingly diverse, no concurrent effort has been made in colleges of education to ensure culturally sensitive and effective teaching practices.

CASE 5: EXPLORING THE ISSUES

1. Addie Taylor is not sure if Ena is having difficulties with learning because of language and cultural differences or because she has a learning disability. To read more about the difficulties in making valid distinctions between English language learners (ELLs) who experience learning problems because of language and cultural difference and ELLs who have a learning disability, read the following article: Wilkinson, C., Ortiz, A., Robertson, P. M., & Kushner, M. (2006, March/April). English language learners with reading related LD: Linking data from multiple sources to make eligibility determinations. *Journal of Learning Disabilities, 30*(2), 129–141. After reading the article, analyze the roles of Addie Taylor and Ena in the case story again, keeping this research in mind. Does Ena have a learning disability, or does she simply have language and cultural differences that make learning difficult for her?

2. Shelley Sheerwin, the counselor in this case story, suggests that Addie Taylor use authentic assessment. According to Eby, Herrell, and Jordan (2006), "authentic assessment tasks are very similar or identical to actual tasks the students routinely accomplish in the classroom setting" (p. 73). These same authors also state that effective authentic assessment is distinguished by the teacher's ability to link grading and reporting criteria with the criteria used in the learning process. Design a lesson plan for an academic subject in your area of certification. Use authentic assessment measures to evaluate what students have learned. At the end of the lesson plan, write a short paragraph explaining why you chose the particular assessment methods you use in your lesson. Give at least one citation that validates your decision. (If you need to refresh your memory regarding authentic assessment before writing your lesson plan, you can get a brief overview by going to http://www.teachervision.fen.com/teaching-methods-and-management/educational-testing/4911.html. This Web site will also give you some related links for planning authentic assessments.)

3. In this case story, Addie Taylor appears to be using a one-size-fits-all approach with students in her classroom. She does not demonstrate that she understands how students differ in their approaches to learning and how she can create instructional opportunities that are adapted to diverse learners. To get another perspective on this, go to Merrill Education's Teacher Prep Web site. Open your preferred browser and type in http://www.prenhall.com/teacherprep. This will take you to the Teacher Prep Web site. Once there, select the *Video Classroom* tab on the left navigation bar; a list of choices will drop down. Select *Multicultural Education* by clicking on it. Then select *Module 7: Language*. Click on *Video 2: Teacher Use of Sign Language*. In this video, the teacher is particularly aware of the need to

create a positive learning climate that takes into consideration the individual differences of her students, especially when it comes to language. What techniques/strategies does the teacher in the video use that Addie Taylor might incorporate into her own classroom? Pay attention to the frequency with which the teacher uses strategies other than sign language, such as eye contact, questioning techniques, cooperative learning, direct and indirect instruction, and so on. How effective will these strategies be with a student like Ena?

4. The school counselor in this case story, Shelley Sheerwin, asks the teacher a series of questions about her student Ena. Sheerwin is trying to gain a better understanding of Ena's *task relevant prior achievements*. According to Borich (2004), task relevant prior achievements "provide a structure for learning that allows larger concepts, principles, and generalizations to be learned at the end of a lesson or unit" (p. 57). Ena's failure to learn concepts at higher levels in a lesson plan may not be indicative of an inability to do so but only of not having learned task-relevant prior behaviors. *Task-relevant behaviors* refer to those facts, skills, and understandings that must be taught if subsequent learning is to occur. Go back to the lesson plan you wrote in step 2 of this section. What task relevant prior achievements would be necessary for Ena to understand the concepts you are trying to teach in your lesson? What questions or activities would help you to be aware of task-relevant behaviors that may be needed for Ena to benefit from your lesson?

5. This case focuses on the teacher's ability to understand how students differ in their approach to learning and on the teacher's ability to create instructional opportunities that are adapted to diverse learners. In the case of Ena, the need is urgent for her to become comfortable with written and spoken English. Northwest Regional Educational Laboratory (NWREL) has an excellent article on strategies and resources for teachers of English language learners. The article discusses "best practices" and gives examples of strategies linked to language acquisition stages. It also gives a sampling of teaching strategies. The article can be found at http://www.nwrel.org/request/2003may/general.html. After reading the article, discuss strategies that might be effective in Addie Taylor's classroom. What is your rationale for choosing some strategies and rejecting others?

CASE 6: GREAT EXPECTATIONS AND CULTURAL CONFLICTS

Thinking Ahead

As you read this case, reflect on the following:

- What is the impact of culture on learning in this case?
- Both Haleema and her teacher are fully engaged in the teaching/learning process. Why isn't it working?
- Haleema's brother attended an intensive English language class, but Haleema was not allowed to attend this same after-school class. What reasons might Haleema's parents have for not allowing her to attend? Should Haleema's school respect these reasons, or should it insist that she be allowed to attend the English language classes?

Haleema said good-bye to her baby sister and joined her two sisters and older brother in the short walk to school. She had lived in Burlington for only ten months and, now well into the second semester of school, she still found the U.S. classroom a confusing but exciting place to be. Haleema had spent the last 4 years in a refugee camp in Kenya and another 4 months in one of the nation's southern states waiting for the move to Burlington. Now settled in the Somali Bantu community in this city, she was attending a U.S. school for the first time in her life. She was old enough to be in fifth grade, but her lack of extensive schooling and English language proficiency caused the school administration to place her in the fourth grade. Haleema didn't mind this at all. The prospects of attending school were exciting enough.

During lunch Haleema sat with two new friends, Alison and Suzanne. The girls were talking excitedly about the weekend, but when the bell for class rang the three girls gathered their books and hurried off to Mr. Darcy's fourth-grade classroom.

"Okay, kids. Come on. Let's get settled," Mr. Darcy began right away. "Ready? Okay. Listen up." Haleema put her head down to hide a giggle. Her family sponsor had explained the meaning of "listen up" to her, but when she translated the words to herself, they still made her laugh.

"We've got to finish up those WebQuests for social studies, and a lot of you are only about halfway through the assignment." Heads nodded in agreement. "Okay then," Bill Darcy continued, "so the people still doing research go in back to your computer stations. If you're still working on your slide show, use the computers near the windows. The rest of you come up here with me, and we'll work on the text for the slide show."

Everyone got up and started moving to one of the assigned places in the room. At first Haleema was confused as to what she should do, but then Alison whispered that she should go in back and finish the research. Haleema's heart started to pound. She knew nearly everyone in the class had already finished this assignment, but she didn't know where to begin. She didn't want her teacher to think she wasn't working hard in school or that she didn't care about this assignment. Mr. Darcy came to the back of the room, and although she was eager for the assistance, this made Haleema more nervous. She quickly adjusted her head scarf and made sure her flowing dress covered her ankles.

"Let's take a look at what you're doing, Haleema," Mr. Darcy said as he leaned over her to look at where she was in the project. Haleema slid her chair over to the side so that Mr. Darcy would not be leaning his body over her. "Okay. So you've already looked at the scenes of colonial Williamsburg. What's next?"

Haleema sat there silently for a few seconds. Then Mr. Darcy said, "Come on, Haleema. You've got to think here. What are you supposed to do next?" Haleema felt totally confused. She thought Mr. Darcy was there to *tell her* what to do next, but now she realized that he expected her to *tell him* what she should do. "Maps?" she ventured shyly.

"No. Not yet," Mr. Darcy answered. He pointed to the handout of Web directions he had given each student. "Skim down the page, and tell me what you've already done," he directed.

Skim was a new word for Haleema. She looked at the paper and tried to pretend she understood what she was supposed to be doing, but she didn't know what the word meant.

Mr. Darcy waited a bit, but it became clear to him that Haleema didn't know what she should be doing. He took the computer mouse and clicked on the site for colonial Williamsburg. "Okay, you're in the site," he said, "and you've already clicked on all of the scenes, right?" Haleema nodded.

"Okay. Then the next direction is to choose one person in colonial Williamsburg and read his or her biography." He clicked on the link that said "Meet the People" and then clicked on the link for biographies. Haleema was delighted to have his help in finding these Web pages. She loved using computers in the classroom but knew very little about how to use one. Alison and Suzanne both had computers at home, and Haleema hoped that her family sponsor would be able to find a computer for her family. She looked forward to this day.

"Do you have your biography page?" Mr. Darcy asked. "In your handout," he added. Haleema sifted through her papers and finally came to one that had a picture of a person with a strange hat in the upper left-hand corner. Next to the picture the word *biography* was written. She flipped the pages of her handout over to reveal only the biography page.

"Okay. Good," Mr. Darcy said. "So now you want to answer these ten questions about—well, I think it's a good idea if you choose George Washington." He clicked on the link for George Washington. "Yeah. This is a good choice, I think," he said. "So answer these ten questions. They will be important for your slide show." Then I'll come back in a bit and see if you need any help." Bill Darcy started to turn away but then turned back for a minute.

"If you finish this and I'm still with another group, go to the next part of the assignment. He pointed to the link for electronic field trips. "You're going to visit the site for mapmakers and watch how they did mapmaking and surveying in the eighteenth century. Okay. You all set, Haleema?"

"Okay, Mr. Darcy," Haleema said. Haleema stared at the screen. She was on the site for George Washington's biography, and the first sentence was "George Washington seems today a figure larger than life—almost as he was when he was a familiar sight in the halls, homes, shops, and taverns of eighteenth-century Williamsburg." Haleema read each word over and over and tried to piece it together to make some sense of it. She scrolled down the page to see how long the biography was. She looked to see what the four other people sitting in the back of the room with her were doing. They seemed to be writing answers to the questions, but one boy looked as confused as she did. Haleema looked around the room to see if she could get Mr. Darcy's attention so he could come back and give her more assistance. He was in front of the room with a small group of her classmates. The students in his group were explaining what they were going to put in their slide shows. "Now would not be a good time to interrupt him," she thought.

Haleema sighed. "I know I won't finish this," she thought. She went back to trying to read the words in the biography.

Haleema remembered that her older brother had told her that when she has having trouble reading she should look at the questions first and then try to find the answer in the reading. Her brother played on the seventh-grade soccer team and talked a lot with his teammates. His teacher had placed him in an after-school intensive English language program, and now he had the best English in the family. Haleema had wanted to go to the intensive English language program, too, but her parents had insisted she come home after school. She decided to try the strategy her brother had suggested.

Haleema slowly read the first question: *Tell us who your person is.* She thought for a minute and then smiled happily. She picked up her pen and wrote "George Washington." Haleema was happy to finally be able to write down an answer. She read the next question on her handout. *When was this person born?* Haleema let her eyes wander slowly through the page until she found some numbers. Carefully she wrote "1-7-3-2." She hoped this was right. There were other numbers to consider, but this was the first group of numbers on the page. Dates of birth were not something discussed very often in her family, but Haleema had learned from Alison's birthday party that Americans paid a lot of attention to them. The next question was *List at least three important things this person has done.* Haleema wrote "Figure larger than life" without hesitation. She wasn't sure what this meant but still felt pleased to write it down. She looked up and saw Mr. Darcy approaching her computer station.

"Hey, Haleema. How's it going down here? Wha'cha got so far?"

Haleema didn't know the word *wha'cha* but did know from the context that Mr. Darcy wanted to see her work. She proudly turned the computer screen toward him and handed him her worksheet.

Mr. Darcy glanced at the three questions Haleema had attempted to answer. "Hey, girl, I don't know," he said in a friendly manner. "We gotta get you on track somehow."

Mr. Darcy's friendly manner indicated to Haleema that he was pleased with her work. "Thank you," she whispered shyly and waited for more instructions.

"Thank you?" Mr. Darcy repeated. "Look, Haleema. I don't know what you're doing back here, but you have to move it along so you finish this project. Get through this page today, okay." He put the worksheet down and walked away briskly.

Haleema fought back tears. She loved school and computers, but she was confused by just about everything. To make it worse, she could never tell if her teacher was pleased or displeased with her work. All she knew was that she didn't know how to do most of the things that everyone else seemed to do so easily in Mr. Darcy's class. She was eager to learn, but she didn't know how.

CASE 5: ISSUES FOR ANALYSIS AND REFLECTION

1. Case 5 is related to the INTASC Standard on Diverse Learners. It addresses three key indicators for this standard: The teacher (a) adjusts instruction to accommodate the learning differences or needs of students (time and circumstance of work, tasks assigned, communication and response modes); (b) uses knowledge of different cultural interactions within the community (socioeconomic, ethnic, cultural) to connect with the learner through types of interactions and assignments; and (c) creates a learning community that respects individual differences. Once you have identified the primary issue, problem, or concern in this case, determine what content knowledge is needed to ensure positive outcomes.

2. What pedagogical knowledge and skills are needed?

3. What must be done to ensure that desired student learning outcomes are obtained?

Use the DEEPS Method to analyze this case. As you work through this case, remember to keep in mind the INTASC Standard for Diverse Learners and the three key indicators listed in item 1.

Determine the primary issue, problem, or concern in this case.

Enumerate the facts that support your belief regarding the primary issue, problem, or concern in the case.

Evaluate the case in order to find all the possible solutions for resolving the issue, problem, or concern.

Problem solve by thinking critically about each possible solution and accepting or rejecting the solution based on its value in ensuring the professional growth of the teacher in relation to the INTASC Standard for Diversity.

Summarize your conclusion/solutions and be prepared to present the best possible solution and your rationale to your professor and colleagues.

CASE 6: WHAT THE RESEARCH SAYS

Three issues are at stake in the preceding case story. The first is Haleema's lack of proficiency with the English language and, as a corollary, familiarity with the culture of U.S. schools. The second is the use of technology as an instructional tool to improve learning, especially when working with diverse populations of learners. Finally, in this case we are introduced to an enthusiastic and dedicated teacher who has not yet learned how to adjust instruction to accommodate the needs of diverse learners in his classroom. Needless to say, in Haleema's case the three issues are intertwined.

The Culture of U.S. Schools and the New Immigrants

According to Tong, Huang, and McIntyre (2006), "it is not uncommon for culturally different students' preferred ways of learning to contrast with ways typically used in our schools and promoted in teaching training programs" (p. 204). Many immigrant children are accustomed to a more direct style of communication in their home and community and are also accustomed to the authority of adults. Their expectation is for classrooms to be teacher centered, with the teacher being the primary provider of information. This is basically a direct instruction model in which there is a "presentation and recitation format with explanations, examples, and opportunities for practice and feedback. The direct instruction presentation-recitation format not only requires verbal explanations from [the teacher] but also teacher-student interactions involving questions and answers, review and practice, and the correction of student errors" (Borich, 2004, p. 180). The child in the case story, Haleema, was confronted with the direct opposite of this. U.S. schools tend to favor a learner-centered, negotiable environment that relies on inquiry-based or problem-solving approaches to teaching and learning. Students are often allowed to learn at their own pace and work collaboratively and noncompetitively. Generally, ideas and opinions, whether right or wrong, are acknowledged positively by teachers. Many immigrant children, upon arrival in the United States, may find these methods confusing.

The Somali Bantu, for example, are a people with strong family and community bonds. Their society is patriarchal, and a great deal of respect is given to elders. For the most part, those who have emigrated to the United States are Muslim, and their religious customs are an important part of their culture. Those who have resettled in the United States are generally from refugee camps, and their political and social backgrounds spill over into the school setting (Bridging Refugee Youth & Children's Services, 2003). Because of the situation prior to resettlement, many children did not attend school at all or did so only infrequently. It was rare for girls to be sent to school because of the dangers of sending them away from the home. This is an important consideration when reflecting on school achievement. Haleema is not only a child who is new to U.S. schools—she is also a refugee child. She is faced with learning a new language and a new culture and even new curricular material. According to individuals who have worked with Somali children new to U.S. schools, it is likely that they "have witnessed the destruction of their communities and the loss of their family members. Approximately 400,000 people died of famine or disease or were killed in the war. Approximately 45% of the population was displaced inside Somalia or fled to neighboring countries, to the Middle East, or to the West, in search of resettlement camps. In addition, for those who were impoverished in their own countries, they likely will experience that poverty in the United States" (Castel & Kurata, 2004). In addition to her problems with the English language, therefore, a "cultural discontinuity" exists between Haleema's culture at home and the culture of the school. "Such cultural differences between students and teachers, along with the teacher's failure to understand the student's culturally learned behavior may result in conflicts that obstruct student learning" (Bae, n.d., p. 2).

Promising Practices

Robert Slavin, researcher and author of numerous books on education, speaks directly to factors that impact achievement, regardless of the linguistic and cultural makeup of the classroom. According to Slavin, these factors must first be in place before teachers begin experimenting with other supplemental methods, including technology, to improve learning. The four factors are as follows:

1. *Quality of instruction*   The degree to which information or skills are presented so that students can easily learn them. Quality of instruction is largely a product of the quality of the curriculum and of the lesson presentation itself.
2. *Appropriate levels of instruction*   The degree to which the teacher makes sure that students are ready to learn a new lesson (that is, they have the necessary skills and knowledge to learn it) but have not already learned it. In other words, the level of instruction is appropriate when a lesson is neither too difficult nor too easy for students. Quite obviously, attention must be paid to student development and to student diversity.
3. *Incentive*   The degree to which the teacher makes sure that students are motivated to work on instructional tasks and to learn the material being presented.
4. *Time*   The degree to which students are given enough time to learn the material being taught (Slavin, 2003).

Technology, such as used in this case story, can be a highly effective tool in the classroom. As Slavin points out, however, technology should be used as a *supplement* to good teaching practice, not as a replacement. All teachers, regardless of the populations they teach, must first master content, pacing, and student–teacher inter-action. Once this is done, experimentation with various methods is more likely to yield positive results. In the preceding case story, it appears that technology was the primary focus of instruction rather than the needs of diverse learners such as Haleema. The teacher, for example, has his students working on WebQuests. A WebQuest is "an inquiry-oriented simulation activity in which some or all of the in-formation students interact with comes from resources on the Internet" (Smaldino, Lowther, & Russell, 2008, p. 185). WebQuests are designed with specific learning out-comes in mind, and students generally follow a predetermined sequence in gather-ing information. The case story about Haleema begins in the middle of the lesson, so it is not known whether or not the teacher provided the introductory information needed for his students to be successful in completing their WebQuests.

A related problem in integrating technology into instruction is time. Technol-ogy is a promising instructional tool, but it is more time consuming than other more traditional methods. Decisions must always be made regarding the time for instruc-tion and the depth of coverage for different topics. The National Council for the So-cial Studies (NCSS) has issued a technology position statement in which it reinforces the idea that technology serves a method to deliver the content of a lesson; it is not the lesson itself. NCSS presents a need "to demonstrate and research how effective use of technology enhances social studies teaching and learning" (NCSS, 2006). The authors of the document point to the need to link research to best practice and "to consider the relationship between the standards movement and the use of such tech-nology, since the acquisition of knowledge cannot occur devoid of the learning and assessment of related skills." As part of its guidelines for integrating technology into classroom instruction, the NCSS adds, "students should use technology as a tool for learning social studies content and skills, rather than using technology for its own sake." In other words, content must come before technology.

Edward Tufte, a professor emeritus of political science, computer science, and statistics, points out the dangers of using technology in place of teaching actual con-tent skills and in place of attending to the strengths and weaknesses of individual students. "Particularly disturbing," Tufte writes, " is the adoption of the PowerPoint cognitive style in our schools" (2003, n.p.). Tufte explains that rather than teaching students to write clear sentences, persuasive arguments, and logical expository es-says, we teach them to write what amounts to infomercials consisting of "10 to 20 words and a piece of clip art on each slide in a presentation of three to six slides—a total of perhaps 80 words (15 seconds of silent reading) for a week of work." Tufte suggests that if we want to use computers to improve student learning, we would be smart to first have a clear view of how learning will happen. For starters, technology should be used to supplement content and not replace it. Even with the possibilities for student engagement that technology offers, the teacher has to plan lessons with the student's prior knowledge in mind.

This sentiment is reiterated by others who state that teacher expertise in content knowledge and pedagogical skills is critical, including skills related to working with diverse learners. Added to this is the need for ongoing professional development and collaboration among teachers and administrators and the community that sur-rounds them. Practices that have been shown to heighten school achievement for di-verse learners include setting high expectations for learning but providing assistance to reach goals; respecting the cultural, ethnic, and religious diversity of students in the classroom; developing English language and reading skills; and involving parents in their child's learning (Quindlen, 2002).

One innovative idea for involving parents who lacked English language proficiency occurred at a school in Baltimore, Maryland. An assembly is held each morning, and parents, students, and teachers are invited to attend. The assembly is essentially a "brag session" in which successes are talked about, achievement is recognized, and resources are made known. Often older siblings will serve as translators for their parents (Quindlen, 2002). This, of course, requires time and competent, dedicated personnel, but what it does is create a learning community that respects individual differences and opens the door for increased cultural interactions within the community.

When it comes specifically to integrating technology into instruction, Smaldino et al. (2008) emphasize that all of the research-based and research-validated principles of effective instruction should be present when integrating technology into instruction. These include the following:

- Assess students' prior knowledge.
- Consider individual differences.
- State objectives.
- Develop metacognitive skills.
- Provide social interaction.
- Incorporate realistic contexts.
- Engage students in relevant practice.
- Provide frequent, timely, and constructive feedback (p. 18).

Special care must be taken not to employ methods that might cause frustration and confusion for newly arrived immigrants. Although it is far more time consuming, to create effective learning environments teachers must be attentive to the cultural context in which students learn. In this regard, "it is not the technology or media, but the instructional strategies that facilitate learning" (Smaldino, 2008, p. 19).

Summary of Research

All teachers, regardless of the populations they teach, must first master content, pacing, and student–teacher interaction. It is important that factors that are research based and research validated be put in place before teachers begin experimentation with other supplemental methods. Methods used to deliver instruction, including integrating the use of technology into the lesson, should be culturally responsive and should be implemented only to significantly improve further learning. Method is never more important than the content being taught. Content and method, however, are necessarily intertwined. A teacher who has a repertoire of methods but little content knowledge will not be effective. By the same token, the teacher who is an expert in content but lacks a suitable means of delivering the subject matter also will not be an effective teacher. Working with today's diverse population of learners requires teachers who understand both content and pedagogy and who can deliver instruction in a variety of culturally responsive ways. Technology should be used as a supplement to good instruction—not in place of it.

CASE 6: TOPICS FOR DISCUSSION

- U.S. schools tend to favor a learner-centered, negotiable environment that relies on inquiry-based or problem-solving approaches to teaching and learning. Students are often allowed to learn at their own pace, work collaboratively and noncompetitively, and generally have their ideas and opinions, whether right or wrong, accepted positively by their teachers. Many recent immigrants to the United States, on the other hand, are used to the authority of adults and to a more direct style of communication in the home and community. These children are confused by the U.S. style of education and, as a result, often exhibit poor academic achievement and poor social interaction skills in the first few years of schooling in the United States.
- Although activities such as WebQuests may motivate students to be more actively engaged in learning, they are also time consuming. Some educators may question whether such activities are worth the time they take when there is so much to be covered in the curriculum. If another method can accomplish the same goal or purpose in a shorter amount of time, doesn't it make sense to choose the alternative method?
- "The United States is facing an unprecedented challenge in serving immigrant youth. Today's immigrants arrive from widely diverse source countries, and are increasingly likely to resettle in nontraditional states and in rural communities, areas that often have the least experience and/or infrastructure to help students learn English and adapt to their new schools and neighborhoods. With immigration levels sustained at well over one million arrivals per year, immigrant students are entering public schools in record numbers. This has tremendous implications for program development, curricula, and funding" (Morse, 2005).
- Teacher preparation programs that serve areas that have large populations of immigrant students are not always responsive to the skills and understanding required to educate culturally and linguistically diverse students.

CASE 6: EXPLORING THE ISSUES

1. Mr. Darcy is an energetic and dedicated teacher, but he is having a difficult time meeting Haleema's learning needs. Eby et al. (2006) delineate five factors that reflective teachers must consider when planning and implementing instruction: comprehensible input; quality of verbal interactions; contextualization of language experiences provided; selected teaching and grouping strategies to reduce student anxiety, and active involvement of students within the classroom (pp. 61–62). Google each of these factors to read more about their impact on learning. Review the case again and make determinations as to which of these factors were or were not part of Mr. Darcy's instructional approach.

2. Haleema's difficulties in school appear to be uniquely related to prior life experiences. She has experienced little formal schooling. She spent several years in refugee camps and was finally permanently settled in a northern city and registered in a school, but without any English language training. She is a student

with limited language proficiency. This is not an unusual situation. DeCapua, Smathers, and Tang (2007) report that between 1993–1994 and 2003–2004 the number of English language learners in the United States increased by 65%. A growing number of students in this population are students who, like Haleema, had a number of interruptions in their formal schooling. These students are sometimes referred to as Students with Interrupted Formal Education (SIFE). To gain insights into how to improve learning opportunities for students like Haleema, go to the following article: DeCapua, A., Smathers, W., & Tang, L. F. (2007, March). Schooling interrupted. *Educational Leadership, 65*(6), 40–46. After reading about factors contributing to SIFE, indications of SIFE, school models that work, and best instructional practices, read the case story again and make some determinations as to what Mr. Darcy might have done differently in his classroom.

3. One of the difficulties Haleema identifies for herself in this case story is that she wants to learn but does not know how. There is some agreement that effective teachers consistently model the following behaviors: awareness of purpose, task orientation, high expectations for students, enthusiasm, clarity/directness. and a positive classroom climate. To some degree, Mr. Darcy models all these behaviors, yet he does not do so effectively. Why is this? What advice can you give him to better connect his assignments and interactions with Haleema's learning needs?

4. Notice that Mr. Darcy does not engage Haleema in any kind of discussion or question-and-answer conversation. Instead, he gives her a series of directions. Do this, then do this, then do this. What are some different types of questions Mr. Darcy might have used to help Haleema understand what was required in her project? How can you determine if a question is effective?

5. One strategy for teaching English language learners is to use what is called *modeled talk*, a technique in which the teacher explains a task step by step and simultaneously models each step of the task. To view an example of modeled talk with English language learners, open your Web browser to Merrill's Teacher Prep Web site and click on *Chapter 9: Modeled Talk, Strategy 27*. In this video, the teacher uses modeled talk to explain a writing assignment to her young students. At the end of the video, she explains the benefits of this strategy and her reasons for choosing to use this strategy. After you have viewed the video and listened to the teacher's explanation, rewrite the part of the case story where Mr. Darcy talks to Haleema about how to complete her assignment. In your revision, create an instructional sequence in which you use modeled talk to guide Haleema through the assignment.

References

Bae, G. (n.d.). Rethinking constructivism in multicultural contexts: Does constructivism in education take the issue of diversity into consideration? Retrieved June 30, 2007, from http://www.usca.edu/essays/vol122004/Bae.pdf

Bennett, C. I. (1995). Preparing teachers for cultural diversity and national standards of academic excellence. *Journal of Teacher Education, 46*(4), 259–265.

Borich, G. D. (2004). *Effective teaching methods.* Upper Saddle River, NJ: Merrill/Prentice Hall.

Bridging Refugee Youth & Children's Services. (2003, August 16). Background in potential health problems for Somali Bantu. Rockville, MD: Office of Global Health Affairs, U.S. Department of Health and Human Services.

Castel, A. F., & Karuta, S. (2004, November). Journey to thinking multiculturally: Journey into the Somali culture. [Electronic version]. *NASP Communique, 33*(3). Retrieved July 24, from http://www.nasponline.org/publications/cq/cq333somali.aspx.

Cochran-Smith, M., Davis, D., & Fries, K. (2004). Multicultural teacher education: Research, practice, and policy. In Banks, J. A. (Ed.), *Handbook of research in multicultural education* (2nd ed., pp. 931–936). San Francisco: Jossey-Bass.

DeCapua, A., Smathers, W., & Tang, L. F. (2007, March). Schooling interrupted. *Educational Leadership, 65*(6), 40–46.

Dunn, S. G. (2005). Philosophical foundation of education: Connecting philosophy to theory and practice. Upper Saddle River, NJ: Merrill/Prentice Hall.

Eby, J., Herrell, A., & Jordan, M. (2006). *Teaching in K–12 schools: A reflective action approach.* Upper Saddle River, NJ: Merrill/Prentice Hall.

Esposito, S., & Favela, A. (2003, March). Reflective voices: Valuing immigrant students and teaching with ideological clarity. *Urban Review, 35*(1), 73–91.

Fuchs, D., Mock, D., & Young, C. L. (2003). Responsiveness-to-intervention: Definitions, evidence, and interventions for the learning disabilities construct. *Learning Disabilities Research and Practice, 18,* 157–171.

Fuller, M. L. (1994). The monocultural graduate in the multicultural environment: A challenge to teacher educators. *Journal of Teacher Education, 45*(4), 269–277.

Garcia, S. B., & Ortiz, A. (2006, March/April). Preventing disproportionate representation: Culturally and linguistic responsive pre-referral interventions. *Teaching Exceptional Children, 38*(4), 64–68.

Gay, G., & Howard, T. (2000). Multicultural teacher education for the 21st century. *Teacher Educator, 36*(1), 1–16.

Harris-Murri, N., King, K., & Rostenberg, D. (2006, November). Reducing disproportionate minority representation in special education programs for students with emotional disturbance: Toward a culturally responsive response to *Intervention* model. *Education and Treatment of Children, 29*(4), 779–799.

Lovelace, S., & Wheeler, T. (2006, Winter). Cultural discontinuity between home and school language socialization patterns: Implications for teachers. *Education, 127*(2), 303–309.

Margolis, J. (2006, March). New teacher, high stakes diversity, and the performance-based conundrum. *The Urban Review, 38*(1), 27–44.

Morse, A. (2005, March). *A look at immigrant youth: Prospects and promising practices.* Washington, D.C.: National Conference on State Legislatures. Retrieved August 1, 2007, from http://www.ncsl.org/programs/health/forum/CPIimmigrantyouth.htm.

National Council for the Social Studies. (2006). *Technology position statement and guidelines.* Retrieved May 1, 2007, from http://www.socialstudies.org/positions/technology.

Quindlen, T. H. (2002, August). Reaching minority students: Strategies for closing the achievement gap. [Electronic version]. *Educational Update, 44*(5). Alexandria, VA: Association for Supervision and Curriculum Development. Retrieved December 29, 2008, from http://pdonline.ascd.org/pd_online/english/eu200208_quindlen.html.

Salend, S., & Salinas, A. (2003, March/April). Language difference or learning disability. *Teaching Exceptional Children, 35*(4), 36–44.

Slavin, R. (2003, March). Elements of effective teaching. *Literacy Today.* Retrieved April 14, 2006, from http://www.literacytrust.org.uk/Pubs/Slavin.html.

Smaldino, S. E., Lowther, D. L., & Russell, J. D. (2008). *Instructional technology and media for learning.* Upper Saddle River, NJ: Merrill/Prentice Hall.

Smolen, L., Colville-Hall, S., Xin, L., & MacDonald, S. (2006, March). An empirical study of college and educational faculty's perceptions, beliefs, and commitment to teaching of diversity in teacher education programs at four urban universities. *Urban Review, 38*(1), 45–61.

Tannenbaum, J. (1996, May). Practical ideas on alternative assessment for ESL students [Electronic version]. ERIC Clearinghouse on Languages and Linguistics. Retrieved December

29, 2008, from http://www.doe.state.in.us/lmmp/pdf/article-alternativeassmnt.pdf.

Tong, V. M., Huang, C. W., & McIntyre, T. (2006, Winter). Promoting a positive cross-cultural identity: Reaching immigrant students. *Reclaiming Children & Youth, 14*(4), 203–208.

Tufte, E. (2003, September). *PowerPoint is evil*. Retrieved April 24, 2006, from http://www.wired.com/wired/archive/11.09/ppt2.html.

Wilkinson, C., Ortiz, A., Robertson, P. M., & Kushner, M. (2006, March/April). English language learners with reading related LD: Linking data from multiple sources to make eligibility determinations. *Journal of Learning Disabilities, 30*(2), 129–141.

4

INTASC Standard 4: Multiple Instructional Strategies

Description of INTASC Standard 4: *The teacher understands and uses a variety of instructional strategies to encourage the students' development of critical thinking, problem solving, and performance skills.*

KEY INDICATORS FOR STANDARD 4

The Teacher

- selects and uses multiple teaching and learning strategies (a variety of presentations/explanations) to encourage students in critical thinking and problem solving.

- encourages students to assume responsibility for identifying and using learning resources.

- ensures different roles in the instructional process (instructor, facilitator, coach, audience) to accommodate content, purpose, and learner needs.

CASE 7: USING STRATEGIES TO ENCOURAGE CRITICAL THINKING AND PROBLEM SOLVING

Thinking Ahead

As you read this case, reflect on the following:

- How can Antoine, the student teacher in this case story, relate this novel to real-life problems? How would this change the questions he asks?
- Are all students equally capable of answering divergent questions? Are all teachers equally capable of formulating divergent questions?
- If divergent questions are asked, how does one separate mere opinion from a truly in-depth and thoughtful response? What are the criteria?

"That was *exhausting!*" Antoine said as he straightened the stack of index cards he had collected from the sixth-graders on their way out of the classroom. "But we got through the key points. I can't believe it!"

Stewart Griffin, Antoine's cooperating teacher, picked up the pile of quizzes from the table in front of the classroom. "You certainly did fly through that material," he said. "Honestly, I thought the lesson was very ambitious—the amount of content you covered, I mean."

"I know!" Antoine replied. "Luckily, we moved through the discussion quickly." Antoine paused briefly, flipping through the index cards. "Cody and Melinda really helped. They answered some of the tougher questions, the ones that could have slowed us down."

"How did the kids do on that 'ticket out'?" Stewart asked. "That technique is great for formative assessments. It's fast, easy, and can provide useful information."

Antoine frowned. "Well, I'm not sure. Some of them are good, but some don't seem to make much sense. I wonder if I should have used other questions after all."

The "ticket out" activity coupled lesson closure with formative assessment. The teacher provided a question that each student answered on an index card and handed to the teacher at the end of the class as the "ticket out" the door. Effective tickets out target a key aspect of a lesson's objectives so that teachers can assess student understanding and modify upcoming lessons based on this formative information.

Stewart read the ticket out question Antoine had written on the board. *How did it help Stanley to imagine getting revenge on the bully at Camp Green Lake?*

Antoine sighed. "A lot of students wrote 'I don't know,' with no explanation," he said. "I really think my other question might have been better."

"What was the other question?" Stewart asked.

"I was going to ask the kids to answer *What is the rule to remember about snakes and scorpions at Camp Green Lake?* When I asked that question in class, Melinda answered right away."

Stewart pointed to the stack of index cards. "Actually, Antoine, *this* question—the one you used—is exactly what I've been trying to encourage you to use in class. It's a divergent question, one that encourages students to think critically, formulate evaluations, and synthesize information and experiences. The other question really just points students to a right or wrong answer. The correct answer only requires reading comprehension."

"I see," Antoine answered. He was pleased to have used an effective question for the ticket out but was frustrated by the students' answers. "They didn't really answer the question," he complained. "Wouldn't it be better to have a formative assessment that the students did well on? I'm sure they would have done a better job answering the other question. And I would know they had read the chapters," he added after a slight pause.

Antoine read over the last card, the one Melinda had written. He smiled as he read her response out loud. "Stanley was the victim of many injustices over which he had no control. He was sent to the camp and had to do hard labor for a crime he didn't commit. But even before he was born trouble started when his great, great grandfather was accused him of stealing a pig. By imagining revenge against all the bullies in his life, Stanley could have some control over his situation—even if it was only imaginary control, it still helped him to cope."

"That's an excellent answer," Stewart said. "Melinda exhibits exceptional critical thinking skills for a student this age. But what about the other students?"

Antoine gestured toward the pile of worksheets on the front table. " I don't know," he said. "Let's see how they did on the quiz."

Stewart hesitated momentarily and then consented. "Okay, let's look them over," he said.

Antoine and Stewart split the stack of papers in half and began correcting them. The quiz Antoine had prepared consisted of 10 questions, each related to a different character in the novel *Holes* by Louis Sachar. Students selected the name of correct characters from a list at the top of the quiz. Working together, Stewart and Antoine finished scoring the papers in less than 15 minutes.

"Well, I definitely feel better now!" Antoine exclaimed. "These students did really well—my lowest score was 70%. How did the kids in your group do?"

"About the same," Steward answered. Antoine noticed that he seemed unusually subdued, especially considering the success of his lesson and the students' performance on the quiz. Hesitantly, he asked if Stewart had more advice for him.

"I'm glad the kids did well on the quiz, Antoine, but we must talk some more about your discussion question and about questions in general." Stewart said. "You covered many key elements of the novel, including symbolism, characterization, and irony. And you did a good job with themes, too."

Antoine nodded. "It's a lot!" he said. "But we did it!"

Stewart stifled a sigh. "Antoine, just because you got through your lesson, it doesn't mean that all the students met your objectives. Can I see your discussion guide?"

Antoine handed the discussion guide to his cooperating teacher. It had a list of 32 questions for discussion. Stewart read the first ones out loud:

What is Camp Green Lake like?

What is the town of Green Lake like?

What does Stanley look like?

What is unusual about Stanley's name?

He stopped reading and glanced at Antoine. "These are all *convergent* questions," he said. "Class discussion based on discussions like these aren't really discussions at all. They are more like a game show where the host calls on contestants and one of them gets the right answer."

Antoine looked crestfallen. "What about the quizzes? The kids did so well. They must have learned *something*."

"Antoine, of course the students learned something. They've learned a lot about this novel. You've done an excellent job presenting material about the novel." He paused for a second to let this compliment sink in. Then he asked, "But why couldn't the kids answer your ticket out question?"

"Well, I don't know. But how do you evaluate answers to questions like that anyway?" Antoine shrugged, raising his palms helplessly. "I'm not sure that I even know a correct answer to that question."

Antoine's frustration provided Stewart with a glimmer of hope. This might be a good place to start. Wasn't it true that a teacher had to be able to think critically himself before he could foster that skill in his students?

"Antoine," he began patiently, "a divergent question should push students to move beyond mere knowledge of content and move toward analysis, synthesis, and evaluation. It's easy to describe Camp Green Lake, but it's more difficult and more interesting to evaluate the actions and thoughts of the characters in the novel or to place that character's actions in different context and imagine how the scenario might differ."

"But then you have the same problem," Antoine protested. "How do you know if the answer is right or wrong? Besides, I know I would never get through the material if I had to listen to all their ideas about every question. I would run out of time."

Stewart wondered how to proceed. With only two weeks left in his placement, Antoine was indeed running out of time.

CASE 7: ISSUES FOR ANALYSIS AND REFLECTION

1. Case 5 is related to the INTASC Standard for Multiple Instructional Strategies. It addresses two key indicators for this standard: The teacher (a) encourages students to assume responsibility for identifying and using learning resources and (b) ensures different roles in the instructional process (instructor, facilitator, coach, audience) to accommodate content, purpose, and learner needs. Once you have identified the primary issue, problem, or concern in this case, determine what other content knowledge is needed by the teacher(s) in this case.
2. What pedagogical knowledge and skills are needed?
3. What can be done to ensure desired learning outcomes are obtained?

Use the DEEPS Method to analyze this case. Keep in mind the INTASC Standard for Multiple Instructional Strategies and the key indicators listed in item 1.

Determine the primary issue, problem, or concern in this case.

Enumerate the facts that support your belief regarding the primary issue, problem, or concern in the case.

Evaluate the case to find all the possible solutions for resolving the issue, problem, or concern.

Problem solve by thinking critically about each possible solution and accepting or rejecting the solution based on its value in ensuring the professional growth of the teacher in relation to multiple instructional strategies.

Summarize your conclusion/solutions and be prepared to present the best possible solution and your rationale to your professor and colleagues.

CASE 7: WHAT THE RESEARCH SAYS

One matter that must be kept in mind in any discussion of effective instructional strategies in our schools is the amount of diversity in U.S. classrooms. The 2007 annual report *The Condition of Education* (National Center for Education Statistics, 2008) shows dramatic increases in the number of children attending K–12 schools and an accompanying dramatic increase in the number of minority students represented in our classrooms. This report states that 42% of public schoolchildren are racial and ethnic minorities. In 1972, this percentage was only 22%. Currently, 22% of school-age children speak a language other than English at home. What this means for today's schools is that the traditional Eurocentric methods of instruction may no longer be adequate. With this in mind, one researcher suggests three broad instructional strategies that can be applied to all classrooms and will help ensure quality of learning for all students, regardless of language or origin (Li, 2002).

- *Offer students opportunities to use their minds*   According to this researcher, the more classroom opportunities require the student to think critically, the better the outcomes will be. In the United States, for example, teachers are more likely to simply state concepts without helping students to understand the ideas behind the concepts. In contrast, in some countries such as China (the native country of the researcher), teachers "often ask students why a concept is so stated and if there are other ways to explain it. After understanding, teachers will then push students to a deeper level of thinking by asking more difficult questions" (p. 331).
- *Engage students in academic tasks*   In the United States, a great deal of attention is given to the affective/social side of learning and less attention is paid to cognitive tasks. Yet, as Li points out, the primary purpose of schooling is to improve learning. Li suggests that teachers in the United States can be better trained to avoid behavior problems among students and to hold higher expectations for all students. The United States has all the resources to offer an effective education and equality of opportunity but is hesitant about establishing high expectations. In many countries, students have much heavier workloads than their counterparts in the United States. Students residing in the United States, on the other hand, have more resources (including space, certified teachers, transportation, breakfast and lunch programs, textbooks, and other materials) than do many students in other countries.
- *Expose students to extended texts*   Students with low socioeconomic status are more likely to have limited exposure to formal texts. According to Li, it is critical that these students become familiar with formal, written material and formal texts as part of the everyday learning environment. Li points out, however, that exposure to formal written material is more likely to happen in countries where a national curriculum has similar expectations for all students. In the United States, curriculum expectations can vary from state to state and from school to school within a specific district. Having the same expectations and standards for all students is seen as a first step toward ensuring equality of educational opportunity (pp. 330–332).

Li's observations regarding the diversity of U.S. student populations and the need to ensure equality of opportunity point to the need for teachers to have a repertoire of instructional strategies at their fingertips. Teachers themselves see this need clearly. In August 2006 the Center for Psychology in Schools and Education (2006), a committee of the American Psychological Association, conducted a survey of 2,334 teachers across 49 states and the District of Columbia. Teachers who participated reported the need for professional development activities related to instructional skills. They reported that, when it comes to instructional strategies, the areas of greatest need for them consisted of enhancing skills to promote critical thinking, to motivate students to learn, and to design and implement a challenging curriculum that includes instructional strategies for problem solving (p. 3).

Implementing any changes will require a change in mind-set for many teachers. According to Aukerman (2006), teachers are accustomed to being the "primary knower" in the classroom and, knowingly or unknowingly, do a lot of the thinking for their students. They must stop doing this if they hope to get students to think for themselves. When the teacher acts as the primary knower, the purpose of questioning is not for the student to think critically about content and pose novel questions of his or her own. The purpose of asking questions in this circumstance is only for teachers to lead their students to their point of view. What has to happen is for the teachers to be genuinely interested in student responses. Questions, in other words, have to be authentic and connected to real-life situations. According to Dewey (1963), it is natural for young children to try to make sense of their world by constantly asking questions and expanding on these questions as they begin to receive answers. They do this effortlessly because the questions are meaningful to their lives, and they are interested in the responses. Once these same youngsters reach school age, however, they are bombarded by questions from their teachers, and the questions all too frequently have no obvious relevance. It is suggested that teachers reflect on their own questioning techniques by asking themselves the following questions:

Are my questions varied and do they encourage a range of responses?

Am I asking higher order questions that encourage students to think deeply?

Are students also generating their own questions?

Who does most of the talking? (Hervey, 2006)

Research also indicates that the use of effective instructional strategies is something that develops over time and with experience. Typically, new teachers enter the field with minimal experience with "best" practices. Because of a shortage of teachers in some areas, there is also a tendency toward "fast track" teacher preparation programs in which candidates complete the program in a very short time. This leaves little room to develop pedagogical skills and knowledge. Effective strategies tend to be learned on the job and by trial and error (Freiburg, 2002). Efforts to reform teacher education programs are currently underway. One suggestion is that "professional development for new teachers should be built on a framework of research-based instructional strategies." The framework of strategies can be categorized into *organizing strategies* (lesson design, pacing, time management, etc.), *instructing strategies* (both teacher-centered methods and learner-centered methods), and *assessing strategies* (both of student learning and of the teacher's professional learning) (Freiburg).

It is important to consider both the class as a whole and the individual student when planning instruction. Knowledge of developmental stages is critical. Whereas some children might be adept at dealing with subject matter at an abstract level, others may be at a concrete level developmentally. The uniqueness and individuality of each learner has to be respected, and simultaneously goals of the class as a whole must be met (VanSciver, 2005). Differentiated instruction offers one means of doing this. Kiernan and Tomlinson (1997) define differentiated instruction as a method in which "all learners focus much of their time and attention on the key concepts, principles, and skills identified by the teacher as essential to growth and development in the subject—but at varying degrees of abstractness, complexity, open-mindedness, problem, clarity, and structure" (p. 6). Differentiated instruction, however, is not a single strategy that can simply be universally adopted for all situations. It is a broad means or method of attempting to meet the needs of learners and, in any attempt to accomplish this, the teachers will need a plethora of supporting strategies. These strategies may range from flexible groupings of students to choice of a variety of projects or activities to variations in the assignments themselves. And, as with all instructional strategies, there should be research-based evidence of their worth (Anderson, 2004). The advantage of differentiated instruction as a framework for other strategies "is that it allows teachers to be responsive rather than reactive to the unique and individual personalities, backgrounds, and abilities, found within students" (Anderson, p. 52). A basic premise behind differentiated instruction is *flexibility* in design. Theroux, for example, states that differentiating instruction can take place in four different ways:

1. *Differentiating the content or topic*   This might take the form of teachers using a pre-test to see what students already know about a topic. Those who have sufficient prior knowledge to understand higher concepts can move ahead quickly. Those who lack important prior knowledge related to the topic can begin with acquiring the needed information or knowledge for further learning.
2. *Differentiating the process/activities*   Students can arrive at the same knowledge, understanding, and concepts in many ways. This might include using graphic organizers, maps, charts, readings, and so on.
3. *Differentiating the product*   Assessment is based on the student demonstrating his or her understanding of content. There can be great variation, however, in how students demonstrate their understanding. It may be as simple as receiving a passing grade on a traditional test or as complex as writing a play, conducting interviews and analyzing for common themes, creating a model of some sort, or drafting a petition and collecting signatures.
4. *Differentiating by manipulating the environment*   This involves changing the classroom environment to meet the needs of individual learners. It can be as complex as addressing the learning styles of students, or it can mean adding additional computers or providing a work area where three or four students can work as a group and it is not necessary to put materials away at the end of the day. (Theroux, 2002)

Differentiated instruction is closely related to Universal Design for Learning (UDL). UDL is inspired by the use of universal design in architecture. For example, the curb cut in sidewalks is designed primarily for easy assess to the sidewalk for individuals with disabilities. Such a design is "universal," however, in the sense that it also benefits the parent with a stroller or the skateboarder or rollerskater. Curb cuts also influence the flow of human traffic. People tend to gravitate toward the curb cut.

Another example is the width of hallways in public buildings. The original intent was to anticipate the needs of an individual who might need to navigate a wheelchair down these hallways. But all people benefit from the wider space when carrying wide packages or even just walking in groups of three or four. At a minimum, UDL has the following characteristics:

1. There are multiple means of representation. In other words, the student is shown a variety of ways to acquire knowledge.
2. There are multiple means of action and expression. Students are allowed alternative ways of expressing what they know. For example, a student may choose to write a paper, give a presentation, give a performance, create a model, and so on.
3. There are multiple means of engagement. A goal for the teacher is always to motivate students to learn. This may occur by paying attention to students' interests, prior knowledge, or anything that makes learning itself relevant to the learner (CAST, n.d.).

UDL and differentiated instruction are highly compatible (and similar) approaches to meeting the needs of diverse learners. Major differences perhaps lie in their origins. UDL was initially an approach for individuals with disabilities, but like differentiated instruction it has proven to be an effective means of tailoring the curriculum to meet the needs of diverse learners.

Summary of Research

Strategies, in short, provide a means for solving problems. Because each instructional problem is unique, the teacher must be able to adapt or modify the strategy to fit the problem (Duffy, 1993). Strategies used effectively are not automatic but the result of an overall plan for constructing meaning. The effective teacher becomes what is known as a *global strategy user* or someone who is content knowledgeable and possesses a repertoire of strategies that can be adjusted, modified, and manipulated to fit the situation (VanScriver, 2005).

CASE 7: TOPICS FOR DISCUSSION

- The 2007 annual report *The Condition of Education* (National Center for Education Statistics, 2008) states that 42% of public schoolchildren are racial and ethnic minorities. Currently, 22% of school-age children speak a language other than English at home. Traditional Eurocentric models of teaching may no longer be adequate.
- Because of a shortage of teachers in some areas, the tendency is toward "fast track" teacher preparation programs in which the candidates complete the program in a very short time. This leaves little room to develop pedagogical skills and knowledge, and graduates of these programs often are not well prepared for their career in teaching.
- When it comes to differentiating instruction, some researchers (Tomlinson et al., 1994) found that novice teachers did recognize differences among students but found it difficult to be responsive to those differences (as cited in Gould,

2004). Other factors found to inhibit novice teachers from differentiating instruction included the lack of emphasis put on differentiated instruction by cooperating teachers, principals, college supervisors, and college professors (Gould, 2004). The inferred message here is that differentiated instruction is much talked about but not really valued.

• According to Allen (2003), the research provides limited evidence that courses in pedagogy contribute significantly to effective teaching—courses focused, for example, on how to teach math or science or focused on building core skills such as classroom management skills.

CASE 7: EXPLORING THE ISSUES

1. Open your preferred browser and type in http://www.prenhall.com/teacherprep. This will take you to Merrill's Teacher Prep Web site. Once you are logged in, select the *Video Classroom* tab on the left navigation bar; a list of choices will drop down. Select *General Methods* by clicking on it. Then select *Module 7: Questioning Strategies.* Click on *Video 1: Higher Order Thinking.* In this video, the teacher leads a high school class through a discussion of Nathaniel Hawthorne's *Scarlet Letter.* What techniques does the teacher in this video use that Antoine, the student teacher in the preceding case story, might have incorporated into his own class?

2. On the Teacher Prep Web site, click on *Articles and Readings* on the tab at the left. Once this window opens, click on *Language Arts Methods.* When this window opens, click on *Content Area Reading Methods* and then on *Module 3: Comprehension Strategies.* Click on *Article 3: What Is High Quality Instruction?* The authors of this article, Weiss and Pasley, are presenting information about math and science classroom instruction, but the information is pertinent to all disciplines. After reading the article, review the five questions at the end of the article and discuss them with your peers.

3. One strategy that is useful for activating prior knowledge about a topic is called the *2-Minute Talk.* For this activity, divide into teams of two. Each person on the team has 2 minutes to share with their partner everything they know about a skill, topic, or concept. At the end of 2 minutes, the first person stops talking and the teammate begins talking. It is okay to repeat some of the things already said. Take differentiated instruction as your topic of discussion. At the end of the 2-Minute Talks, present what you know to the class as a whole. How effective was this strategy in activating prior knowledge?

4. Now that you have activated prior knowledge regarding differentiated instruction, write a lesson plan in which you use higher order thinking to discuss a suitable work of children's literature. Make sure you also pay attention to the principles of high quality instruction that you read in item 2.

5. UDL and differentiated instruction are highly compatible. Create a chart that shows the similarities in these two approaches. Create a separate chart that shows the differences between UDL and differentiated instruction. Share both charts with your classmates. Reach consensus as to whether UDL and differentiated instruction are basically the same approach with the same principles and expectations—but with different names.

CASE 8: MR. O'DAY AND TAKING RESPONSIBILITY

Thinking Ahead

As you read this case, reflect on the following:

- Does school have to be fun for significant learning to occur?
- Even preservice teachers have a difficult time taking responsibility for their own learning. How do you get young children to take responsibility?
- What is the difference, if any, between learning that is relevant and learning that is utilitarian?
- What do the conversations John O'Day has both with himself and with his students reveal about his approach to teaching? Do his beliefs and personality traits support diverse learners, or do they hinder learning?

"It was lots of fun last year with Mr. Hanson. That Mr. O'Day is so boring."

"Yeah," came the quick reply. "All we do in class is work. There's never any fun like last year."

John O'Day sat staring absently out the window and playing back these words in his mind. One of his fourth-grade students had said them at the end of the day as they lined up for dismissal. The student had no trouble finding someone to agree with him.

"What can we do but work?" Mr. O'Day thought. "We're almost through October, and everyone is so far behind." He let his thoughts shift to his last year's class. "Those kids were easy," he thought. "They were so willing to take responsibility for their own learning." He thought about his students now and the difficulty he had getting them engaged in lessons. "As a class they're more immature than last year's group," he mused. "And there are a few more kids this year that are fairly new to this country." He smiled to himself as he thought about the work before him. "Half the class doesn't know the difference between a subject and a predicate, and a good many of them are reading below grade level."

Mr. O'Day rested his head in his hands and thought despondently, "There's got to be some way to get kids excited about learning. It doesn't have to be fun necessarily, but it should at least be interesting for them."

Mr. O'Day spent the weekend rereading the learning standards for Grades 2 and 3. He resolved to tackle the deficits in his students' understanding. "I've got to get them thinking and problem solving," he thought, still feeling the sting of the comment made at dismissal. "I don't want them to hate school. I want them to believe it's worth showing up every day."

Mr. O'Day had been relying on an interactive lecture style of instruction so as to quickly cover required course material. Even though he knew it would take more instructional time, he decided to switch to an approach that incorporated more student inquiry and put the responsibility for learning on his students. "It will take more time," he said to himself, "but I need to get these kids involved. I'll just have to be very careful not to skip over any of the necessary content."

On Monday, Mr. O'Day experimented with a science lesson that met both second and third-grade standards. The lesson had to do with the environment and survival of the fittest. Mr. O'Day had all the children in his class pretend they were deer in a hardwood forest. Most of the deer were healthy, but some had injuries, such as a broken leg, loss of eyesight, or other such injuries. To make this more effective, Mr. O'Day blindfolded some students or tied an arm or leg so they couldn't be used. Then he scattered plastic chips along the floor and instructed "the deer" to gather food for the day. Among much laughter, the children crawled along the floor and gathered as many chips as possible. When everyone had returned to their seats, Mr. O'Day asked his students to describe their experiences and to tell the class how many chips each had managed to gather. In return, Mr. O'Day told each student how many chips they would have needed for survival. For example, if one of them collected as many as 30 chips, it was an indication that he or she was strong and healthy enough to survive another year.

A hand shot up. "Mr. O'Day," a student said enthusiastically, "there's lots of things besides food. You could die anyway. What about wolves that chase the deer—or hunters?"

"A very good point," Mr. O'Day replied. "Anyone want to try and answer this question?"

A student near the front of the class quickly shouted out, "Hey, the healthy deer can run faster!"

"Okay, that's good," Mr. O'Day replied. "But how about raising a hand next time?" he added with a smile.

"The first student, without raising his hand either, shot back, "Oh yeah, you can run. But there's still a chance you'll get shot by hunters. Bullets move faster than deer, you know." The class laughed appreciatively.

"Robert is making some good points for us," Mr. O'Day said. "Are there other things we should be considering?"

Several hands went up. Mr. O'Day waited a few seconds for a few more hands to appear and then called on one of his students. "There's really a lot of things, Mr. O'Day," the student said thoughtfully. "Sometimes there's not enough water, or there's too much snow to find food, or you just get too cold. Yeah, lots of stuff really."

"Maybe we can start making a list of what allows some animals to survive and not others," Mr. O'Day said. "Any idea how we might organize our list?"

Students suggested several graphic organizers that could be used. In the end, the class settled on a simple two-column list: one column for factors that increase the possibility of survival and another column for factors that decrease possibilities. "Let's just brainstorm for now," Mr. O'Day said. "Turn around to the people sitting next to you and come up with as many ideas as you can in the next five or six minutes."

Mr. O'Day watched with satisfaction as his students huddled together to work on the assignment. "They're really enjoying this," he thought.

"Hey, Mr. O'Day," one student called out, interrupting his thoughts, "whadda you think we make another chart of the number of us who survive the next year and the number who won't do so good? You know, when we were deer?"

"I think that's a great idea, Sam," Mr. O'Day said happily. He had planned to talk about how what his students were doing now connected to their lesson last week on different types of graphs. But to his delight, one of his students had already made this connection independently.

"You know what, Mr. O'Day?" another student in the same group volunteered. "If we're going to make that chart about when we were deer, we should say what kind of injuries each of us had."

"Why do you think that, Maria?" Mr. O'Day asked, with the intention of getting her to articulate her understandings.

"Ummm—I'm not sure," she replied hesitantly, shrugged her shoulders, and went back to helping with the chart.

Mr. O'Day persisted, hoping that if he asked the right questions he could get Maria to verbalize the understanding behind her own question. "Were you a healthy deer or an injured deer in the game we played, Maria?" he asked gently.

"She had a broken leg, too, Mr. O'Day," Sam chimed in. "Not like me though. I had a broken leg *in back* and a broken leg *in front*." The two children laughed together. "Yeah," Maria said, "you were messed up! I got lots more chips than you!"

"More than my four chips?" Sam retorted. "That's not saying much!" They laughed again.

Mr. O'Day smiled. "So what do you think, Maria? Does this tell you anything about injuries and survival?"

"Better to be able to move at least a little," Maria replied quickly, still smiling. "Yeah," she said more to herself now than to her teacher. "You got to be able to get at least a little food to survive."

Mr. O'Day smiled in acknowledgment before returning to the front of the class to discuss the students' ideas. "This is working even better than I hoped it would," he thought happily.

CASE 8: ISSUES FOR ANALYSIS AND REFLECTION

1. Case 8 is related to the INTASC Standard on Multiple Instructional Strategies. It addresses two key indicators for this standard: The teacher (a) selects and uses multiple teaching and learning strategies (a variety of presentations/explanations) to encourage students in critical thinking and problem solving and (b) ensures different roles in the instructional process (instructor, facilitator, coach, audience) to accommodate content, purpose, and learner needs. Once you have identified the primary issue, problem, or concern in this case, determine what other content knowledge is needed to ensure positive outcomes.
2. What pedagogical knowledge and skills are needed?
3. What must be done to ensure that desired student learning outcomes are obtained, not just for this one lesson but throughout the academic year?

Use the DEEPS Method to analyze this case. Keep in mind the INTASC Standard on Multiple Instructional Strategies and the key indicators listed in item 1.

Determine the primary issue, problem, or concern in this case.

Enumerate the facts that support your belief regarding the primary issue, problem, or concern in the case.

Evaluate the case to find all the possible solutions for resolving the issue, problem, or concern.

Problem solve by thinking critically about each possible solution and accepting or rejecting the solution based on its value in ensuring the professional growth of the teacher in relation to multiple instructional strategies.

Summarize your conclusion/solutions and be prepared to present the best possible solution and your rationale to your professor and colleagues.

CASE 8: WHAT THE RESEARCH SAYS

This case story focused on two indicators that the teacher is effectively using multiple instructional strategies to ensure student learning: (a) the teacher selects and uses multiple teaching and learning strategies (a variety of presentations/explanations) to encourage students in critical thinking and problem solving and (b) the teacher ensures different roles in the instructional process (instructor, facilitator, coach, audience) to accommodate content, purpose, and learner needs. Mr. O'Day, an experienced and effective teacher, is able to shift easily from one instructional strategy to another to meet the needs of learners in his classroom. It is impossible, in fact, to talk about the effective use of instructional strategies without first talking about components of effective teaching. As one researcher writes in reference to finding qualified teachers, "a great curriculum in the hands of a mediocre teacher— even one with a credential—is nothing more than a mediocre curriculum" (Pillsbury, 2005, p. 34).

Too often students see schools as a place to go and receive a credential or diploma verifying their attendance, as opposed to viewing schools as a place where learning takes place. John Dewey, the famous 20th-century philosopher and educator, makes an important distinction in this regard in relation to education and schooling. For Dewey, education takes place constantly, and schooling is only one of the environments where education occurs. Nonetheless, the school provides a unique environment. It is a place where we are able to control the experiences of the individual and provide structured opportunities that lead to desired outcomes (Dewey, 1963). One way for us to ensure desired learning outcomes is to graduate from our schools of education teachers who are highly effective in the classroom, including effective in their ability to use a variety of instructional strategies to meet the needs of diverse learners.

Research related to teaching generally concludes that effective teachers are those who "understand the larger social context in which they are working" (Reeves, 2007, p. 294). Effective teachers, in other words, are those who understand that academic and social achievement do not occur apart from societal structures. Governments, markets, property rights, laws, implicit and tacit practices, and patterns of inequity because of race, gender, religion, sexual orientation, and disability all have a huge impact on what happens in the classroom (p. 294). What this means is that teachers have to be able to successfully implement a variety of instructional strategies to meet the needs of all learners in the classroom. Possessing knowledge is simply not enough; teachers must also have the skills to put knowledge and theory into practice (Grant & Gillette, 2006, p. 297). Besides the dispositions and understanding teachers bring to the classroom, other critical "qualities of effective teachers include the teachers' classroom behavior, subject matter knowledge, time spent on teaching content, classroom management skills, task setting, task content, and, very importantly, pedagogic skill" (Wray, Medwell, Fox, & Poulson, 2000, p. 77).

Over three decades ago, Porter and Brophy (1988) stated that one of the reasons for so much variation in teacher effectiveness may well be related to the number of goals the teacher sees as important. Once the classroom door is closed, teachers generally have a great deal of autonomy to determine how the day will be spent. If teachers decide to spend instructional time as comfortably and as pleasantly as possible for themselves—that is, by not engaging students in meaningful learning that challenges them cognitively—the results will be a compromised curriculum. At the other end of the spectrum may be teachers who are too goal driven. These teachers expect to accomplish more goals than are possible given the time constraints of the typical school day. If too many goals are included in the instructional plan, what is likely to happen is that nothing will be covered thoroughly. Some of the blame for this can be placed on teacher preparation programs. When it comes to ensuring effective teaching and the use of multiple instructional strategies, teacher preparation programs must focus not only on theories of education and lesson and unit planning but also on how to effectively execute those plans (Polk, 2006, p. 28). Much of what these researchers say underlies concerns we struggle with today. The pressure to cover content, engage students in constructing understandings related to content, and to demonstrate student learning through a variety of assessment measures can be overwhelming if the novice teacher is not provided with appropriate mentoring and resources.

Research points to the need for "site-based, on-going, rich teacher collaboration across experience levels" that begin with teacher induction into the profession (Johnson & Kardos, 2002, p. 12). This, however, is all too often exactly what does not happen with new teachers. Even opening-day orientation sessions are, according to one writer, more likely to focus on "an indoctrination to the district, to the union . . . benefits and health care." As one teacher stated, "in terms of what was expected of her as a classroom teacher, the message was *There's your classroom. Here's your book. Good luck* (p. 13). Teachers themselves report that what they want and need is "experienced colleagues who will take their dilemmas seriously, watch them teach and provide feedback, help them develop instructional strategies, model skilled teaching, and share insights about students' work and life" (p. 13).

The transition from emphasizing such isolated skills as moving around the classroom, making eye contact, or showing enthusiasm for subject matter to looking broadly at effective teaching and the use of multiple instructional strategies to meet learner needs is not an easy one. The question can rightfully be asked whether it is or is not possible to teach effective teaching. Current research indicates that not only is it possible but that it is also desirable and essential in order to improve student learning in ways that are equitable for all learners. Silcock (1993), for example, points to an extensive study of the primary English school (ILEA, 1988) in which it was concluded that "consistent, well-structured, challenging teaching, with maximum high-level pupil-teacher interaction ensuring that pupils work industriously, was found to make schools successful" (Silcock, p. 13). Silcock points out rather humorously, however, that this should surprise no one. No one would suggest that teachers should lack content knowledge, be unprepared, uninterested, uncaring, or encourage students to be off task. Yet along with many outstanding teachers, annually we graduate a number of preservice teachers from our teacher preparation programs who lack the knowledge and skills to be effective teachers. The question really is how do we translate what we know about effective teaching into teaching teachers. The answer is that this is not easily done. It is not as simple as revising the curriculum and practices of teacher preparation programs.

Teachers, in fact, encounter a great diversity of personalities and learning styles in their classrooms. Silcock (1993) suggests that providing opportunities to learn might require "particularly sensitive and flexible ways of dealing with the widely different circumstances learners introduce into the classrooms, rather than the consistent use of pedagogical skills" (p. 20). Effectiveness, Silcock explains, depends as much on behaviors of the learner as it does on behaviors of the teacher. And, because human beings are dynamic rather than static creatures, behaviors are constantly changing and developing. As it is often stated in debates over teacher effectiveness and the use of effective instructional strategies, teachers can provide opportunities to make learning possible; students must make learning a reality by putting in the time, effort, and critical thinking for new learning to occur.

Summary of Research

No one would question that teachers have a huge impact on student learning. Effective teachers are described as those who provide opportunities for learning and see instruction as their primary goal. They also understand that the context in which learning occurs has an influence on the achievement of learners. The teacher's ability to set *appropriate* curriculum goals and objectives may be an important factor in teacher effectiveness. Failing to establish high expectations and challenging instruction will likely result in a compromised curriculum. On the other hand, too many goals may result in a lack of depth in which instruction becomes "mentioning without teaching."

Ultimately, the learner has to take responsibility for his or her own learning. The teacher can provide opportunities for learning, but they are of no value if the student does not make the best use of these opportunities to improve knowledge and skills.

CASE 8: TOPICS FOR DISCUSSION

- Online courses are a quick and easy way to obtain credits and are as valuable as attending a class in person.
- When teachers are observed by their supervisors, the supervisor often has a checklist that notes such specifics as making eye contact, walking around the room, allowing wait time after questions, and so on. None of this guarantees that the teacher is effective.
- We graduate a number of preservice teachers from our teacher preparation programs who lack the knowledge and skill to be effective teachers. The question really is *How do we translate what we know about teaching into teaching teachers?*
- "A great curriculum in the hands of a mediocre teacher—even one with a credential—is nothing more than a mediocre curriculum" (Pillsbury, 2005, p. 34).

CASE 8: EXPLORING THE ISSUES

1. Visit an elementary classroom and observe instruction in at least three different subject areas. Take notes as to whether or not the teacher uses probes to get students to give higher level responses or if the teacher is satisfied with lower level responses. Discuss your findings with a group of your peers.
2. Design a lesson plan around this hypothesis: "Adding table salt to water will cause the water to boil at a higher temperature." For your lesson plan, write out what prior knowledge or experience students will have to have to understand this concept. Also, write out the questions you will use to get students to think critically about the hypothesis. Then design your lesson, making sure to include needed experiences for students.
3. Divide into groups of three or four. Discuss concerns you have about teaching a diverse group of students in your classrooms. Once you have a list of concerns, discuss strategies you might use to ensure quality teaching and learning.
4. Open your preferred Web browser to http://www.prenhall.com/teacherprep. This will take you to back to Merrill's Teacher Prep Web site. Once you are logged in, select the *Video Classroom* on the left navigation bar; a list of choices will drop down. Click on *Science Methods*. When this opens, click on *Module 5: Questioning Strategies* and then open *Video 1*. The teacher in this video had students prepare questions related to the lesson and is now recording his students' questions so that they can begin to find answers. As you watch the video, think about the quality of questions the students are asking: *What is the purpose of the dark streak along the back of earthworms? How do worms have babies? How do worms defend themselves? Is it true that worms have two hearts?* Students are obviously interested and engaged in this material. What other strategies do you think the teacher will use to keep students involved at this level? What state or national goals does this lesson meet?
5. Do some research on earthworms and see if you can find answers to the questions asked by children in the video. Then write a lesson plan in which you direct children in your class to find these same answers on their own or in small groups. Be sure to give clear directions as to which resources are needed (library, Internet, specific and age-appropriate information books, etc.).

References

Allen, Michael. (2003). Eight questions on teacher preparation: What does the research say? Education Commission of the States. Retrieved December 17, 2008, from http://www.ecs.org/ecsmain.asp?page=/html/educationIssues/teachingquality/tpreport/index.asp.

Anderson, M. (2004, February). Summer school for teachers. *School Library Journal, 50*(2), 36–37.

Aukerman, M. (2006, October). Who's afraid of the big bad answer? *Educational Leadership, 64*(2). Retrieved January 28, 2007, from http://www.ebscohost.com. CAST. (n.d.). *What is Universal Design for Learning?* Retrieved August 30, 2008, from http://www.cast.org/research/udl/index.html.

Coalition for Psychology in Schools and Education. (2006, August). *Report on the teacher needs survey.* Washington, DC: American Psychological Association, Center for Psychology in Schools and Education. Retrieved January 6, 2009, from http://www.apa.org/ed/cpse/tns_execsummary.pdf.

Dewey, J. (1963). *Experience and education.* New York: Collier Macmillan.

Duffy, G. (1993, January). Rethinking strategy instruction: Four teachers' development and their low achievers' understanding. *Elementary School Journal, 93*(3), 231–247.

Freiburg, J. H. (2002, March). Essential skills for new teachers. *Educational Leadership, 59*(6). Retrieved January 1, 2007, from http://www. ebscohost.com.

Gould, H. (2004, December). *Can novice teachers differentiate instruction? Yes, they can!* Retrieved January 5, 2009, from http://www. newhorizons.org/strategies/differentiated/ gould.htm.

Grant, C. A., & Gillette, M. (2006). A candid talk to teacher educators about effectively preparing teachers who can teach everyone's children. *Journal of Teacher Education, 57*(3), 292–299. Retrieved February 11, 2007, from http://www. ebscohost.com.

Hervey, S. (n.d.). (2006). *Who asks the questions?* [Electronic version]. *Teaching PreK-8: Professional Development and Classroom Activities for Teachers, 37*(1). Retrieved February 10, 2007, from http://www.teachingk-8.com/archives/ articles/who_asks_the_questions_by_sheena_ hervey.html.

ILEA. (1988). Factors influencing primary schools' effectiveness. In M. Clarkson (Ed.), *Emerging issues in primary education.* Sussex, England: The Falmer Press.

Johnson, S. M., & Kardos, S. (2002, March). Keeping new teachers in mind. *Educational Leadership, 59*(6), 12–16.

Kiernan, L. J., & Tomlinson, C. A. (1997). *Why differentiate instruction?* Alexandria, VA: Association for Supervision and Curriculum Development.

Li, N. (2002, Winter). Toward educational equality within the context of school teachers' managing. *Education, 132*(2), 239–242. Retrieved January 30, 2007, from http://www.ebscohost.com.

National Center for Education Statistics. (2008). *The condition of education 2007.* Retrieved December 17, 2008, from http://nces.ed.gov/ pubs2007/2007064.pdf.

Pillsbury, P. (2005, October). Only the best. Training outstanding teachers. *Leadership, 35*(2), 36–38.

Polk, J. (2006, March). Traits of effective teachers. *Arts Education Policy Review, 107*(4), 23–29.

Porter, A. C., & Brophy, J. (1988). Synthesis of research on good teaching: Insights for the work of the Institution of Research on Teaching. *Educational Leadership, 45*(8), 74–85.

Reeves, D. (2007, May). New ways to hire educators. *Educational Leadership, 64*(8), 83–84.

Silcock, P. (1993). Can we teach effective teaching? *Educational Review, 45*(1), 13–20.

Theroux, P. (n.d.). *Differentiating instruction.* Retrieved January 5, 2009, from http://members. shaw.ca/priscillatheroux/differentiating.html.

Tomlinson, C. A., Tomchin, E. M., Callahan, C. M., Adams, C. M., Pizzat-Tinnin, P., Cunningham, C. M., et al. (1994). Practices of preservice teachers related to gifted and other academically diverse learners. *Gifted Child Quarterly, 38*(3), 106–114.

VanScriver, J. H. (2005, March). Motherhood, apple pie, and differentiated instruction. *Phi Delta Kappan, 86*(7), 534–535.

Wray, D., Medwell, J., Fox, R., & Poulson, L. (2000, February). The teaching practices of effective teachers. *Educational Review, 52*(1), 75–84.

5

INTASC Standard 5: Motivation and Management

Description of INTASC Standard 5: *The teacher uses understanding of individual and group motivation and behavior to create a learning environment that encourages positive social interaction, active engagement in learning, and self-motivation.*

KEY INDICATORS FOR STANDARD 5

The Teacher

- encourages clear procedures and expectations that ensure students assume responsibility for themselves and others, work collaboratively and independently, and engage in purposeful learning activities.

- engages students by relating lessons to students' personal interests, allowing students to have choices in their learning, and leading students to ask questions and solve problems that are meaningful to them.

- organizes, allocates, and manages time, space, and activities in a way that is conducive to learning.

- organizes, prepares students for, and monitors independent and group work that allows for full and varied participation of all individuals.

- analyzes classroom environment and interactions and makes adjustments to enhance social relationships, student motivation/engagement, and productive work.

CASE 9: ZERO TOLERANCE AND MOTIVATION

Thinking Ahead

As you read this case, reflect on the following:

- What does the research say about "best practices" for working with children who are at-risk for learning failure?
- How do motivation theories related to extrinsic and intrinsic rewards account for the behavior of the young boy in this case?

- Would the teacher in this case be more likely to make appropriate decisions if she knew more about theories of motivation and discipline models, or is her own sense of caring and compassion sufficient?
- The conversations in this case story hint that the social worker, the teacher, and the principal each have different levels of self-efficacy when it comes to effective classroom management. How can beliefs regarding one's own self-efficacy influence outcomes for the child in this story? Think about this both in short-range and long-range terms.

Karen pressed her eyelids with her fingertips, trying to hold back tears. "Why can't they put him in a foster home or something?" She looked up at Lydia, the school's social worker.

"That's easier said than done," Lydia replied. "And foster care is not always the best solution either. Believe it or not, this is not among the worst case I've seen, even right here at Creekview Elementary. It can be a lot worse. A *lot* worse."

Karen, a fifth-year teacher, didn't want to think about worse cases. This case was cause for enough worry. She flipped through Joey's records. In an attempt to understand her student's academic difficulties, Karen had asked to see Joey's files from the previous year. She was surprised to be handed a thick file containing personal and psychological information, a file that also documented physical and emotional abuse by his mother and stepfather.

The County Child Protection Services Agency had mandated several interventions, including required parenting classes. Whatever his mother and stepfather did at these classes, it seemed to have convinced the county to let them maintain custody and full guardianship, but it was clear that Joey's home life was not conducive to healthy social and emotional development, much less academic achievement. In fact, given his chaotic and abusive family conditions, it seemed miraculous that Joey managed as well as he did in school. A recent behavioral incident with Joey, however, was what caused Karen to seek assistance from Lydia. Lydia was familiar with Joey's family situation and also administered his case file. Karen knew her school was fortunate to have a full-time social worker at her school. In other districts, this often was not the case.

Karen set the thick file labeled "Williams, Joseph" on the corner of Lydia's desk. She couldn't help thinking how peaceful her office seemed compared to the chaos just outside her door. "We move these kids back and forth from one confusing situation to another," she thought and let out a long sigh.

Lydia smiled. "Are you all right?" she asked. "I know it's been a rough week."

Karen swallowed and sat up straight. "I guess I'm still not used to this," she said. "I mean they are still so young, and they face all these problems every day. Sometimes we talk about motivating them to do better in school, but it seems like the whole system is against them."

Lydia nodded. "I know. Some of the kids seem practically heroic at times." She looked up, waiting for Karen to make eye contact. "I know this is a cliché, Karen, but there really are no easy answers."

"I know, I know." Karen replied. "And I do understand the policy. Maybe it helps the school as a whole, but I know it's not going to help Joey."

Karen thanked Lydia for her time and walked out into the hallway. She was immediately thrust into the pandemonium that seemed to characterize Creekview Elementary. Classroom doors burst open and slammed shut. Children shoved and shouted. Teachers' voices could be heard calling "Stop that! Keep your hands to yourself! Come back in here and sit down! Right now! I said right now!" The noise was relentless.

It was exactly this constant disorder that was the main reason the principal had a new assistant principal appointed at Creekview Elementary. The assistant principal, a former military officer who had since earned certification as a school administrator, had the primary task of bringing order to the classrooms and hallways so that motivation and management became routine. As part of his overall plan, the new assistant principal had instituted a zero tolerance policy. He had introduced the new policy at a faculty meeting 4 weeks earlier, and most teachers were enthusiastic supporters of the policy. At the time, Karen had liked the idea, too. Now, when faced with applying this policy to one of her own at-risk students, she was not so sure it was such a good idea. She knocked almost mechanically on a door that had a window recently stenciled with "Mark Gardner, Assistant Principal."

Mark looked up from the papers on his desk and signaled for Karen to come in. "Hey, Karen. How are you?" Despite his short time on the job, Mark had impressed everyone by learning the names of the whole faculty, every staff member, and almost all the students. Creekview Elementary had nearly 400 students in the building, so this was no small accomplishment.

Karen slid into one of the three chairs that faced Mark's desk. She smiled at the symbolism of the three chairs. "Meetings," she thought. "Meetings that usually include a student, a parent, and a teacher." This time it was just her trying to avoid needing the three chairs. "I'm fine, Mark," she said. "How are things going with you?"

Mark laughed out loud. "You're stalling," he said, still laughing. "I know you're here about Joey." Mark was right. He had developed a reputation for uncompromising application of discipline policies, and Karen was still trying to find a way to save Joey from suspension. Joey's behavior had been unacceptable all year, but lately it had worsened. He had pinched Sarah twice on Monday, thrown a pencil at Ahmed this morning, and this afternoon had pulled a chair out from under Jessie. In addition, Jessie had injured his foot in the sudden fall, and the nurse had to send him home with a note that it was probably just sprained but a doctor should be consulted. Joey had been sent to the "ice room," a supervised room that was used for students who needed a time-out period. It had earned its name from students who said you go there to "chill out." Karen knew that unless she could provide some very good reason not to suspend Joey, he was going to end up with a 3-day suspension.

None of these recent incidents painted a complete picture of Joey, however. He had a sparkling personality, a good sense of humor, and natural leadership qualities. His classmates constantly sought him out to participate in games and to be part of their team in group discussion. Although he was only 7 years old, he had advanced skills in the use of computer technology. Karen knew he didn't have a computer at home so wasn't sure how he acquired these skills, but it was always Joey who quickly fixed a classroom computer that didn't seem to be working, and he was the one who seemed to know all the latest high-tech computer games. For all his problems,

Joey also stood out among the rest of the second-grade students because of his accomplishments. Karen decided to plead her case.

"What happened today," she began, "is not all there is to Joey."

"It's what there is to Joey today," Mark retorted. "I know how much you care about Joey, but letting him get away with that kind of behavior is not helping him. He's growing up, and he has to learn to follow rules or someone will get hurt more than Jessie did this afternoon."

"You know what his home is like," Karen said. "Home is not a safe place for Joey."

"It seems like school is not a safe place either when Joey is here," Mark answered. "You want Joey to settle down and do consistently better in school. How is that going to happen if you let him get away with the kind of behavior he's been displaying all week."

"And how does sending him home for three days help him do better?" Karen answered hotly. Mark leaned back in his chair. "Okay," he said. "I've laid out a plan for this school. If you have a better plan, I'm all ears. What's your plan?"

Karen felt the tears welling up in her eyes again. What *was* her plan to help Joey and other kids like him? All she could think about at this point was that sending Joey home for 3 days to abusive parents was the worse thing that could happen to him. Mark sat quietly, waiting for Karen's response.

CASE 9: ISSUES FOR ANALYSIS AND REFLECTION

1. Case 9 is related to the INTASC Standard for Motivation and Management and to the following two key indicators for this standard: The teacher (a) encourages clear procedures and expectations that ensure students assume responsibility for themselves and others, work collaboratively and independently, and engage in purposeful learning activities and (b) analyzes the classroom environment and interactions and makes adjustments to enhance social relationships, student motivation/engagement, and productive work. Once you have identified the primary issue, problem, or concern in this case, determine what other content knowledge is needed to ensure positive outcomes.
2. What pedagogical knowledge and skills are needed?
3. What must be done to ensure that desired learning outcomes are obtained?

Use the DEEPS Method to analyze this case. Keep in mind the INTASC Standard for Motivation and Management and the key indicators listed in item 1.

Determine the primary issue, problem, or concern in this case.

Enumerate the facts that support your belief regarding the primary issue, problem, or concern in the case.

Evaluate the case to find all the possible solutions for resolving the issue, problem, or concern.

Problem solve by thinking critically about each possible solution and accepting or rejecting the solution based on its value in ensuring the professional growth of the teacher in relation to motivation and management.

Summarize your conclusion/solutions and be prepared to present the best possible solution and your rationale to your professor and colleagues.

CASE 9: WHAT THE RESEARCH SAYS

The preceding case story has an interesting focus on concerns related to zero tolerance policy in schools. On the one hand, the teacher in this case is faced with the dilemma of reporting one of her students for various behavioral infractions and knowing that this will result in rigid enforcement of the school's zero tolerance policy and the student's suspension. On the other hand, the teacher can continue to try to work with the student and encourage appropriate behavior. It is a dilemma that most teachers will have to face at some point in their careers.

Research on zero tolerance policies is varied, with some research supporting at least the spirit of such policies and others claiming the policies are detrimental and do nothing to improve student behavior. *Zero tolerance* basically is a disciplinary policy in which incidents involving weapons or drug and alcohol possession, fighting, swearing, threats, or other forms of disruptive behavior result in the enforcement of "zero tolerance" policy—that is, anyone involved in the behavioral incident is punished, not uncommonly by suspension or expulsion from the school (Skiba & Knesling, 2001).

This policy is an understandable reaction to the need to maintain safe classrooms while simultaneously teaching all children. Teachers are under considerable pressure to meet the needs of diverse student populations, ensure learning, prepare students for the high stakes testing so common today, and attend to the affective side of learning as well (Baker, 2005). Instituting a zero tolerance policy, although it may unfairly target some students for minor infractions, is believed by some teachers to at least decrease the number of serious offenses in schools. To bring more balance to this policy, however, some research calls for revised approaches in which policies are clearly explained, due process is ensured, alternative education is available if the student is suspended from school, and the impact of zero tolerance policies on improving the school climate are periodically evaluated (p. 62). The fear is that without this more balanced approach, zero tolerance will disproportionately target racial minorities and low income students. The research on who gets suspended or expelled as a result of zero tolerance policy, in fact, shows this to be true (Baker).

A major concern with zero tolerance policy is its rigidity. As with the young boy in this case story, extenuating circumstances can be relevant when it comes to wrongdoing. As well, the degree of wrongdoing should also be considered when determining the consequences for behavior. One researcher (Kajs, 2006) suggests that school administrators should take into consideration factors such as the student's age and grade level, any special considerations such as disability or recent traumatizing events, the seriousness of the offence, circumstances of the offense (was it intentional or accidental), the student's prior history of disruptive incidents, the student's socioemotional development, and the overall impact of the behavior on the school learning environment (p. 23). Rather than applying a one-size-fits-all policy across the board, applications of fairness and consistency should be the priority.

Interestingly, in spite of the controversies surrounding zero tolerance policy, little evidence seems to support its benefits. The literature is replete with examples of this policy being applied in what seem almost foolish circumstances. One story tells of a 5-year-old boy being suspended from school for having a 5-inch plastic axe attached to his city fireman Halloween costume. In another news report, a young girl had a lightweight 10-inch jewelry chain attaching a charm to her wallet; the school ruled that chains are considered weapons, and the girl was suspended. In another case, a teenage boy was suspended for having a plastic lunch knife in his backpack (Skiba & Knesling, 2001). In each of these incidents, the intention was to send a clear message that inappropriate behavior of any kind will not be tolerated. In all these cases, however, the incidents were minor and would not on their own have a negative impact on the learning environment, and they do take up a good deal of time and resources that might better be spent in other endeavors. As one researcher wrote, "targeting both minor and major disciplinary events equally will, almost by definition, result in the punishment of a small number of serious infractions and a much larger percentage of relatively minor misbehavior" (Skiba & Knesling, 2001, p. 26). Skiba and Knesling do concede that zero tolerance policies—even if applied equally to all students regardless of the degree of infraction—might be of value if they could be shown to improve school behavior and decrease incidents of misbehavior. Without such evidence, zero tolerance is not justified. According to Skiba and Knesling, "there is yet to be a credible demonstration that zero tolerance has made a significant contribution to school safety or to improved student behavior . . . faced with an almost complete lack of evidence that zero tolerance is among the strategies capable of accomplishing that objective, one can only hope for the development and application of more effective, less intrusive alternatives for preserving the safety of our nation's schools (p. 38).

The teacher's own feelings of self-efficacy appear to be a factor when it comes to using a variety of approaches to ensure a positive classroom climate. In one study (Baker, 2005), 345 teachers reported their feelings of self-efficacy regarding their classroom management skills. They were also asked to self-report their perceptions of their ability to implement a variety of management skills, depending on learner needs. Approximately half the teachers had 15 or more years of experience in the classroom and about 20% of the teachers had 5 or fewer years of experience. Generally speaking, all the teachers in the survey were comfortable establishing appropriate rules for students and relying on their colleagues for advice and help when needed. When challenged by difficult or defiant students, however, teachers reported that they felt less confident. Baker concluded that teacher preparation programs must pay more attention to training preservice teachers in the use of meaningful disciplinary techniques. Once in the schools, all teachers should be presented with opportunities to upgrade their skills. Administrative support in the form of external validation of the teacher's efforts and guidance is also essential. According to this researcher, all teachers are far more likely to deal positively with challenging situations when their efforts are supported and appreciated.

One promising technique related to classroom management comes from William Glasser, author of *Reality Therapy* and *Control Theory in the Classroom*. Glasser notes that most behavioral changes that occur in schools are short-term changes. Once the stimulus for behavior is withdrawn, the child reverts back to his or her previous behavior. This, according to Glasser, is because motivation must come from within and not be a result of external forces and policies, such as the zero tolerance policy (Glasser, 1986, p. 13). Glasser explains further that it is human nature to do what brings us satisfaction. Even if students have problems outside of school, live in poverty, or are otherwise in an unhappy or misfortunate life situation, they will do well in school if they find it satisfying and *internally* rewarding to do so (p. 21).

Glasser, in other words, would not be as concerned as the teacher in this story with the history of the boy in question. He would be much more focused on his current school placement.

Marshall, Weisner, and Cebula (2004) support this approach. These researchers state that the only way to promote responsible behavior is by motivating students internally. External rewards and punishments always carry with them the added message that good behavior on its own is not sufficient; it has to have some external acknowledgment added to be of any value. Glasser's reality therapy, on the other hand, holds individuals (both students and teachers) responsible for their own actions. Although behavior may be influenced by past experiences, it is the present behavior that is a concern. Marshall, Weisner, and Cebula (2004) also note that all behavioral problems are relationship oriented. If the student does not feel valued and psychologically and emotionally safe in the classroom, then learning is impeded (p. 26). Along these same lines, another researcher notes that the problems with policies such as zero tolerance is that the focus is on the negative side of behavior: what the child did not do, rather than what the child can do. This researcher (Rubin, 2005) also stresses the need for a strong teacher–student bond in which the student feels valued as a member of the class. It is up to the teacher, Rubin writes, to create an effective teacher–learner environment in which children understand the impact of their behavior on one another and on the classroom as a whole.

With this in mind, Rubin lists several pitfalls of one-size-fits-all approaches (such as zero tolerance policy) when it comes to classroom management:

1. Viewing misconduct as an opportunity to do something to a student and or to his or her family rather than as an opportunity to engage in relationship-building, problem solving, skill-development, and support (as cited in Jones & Jones, 1998; Kohn, 1996; and Marshall, 2003).
2. Establishing school-wide policies and procedures that heavily invest precious human and material resources on reactions and interventions rather than on pro-action and prevention.
3. Practicing strategies that many times are punitive and disrespectful, that rely on taking something away while employing humiliations and exclusion.
4. Fostering an obedience-oriented ethos that stresses arbitrarily developed and adopted rules of behavior that are fueled by fear and reward and teach students to be responsive to the most persuasive voice (the antithesis of critical and creative thinking) (Rubin, 2005, p. 243).

In brief, the opportunity to engage in self-reflection and self-evaluation should be part of any disciplinary system. Zero tolerance is a short-term fix that does not ensure appropriate behavior outside of this structure.

Summary of Research

Zero tolerance policy has been established in many schools to give a clear message that inappropriate behavior of any kind will not be tolerated. This policy, however, has resulted in suspensions and expulsions from schools for students who have committed no infraction at all or only minor infractions. Some researchers believe that zero tolerance policy places far too much emphasis on negative behavior and takes time away from building effective teacher–learner environments that value only learners and in which students feel emotionally and psychologically secure. In addition, no conclusive research shows that schools have a decrease in disruptive behavior as a result of zero tolerance policy.

It has been suggested that teacher preparation programs can do much more to train preservice teachers in effective classroom management techniques. Ongoing opportunities to upgrade knowledge and skills also should be available to teachers once they begin their careers.

CASE 9: TOPICS FOR DISCUSSION

- Even if students have problems outside of school, live in poverty, or are otherwise in an unhappy or misfortunate life situations, they will do well in school if they find it satisfying and *internally* rewarding to do so (Glasser, 1986, p. 21).
- Zero tolerance is an ineffective method of reducing drug and alcohol abuse among middle school children. If they want to use drugs or alcohol, they will.
- Students of color, specifically African American students, tend to be disproportionately affected in a negative way when schools implement zero tolerance policies.
- When it comes to disruptive behavior in the classroom, whether intended or not, the teacher and not the chief school administrator should have the final say in how the discipline case is handled.

CASE 9: EXPLORING THE ISSUES

1. Make a list of 10 behaviors that you would not tolerate in your own classroom. When you are finished, prioritize behavioral concerns from most serious to least serious. Share your list with three or four other students and see if you can come to agreement on one list that is prioritized from most serious to least serious behaviors. Discuss why it is difficult to agree on this.

2. Open your preferred Web browser to http://www.prenhall.com/teacherprep. This will take you to Merrill's Teacher Prep Web site. Once you are logged in, click on *Articles and Readings.* When this opens, click on *Module 7: Maintaining Appropriate Student Behavior.* When this opens, click on *Article 3: The Caring Classroom's Edge* by Lewis, Schaps, and Watson. After reading the article, answer the four questions at the bottom of the page. How might the authors' ideas have helped the teacher in this case story to make a decision?

3. Pretend that you are the teacher of a second-grade inclusive class in which three of your students have serious emotional and behavioral disorders. Design a lesson plan that requires hands-on activity. Provide direction in your lesson plan as to how to deal with the disruptive behaviors of these three students (should they occur) while still ensuring that content is covered.

4. Read the article on student rewards entitled *Punished by Rewards? A Conversation with Alfie Kohn,* which can be found at http://www.alfiekohn.org/teaching/pdf/Punished%20by%20Rewards.pdf. After reading this article, write a response to it. State in your response your reasons for agreeing or disagreeing with the author.

5. Open your Web browser to http://www.prenhall.com/teacherprep. This will take you to Merrill's Teacher Prep Web site. This time, click on *Video Classroom* and go to *Classroom Management*. Click on *Module 5: Maintaining Appropriate Student Behavior*. Watch *Video 1: Empowering Students to Resolve Conflicts*. After watching this video, think again about the article on the caring classroom (item 2). How closely does this teacher's method of resolving conflict resemble principles of the caring classroom? Write down at least two questions or concerns you have about this method and then discuss them with your peers.

CASE 10: THE ROLE OF MENTORS IN MOTIVATION AND MANAGEMENT

Thinking Ahead

As you read this case, reflect on the following:

- What should the role of a mentor be in teacher induction programs?
- How do motivation theories related to extrinsic and intrinsic rewards account for the behavior of both teachers in this case?
- How could both teachers change their behavior to benefit more from this mentoring relationship?

"It's not supposed to be this way," Sara thought as she sat glumly at her desk in Room 104 of Franklin Middle School. It was late Tuesday afternoon. The students were long gone. Sara stared absently out of her classroom window at the falling rain, which she was certain was turning to sleet.

Sara was waiting for the arrival of her mentor, a colleague assigned by district contract to work on a confidential basis with first-year teachers. The contract required Sara and her mentor to meet once a month, and this was the third meeting of the school year. Sara had arrived 15 minutes early. "If nothing else," she thought, "at least I'm on time and ready."

To say that Sara had a Type A personality would be an understatement. She had graduated from her teachers college program the previous spring with a degree in sociology and certification as an elementary teacher. She was one of a few students in her class who graduated summa cum laude. Competition for teaching positions was stiff in the county in which she lived, but Sara had excellent interview skills and a remarkably well-developed portfolio. The brief teaching segment she did for the interview team was flawless. She was hired immediately. The rumor after Sara left the room was that the principal initiated the post-interview discussion by simply saying, "Wow!"

After being hired, Sara spent the next 2 months preparing for her Grade 3 class. She familiarized herself with class texts and trade books, reviewed the newly aligned primary school curriculum, purchased supplemental materials, and planned elaborately detailed lessons and units that aligned perfectly with state and national standards. When the school year finally began, Sara was ready—or so she thought.

As the exciting early days of school turned into weeks, Sara realized her students were becoming increasingly disruptive. She was having a difficult time getting their attention. The transitions from one activity to another seemed to take longer and longer, and a growing number of students appeared to be disengaged from class work, although they appeared to be thriving socially. The poor behavior of her class was most evident when Sara took her students to a public place, such as the auditorium for an assembly or the lunchroom or even the playground. When compared to classes of her colleagues, Sara's students were clearly the most poorly behaved. It was not uncommon for another teacher to step in quickly and reprimand her students if they were misbehaving. Sara took this as a sign that her colleagues had already lost confidence in her.

Sara thought this over now with some bitterness. She had been told repeatedly in her teacher preparation program that good planning was a key element of good classroom management. If lessons were well planned, students would be engaged and discipline problems would be minimized. "But my lessons *are* well planned," she thought, "and I still have discipline problems. Teaching is not what I thought it would be." She shifted in her chair, dreading the meeting with her mentor.

Sara's mentor was another primary-level teacher, a 15-year veteran named Marilyn who just at that moment appeared in the doorway.

"Sorry I'm late," Marilyn said. "I had to return a parent phone call, and it lasted longer than I thought. How's it goin'?"

Sara had planned to be calm and positive, but the question struck a chord and Sara found herself recounting all that had happened the past week, including the numerous discipline problems in her class.

"It sounds like you're having a tough time," Marilyn replied when Sara finally stopped speaking. "Let me ask a question. Do you have a written management plan for your class?"

Sara brightened. "Sure," she said. "It's right here." She pulled a 12-page plan from the "Discipline" section of the portfolio she had with her.

Marilyn skimmed over the plan. "Okay," she said. "It's here in your portfolio, but have your students seen this plan?"

Sara wasn't sure how to answer. She flipped through the rules and discipline procedures that she had written. Finally, she looked up and answered, "No, but I've told them what I expect from them. A plan like this is not really written for students, especially first-grade students." Sara hesitated, not sure of whether she should defend herself or just wait for advice.

Marilyn jumped in right away and said, "Good classroom management is not just something on paper, Sara. It's not a function of a great personality either."

"I know, I know," Sara stammered.

Marilyn ignored Sara's discomfort and continued. "From my experience, good classroom management consists of two parts: clear rules and procedures and, second, a well-thought out discipline approach if those rules and procedures are violated."

"I know what you're saying," Sara answered, " but I don't want my class to just be about rules. I want my students to have fun learning."

Marilyn sighed. "Well, let's talk about the problem yesterday with your silent reading."

"You mean when we were having the daily SSR—you know, the Sustained Silent Reading period. I guess that was a disaster. I just couldn't get my students to read quietly."

"So how did you handle it?" Marilyn asked.

"I really want them to get in the habit of reading quietly," Sara said, so after telling them a couple of times what was expected, I thought offering an incentive would be a good idea. I told them if they were quiet for the SSR, we would have a pizza party on Friday."

"Did it work?" Marilyn asked. "Was everyone quiet?

"Mostly they were," Sara said enthusiastically. "There were a few—maybe just four or five—who just couldn't stay focused, though. They kept whispering to each other every few minutes." Sara paused for a second and then said, "I would give them the 'teacher look,' you know—that sort of stern look that they had better stop." Sara smiled. "But it only worked for a minute or so, and then they were right back whispering."

"And when Friday came?" Marilyn asked. "You had the pizza party or not?"

"No, we had the party," Sara replied at once. "Most of my students did what they were asked. It was only those four or five who didn't."

Marilyn looked directly at Sara. "Listen, Sara," she said, "as your mentor I have to tell you that other teachers have commented on how poorly your class behaves. You must get a grip on this whole classroom management and student discipline thing. The two concepts are not interchangeable."

"I'm lost," Sara said, now close to tears again. "What do you mean they're not interchangeable?"

"Let's begin with procedures and expectations," Marilyn said. "What are your class rules for collecting homework? Or for moving as a class down the corridor?"

"I tell them to keep their hands to themselves," Sara replied promptly, "and to treat others the way they want to be treated."

"That's at least a start," said Marilyn, "but there's more to classroom management than that. Unless you have a clear set of procedures and then *practice* those procedures in your class, your students are going to become disruptive. They're only eight years old, Sara."

"Okay," Sara said. "I can develop a set of procedures."

"But that's not all," Marilyn answered. "Effective classroom management will minimize discipline problems, but it won't eliminate them altogether. Classroom management is *your* responsibility. Discipline involves *students'* behavior and the consequences connected to that behavior."

Sara could feel the tears welling up in her eyes as Marilyn continued talking. "No matter how good your classroom management plan is, Sara, you will still have discipline problems. It's part of the job. All teachers have discipline problems every day, and you really need to develop some skills in this area." Marilyn paused to give Sara a chance to reply. Sara wanted to reply, but she was too busy fighting back tears.

"Let's meet again next Tuesday," Marilyn said, a little more gently. "We have some work to do. I'll see you then, okay?"

After Marilyn left the room, Sara ran her hands over her management plan and thought about the effort she had put into developing it. "Was it all a waste of time?" she wondered. "Is it possible I chose the wrong profession?"

CASE 10: ISSUES FOR ANALYSIS AND REFLECTION

1. Case 10 is related to the INTASC Standard for Motivation and Management and to the following four key indicators for this standard: The teacher (a) engages students by relating lessons to students' personal interests, allowing

students to have choices in their learning and leading students to ask questions and solve problems that are meaningful to them; (b) organizes, allocates, and manages time, space, and activities in a way that is conducive to learning; (c) organizes, prepares students for, and monitors independent and group work that allows for full and varied participation of all individuals; and (d) analyzes classroom environment and interactions and makes adjustments to enhance social relationships, student motivation/engagement, and productive work. Once you have identified the primary issue, problem, or concern in this case, determine what other content knowledge is needed by the teacher(s) to ensure positive outcomes.

2. What pedagogical knowledge and skills are needed?
3. What must be done to ensure that desired student learning outcomes are obtained?

Use the DEEPS Method to analyze this case. Keep in mind the INTASC Standard for Motivation and Management and the key indicators listed in item 1.

Determine the primary issue, problem, or concern in this case.

Enumerate the facts that support your belief regarding the primary issue, problem, or concern in the case.

Evaluate the case to find all the possible solutions for resolving the issue, problem, or concern.

Problem solve by thinking critically about each possible solution and accepting or rejecting the solution based on its value in ensuring the professional growth of the teacher in relation to motivation and management.

Summarize your conclusion/solutions and be prepared to present the best possible solution and your rationale to your professor and colleagues.

CASE 10: WHAT THE RESEARCH SAYS

This case story raises the question of what the role of a mentor is in ensuring a smooth induction into the profession of teaching. More important for this standard is the role of mentorship in addressing four of the key indicators related to motivation and management:

- Encouraging clear procedures and expectations that ensure students assume responsibility for themselves and others, work collaboratively and independently, and engage in purposeful learning activities
- Engaging students by relating lessons to students' personal interests, allowing students to have choices in their learning, and leading students to ask questions and solve problems that are meaningful to them
- Organizing, allocating, and managing time, space, and activities in a way that is conducive to learning
- Organizing, preparing students for, and monitoring independent and group work that allows for full and varied participation of all individuals

The literature related to this topic brings into question whether or not mentors, although well intentioned, are sufficiently trained to provide the kind of mentorship that novice teachers need to be successful. According to Smith (2005), for example, teacher preparation programs last a relatively short time, often only a year. Although preservice teachers may excel while in the program, this short time is not enough to allow for the testing of beliefs in practice. Preservice teachers eventually enter the field and have to come to terms with the realities of practice, and this may cause, as in this case story, cognitive dissonance and distress. Smith contends that mentors of novice teachers must value, support, and encourage a wide repertoire of skills to encourage a sense of self-efficacy in these new teachers. Mentors also must provide positive support that has a goal of reducing fear of failure. The desire of most novice teachers, according to this researcher, is to be highly qualified and respected professionals in their chosen career. The actualizing of this is dependent, of course, upon accomplishments and the avoidance of failure (p. 210). The novice teacher in this case story feels a strong sense of failure, along with confusion over why all she had learned in her teacher preparation program and had been lavishly praised for mastering is now seemingly not valued at all. The case story leaves us with two important questions: (a) What can the mentor do to promote the professional growth of this new teacher and help her with motivation and management concerns? (b) What can the novice teacher do herself to further develop her skills and understanding when it comes to motivation and management?

One of the growing concerns about mentorship programs for novice teachers is the focus of mentoring activities. In an analysis of what actually happens in a mentorship program, for example, researchers found that more than two thirds of the conversations between mentors and novice teachers consisted of the mentor reiterating observable events, such as a student being disruptive, students not raising their hands before talking, and so on. Although positive and encouraging in intention, this kind of reiteration of the obvious by mentors did little to enhance the professional knowledge of the novice teacher (Edwards & Protheroe, 2004, p. 185). Research suggests strongly that mentors must do more than focus on isolated details or on observations of whether or not students complete various tasks and the attitudes with which they complete these tasks. What mentors must do is help novice teachers to develop the capacity to "interpret a learner's abilities and needs [and recognize] how to use the resources available to respond to their needs and connect the learner to the curriculum" (p. 194). This requires a shift from the traditional role of the mentor as someone who observes student task completion and reports this information back to the novice teacher. The novice teacher in this case story is struggling with motivating her students and with managing classroom behaviors. The mentor, although no doubt well intentioned, merely points out what the teacher already knows: that she is doing poorly in both of these areas.

Other research shows that purposeful mentoring designed to enhance professional knowledge and skills during the first year of practice may be the key factor in ensuring teacher quality and teacher retention. Good mentors are those who help novice teachers to gain perspective; implement effective strategies related to instruction, motivation, and classroom management; avoid isolation; and manage the workload (Fluckinger, McGlamery, & Edick, 2006, p. 9). Of great importance, good mentors help novice teachers to see that these are not isolated skills and that one is integral to the other. Skill in classroom management does not exist apart from general effective teaching. Mentors must help novice teachers to make connections that will help them "to make increasingly informed interpretations of pupils, curricula, and classrooms" and "to continuously extend their repertoire of appropriate responses" (Edwards & Protheroe, 2004, p. 186). Novice teachers themselves report that they all enter the classroom with fears that motivating their students and maintaining classroom order and discipline will be problematic. They report that among characteristics they valued most in their mentors were all of the following: nonjudgmental sharing of how they handled similar problems related to motivation and management, encouraging risk taking, modeling effective strategies, team teaching with them to more effectively model strategies, sharing and modeling best practices such as asking reflective questions, modeling effective instruction, and providing additional curriculum resources. Novice teachers also valued mentors who provided opportunities to get support and feedback from other professionals in their teaching area. All this, according to the novice teachers, helped them to develop perspectives on quality teaching and on the interconnectedness of all aspects of quality teaching, including motivation and management (Fluckinger, McGlamery, & Edick, 2006; Jackson, 2004). The mentor in this case story, on the other hand, uses criticism as her primary method of interaction, and it is easy to see that the novice teacher in the story already is experiencing a sense of failure to the extent that she is questioning her career choice.

Novice teachers eventually must move from dependency on a mentor to independent behavior and the ability to rely on their own judgments when making decisions about students and curriculum (Smith, 2005). One researcher suggests that the pressures of teaching often override the time needed for self-reflection to bring one to this stage. All teachers are pressured by the demands of standardized testing, budget constraints, time to cover material, the need for remediation, meeting the needs of individual learners, and so on. Early in their careers, however, teachers must be provided with, and take advantage of, multiple opportunities to collectively explore personal and professional beliefs and how these not only impact teaching but also impact the teacher's passion and purpose for choosing teaching as a career (Intrator & Kunzman, 2006). To develop the capacity to ensure student learning and minimal classroom discipline problems, in other words, the novice teacher in this case story must explore opportunities outside the mentor relationship. All teachers need a safety net in which they can discuss their successes and failures without fear of judgment. By joining with other experienced and inexperienced teachers, novice teachers have an opportunity to "share insights based on real world experiences and demonstrate a deeper understanding of the enormous responsibilities" in the profession of teaching (Jackson, 2004, p. 17). Mary Bafumo, a program director for the statewide Council for Educational Change in Florida, encourages this type of reflective activity. Bafumo states that it is easy to develop routines and fail to analyze whether or not they are accomplishing the desired student learning outcomes. Bafumo gives the example of learning the rhythm of a song incorrectly and then singing it over and over until the pattern becomes ingrained. It is very difficult to relearn the song correctly. It is much easier to repeat the pattern already learned. It is important for teachers to be alert to the possibility of developing instructional routines that are not effective. When it comes to the motivation and management of students, reflection is necessary, and this reflection includes paying attention to what is working in classrooms. In the preceding case story, the novice teacher relies on earlier learning, and it is difficult for her to break the pattern of procedures that earned her praise as a student. By interacting with other teachers and discussing her concerns and successes, she can begin to evaluate her "skill in instructional practice, classroom management, and classroom curriculum" and then take steps to grow in the direction needed (Bafumo, 2006, p. 12).

One school has designed a course in which preservice teachers are given early induction into this type of self-reflection and group interaction. Preservice teachers spend the morning in a school observing and then return to their classrooms to discuss their observations. Over a 4-week period they move from merely observing to assisting individual students with course work. They then return to their own college classroom to discuss problems they had with motivation and management and obtaining desired learning outcomes. The professors in this course encourage the preservice teachers to reflect on and share with each other what was and was not effective in the schools they visited. By the time these preservice teachers enter their full student teaching practicum, they have already developed skills in self-reflection and have learned to profit from the experiences and insights of their colleagues (Jackson, 2005). Some evidence indicates, nonetheless, that novice teachers often are overly concerned with appearing successful at their new job of teaching. Concerns such as self-image, classroom management issues, mastering materials for instruction, and being able to follow school-related procedures (a lack of knowledge of which often gives the appearance of weak management skills) can take up much time for a novice teacher. It is only after the first 2 or 3 years of teaching that new teachers shift their focus from themselves to a concern with student learning outcomes. What is encouraging is that evidence also indicates that support from properly trained mentors and opportunities to build networks with other experienced and inexperienced teachers can have a strong impact on the development of understandings related to instructional strategies, classroom management, and curriculum (Athanses & Achinstein, 2003, p. 1486).

Summary of Research

Mentors of novice teachers may lack sufficient training to encourage the development of professional growth in their mentees. It is important for mentors to help novice teachers develop self-efficacy and to help them make increasingly informed decisions about the practice of teaching.

Novice teachers must also move from dependence on a mentor to a wider circle of support that includes colleagues and other professionals. Sharing failures, accomplishments, and general concerns provides an opportunity to better understand the interrelated demands of instruction, classroom management, and curriculum.

CASE 10: TOPICS FOR DISCUSSION

- It is questionable whether teacher-mentors are sufficiently trained to provide the kind of mentorship that novice teachers need to be successful.
- Although a body of literature relates to mentoring novice teachers, the reality is that teachers are on their own from the time they enter their teacher training programs until they retire from their teaching career.
- It is time for schools to move from a master teacher to teacher hierarchical model to more of a teacher to teacher collaborative model. The hierarchical

model is demotivating, whereas a collaborative model encourages, supports, and excites commitment to the profession of teaching.
- To ensure that teachers are well prepared, teacher preparation programs should last a minimum of 2 years followed by 2 years of supervised internship.

CASE 10: EXPLORING THE ISSUES

1. Imagine yourself as a novice teacher. Describe the characteristics you would want to have in a mentor during your first year of teaching. In what areas would you hope to have help?
2. Teachers are often told they must provide a supportive environment to help their students to learn. What are the characteristics of a supportive environment for students? How do these characteristics vary from a supportive environment for teachers? Interview two teachers at two different grade levels to ascertain what they believe to be supportive or not supportive in the schools in which they work.
3. Open your Web browser to http://www.prenhall.com/teacherprep. This will take you to Merrill's Teacher Prep Web site. Once you are logged in, click on *Strategies and Lessons*. When this opens, click *on Classroom Management* and then on *Module 5: Managing Problem Behaviors*. When this window opens, click on *Beane's 8 Steps to Conflict Resolution*. After reading these steps, write a simulation in which the person acting as the teacher goes through each of these steps to resolve conflict. Act out the simulation in front of your classmates and determine whether or not they believe the "teacher's" actions are realistic for the classroom.
4. Open your Web browser again to http://www.prenhall.com/teacherprep, and this time go to *Video Classroom*. Click on *Educational Psychology* and then on *Module 10: Motivation*. Watch *Video 2: Discussion of the Properties of Air*. After watching this video, break into groups of three to five and discuss what characteristics of the teacher motivated the students to learn and what characteristics may have suppressed motivation.
5. Have each person in your group share a school incident in which they were highly motivated to master some content. Discuss the factors that led to this motivation.

References

Athanses, S., & Achinstein, B. (2003, October). Focusing new teachers on individual and low-performing students: The centrality of formative assessment in the mentor's repertoire of practice. *Teachers' College Record, 105*(8), 1486–1520.

Bafumo, M. E. (2006, October). Changing teaching practices. *Teaching Pre K-8, 37*(2), 10–12.

Baker, P. H. (2005, Summer). Managing student behavior: How ready are teachers to meet the challenge. *American Secondary School, 33*(3), 51–64.

Edwards, A., & Protheroe, L. (2004, June). Teaching by proxy: Understanding how mentors are positioned in partnerships. *Oxford Review of Education, 30*(2), 215–225.

Fluckinger, J., McGlamery, S. & Edick, N. (2006, Spring). Mentoring teachers' stories: Caring mentors help teachers stick with teaching and develop expertise. *Delta Kappa Gamma Bulletin, 72*(3), 8–13.

Glasser, W. (1986). *Control theory in the classroom.* New York: Harper & Row.

Intrator, S., & Kunzman, R. (2006, March). Starting with the soul. *Educational Leadership, 63*(6), 38–42.

Jackson, D. H. (2004, Winter). Nurturing future teachers. *Delta Kappa Gamma Bulletin, 70*(2), 15–17.

Jones, F. V., & Jones, L. S. (1998). *Comprehensive classroom management: Creating communities of support and solving problems.* Boston: Allyn & Bacon.

Kajs, L. T. (2006, June). Reforming the discipline management process in schools: An alternative approach to zero tolerance. *Educational Research Quarterly, 29*(4), 16–27.

Kohn, A. (1996). *Beyond discipline: From compliance to community.* Alexandria, VA: Association for Supervision and Curriculum Development.

Marshall, M. (2002). *Discipline without stress, punishments or rewards: How teachers and parents promote responsibility and learning.* Los Alamitos, CA: Piper Press.

Marshall, M., Weisner, K., & Cebula, M. L. (2004, September). Using a discipline system to promote learning. *International Journal of Reality Therapy, 24*(1), 23–33.

Rubin, R. (2005, Fall). A blueprint for a strengths-based level system in schools. *Reclaiming Children and Youth, 14*(3), 143–145.

Skiba, R., & Knesting, K. (2001, Winter). Zero tolerance, zero evidence: An analysis of school-discipline practice. *New Directions for Youth Development, 2001* (92), 17–43.

Smith, J. D. N. (2005, August). Understanding the beliefs, concerns, and priorities of trainee teachers: A multi-disciplinary approach. *Mentoring and Tutoring, 13*(2), 205–219.

6

INTASC Standard 6: Communication and Technology

Description of INTASC Standard 6: *The teacher uses knowledge of effective verbal, nonverbal and media communication techniques to foster active inquiry, collaboration, and supportive interaction in the classroom.*

KEY INDICATORS FOR STANDARD 6

The Teacher

- models effective communication strategies in conveying ideas and information and when asking questions (e.g., monitoring the effects of messages; restating ideas and drawing connections; using visual, oral, and kinesthetic cues; being sensitive to nonverbal cues both given and received).

- provides support for learner expression in speaking, writing, and other media.

- demonstrates that communication is sensitive to gender and cultural differences (e.g., appropriate use of eye contact, interpretation of body language and verbal statements, acknowledgment and responsiveness to different modes of communication and participation).

- uses a variety of media communication tools to enrich learning opportunities.

CASE 11: THE TECHNOLOGY PROJECT

Thinking Ahead

As you read this case, reflect on the following:

- Is "the best teacher ever" entitled to make mistakes and be excused for them?
- Should the teacher in this case have stayed home since she knew she was too distracted to teach well? Would you have

the same response if the case involved a lawyer or a doctor at his or her
workplace?
- How do we decide what is "just a bad day" and what is "poor teaching"?
- Why are we so willing to attribute some mistakes to "just a bad day" when it
comes to teachers and principals but are adamant when it comes to holding
doctors, police officers, and lawyers accountable for their actions?

Darlene Ellis sat nervously sipping her tea and waiting for the phone to ring.
She was expecting two calls, and neither one would carry good news. Her sister had
undergone surgery a week earlier for breast cancer, and the whole family was waiting
to hear the biopsy results from the medical lab. Darlene hoped that the cancer had not
metastasized to other parts of her sister's body. The other call would be from the
school principal, Phil Brentwood. Darlene was distraught the day she heard her sister
was in the hospital. She probably should not have gone to school at all, but she did.
She loved teaching and thought being with her third-grade students might get her
mind off her sister's illness. But by mid-afternoon she was tired and weary and overly
anxious about her sister. She angrily told four boys who were taking advantage of her
lack of attention to go to the computer area and finish researching information on the
explorers they had been assigned. With that, she went back to her reading group.
Twenty minutes later she turned her attention back to the four boys, who were whispering and giggling at the computers. She got up and went over to reprimand them,
only to find that they had navigated onto a soft porn Internet site. She shut off the
computers and sent the boys back to their desks. By the end of the day, the boys had
told everyone what they had discovered. By the next morning, the school principal
had received at least 10 calls from parents who had heard about the incident. Darlene
wished she had told Phil Brentwood herself what had happened.

The phone rang and, as Darlene expected, brought no good news. The cancer
had already spread to the lymph nodes, and her sister had to undergo intensive
chemotherapy followed by radiation. Fifteen minutes later the phone rang again.
This time it was Phil Brentwood asking Darlene to meet with him early Monday
morning and to be prepared to meet with the assistant superintendent and union
representative in his office after school on the same day. Later that evening Darlene
got two more phone calls, both from parents of the boys in her classroom who had
been surfing the pornography site on the Internet. "That's all they talk about," one
parent complained. "Don't you pay attention to them when they're working, or do
you just go off and do whatever you feel like doing?"

The next morning Darlene met with her principal. "I'd like to explain things,"
she began, "I can't be everywhere in the classroom, and it honestly never occurred to
me that the boys would find a site like that."

"Did you give them any guidelines for the lesson?" Phil asked. "Had you bookmarked the sites the children were expected to use?" Darlene said that she had but
this would not prevent her students from navigating to other sites.

"Did you even read the school policy for technology?" Phil asked, more angrily
now. "I know it's a work in progress, but everyone agreed to stick with the existing
policies until we all gained more experience with incorporating technology into the
curriculum."

Darlene tried to control her frustration but found herself blurting out her feelings. "I'm fed up with this technology stuff," she retorted. "And those boys knew better anyway. Why are you talking to me about it? You should be talking to them—and to their parents, too," she added. "They need to take some responsibility themselves for having their children behave like that."

Phil Brentwood had also reached the breaking point. "I'm talking to you," he said sternly, "because it's your class. You are the one in charge of instruction in your class. Do you know how many phone calls I've fielded between yesterday and today? I've talked to just about everyone from the superintendent to the janitor about this. So don't just tell me you can't be everywhere. It's your classroom. You're supposed to be everywhere."

Darlene and the principal sat quietly for a few seconds, trying to collect themselves. Finally, Phil asked gently, "Is there anything else wrong, Darlene? I've never seen you react this way. You've taken me completely off guard."

Darlene tried hard to hold back tears, but they came anyway. "My sister is in the hospital," she cried, "and I hate all this technology. I feel like I don't know how to teach anymore."

By the time the meeting ended, Darlene and Phil had talked about Darlene's sister and had reviewed the classroom Internet incident. Phil also cautioned Darlene to carefully review the school's policy on technology and to implement those policies in her classroom. They parted on civil but not necessarily friendly terms. As she was going out the door, Phil stopped her for a moment and said, "Darlene, I don't know what to do in this case. It's really something that got out of hand and the phone calls went all the way to the superintendent's office. We have a lot of angry parents out there. Whether they should be or not is another story." Darlene nodded in acknowledgment of his words and said simply, "Well, I'm sorry for all the trouble this has caused." With that, she walked down the hall to her classroom.

When the children left for lunch, Darlene sat with her friend and classroom aide, Alexsandra Zaric. "How did it go?" Alexsandra asked.

"About as bad as possible," Darlene sighed. "I lost my temper. Phil lost his temper. We both tried to be civil. There have been so many phone calls that the superintendent and assistant superintendent are involved and, worst of all, all the kids know about this and are taking advantage of it."

"I know," Alexsandra said. "When the teacher gets in trouble instead of them, it's a happy day."

Darlene laughed at her friend's characterization. "Oh, look," she said, "of course I should have been supervising them. I could have at least glanced down there once in a while. But, you know, this whole Internet thing creates its own problems."

"Sure," Alexsandra said, "It makes the kids stupid."

Darlene laughed again. "What do you mean?" she asked.

"Oh, come on," Alexsandra said. "Look at countries that don't have all this technology to play around with. That means the kids have to do some work in their classrooms. In my country we used to joke about how the United States and Canada are so rich the children can just play when they go to school."

"It's not all play," Darlene mused. "But I suppose in a lot of ways it's not as rigorous as you might expect."

"Not even a little bit as rigorous," Alexsandra answered quickly. "But we don't have as much diversity as you do either. And we also don't have so many children from so many different economic backgrounds in the same school."

"Yeah," Darlene said, "Maybe we just use that as an excuse, though. I really do think technology has some real value. There's so much information available so quickly on the Internet. But I think the Internet leads to a lot of superficial learning. All sites are created equal, you know. How do the kids figure out what's of value and what's not?"

"They don't," her friend answered. "In fact, they don't figure out anything at all. There's so much information available that the older kids can just cut and paste it into a report and the teachers never know they didn't write it themselves. I'm already seeing that with my daughter."

"Oh my goodness!" Darlene exclaimed. "That's something else I haven't thought about. It never occurred to me to check and see if the kids were just copying papers or if it's their own work. I feel like I'm in a time warp."

"They're only eight years old now," Alexsandra answered. "They're not too sophisticated when it comes to cheating yet. But just give it a couple of years. I can't even convince my daughter that it's not okay to copy things from the Internet."

"Well, maybe I can turn the conversation around to this in the meeting with the assistant superintendent," Darlene wondered out loud. "I don't mind admitting I should have supervised the students more carefully, but I hope I can get him to see that if we put too much focus on this technology we're going to be graduating a lot of shallow kids who have no critical thinking skills."

"Good luck with that plan," Alexsandra quipped.

At the end of the school day, Darlene went promptly to Phil Brentwood's office. The assistant superintendent and union representative were already there chatting amiably with Phil. She could feel the mood shift as she walked in. After introductions, the assistant superintendent got right to the point.

"I think this whole incident has been blown way out of proportion, Mrs. Ellis," he began. "We all know that things like this will happen occasionally. Sometimes it amounts to nothing, but this time the phone calls have been flying in so we have to deal with it."

"I understand," Darlene answered. "I'm sorry we're at the point we are, and I wish I had supervised the students more closely."

"That's part of the problem, isn't it?" the assistant superintendent said. "You seem to think of technology environments as different from other classroom environments. But it's all the same. All the students in the classroom are under your supervision all the time, even at the computers."

Darlene bristled inwardly at the assistant superintendent's tone but retained her appearance of composure.

"Your school has a written policy on technology usage," the assistant superintendent continued. "Here, let me read you something." His eyes skimmed down the page until he came to the section he wanted. "Ah yes," he muttered. "listen to this: 'Unsupervised Internet surfing by students is not allowed. Students are restricted to sites that the teacher selected and bookmarked. These recommendations support our efforts to provide a safe and secure learning environment for your child in the classroom.'"

The assistant superintendent looked up. "Are you familiar with these policies, Mrs. Ellis? These are the same policies that were sent home with every child at the beginning of the year."

"I am familiar with them," Darlene answered. "I just had a lot on my mind that day, I guess, and was not paying as much attention as I normally would."

"And that's the source of our problems today, Mrs. Ellis," the assistant superintendent replied, any pleasantness gone from his voice. "We're all here to talk about you not following school policy and about you not supervising your students properly during the school day."

Darlene was stunned. All thoughts of engaging in a broader discussion about technology left her mind. Was it possible that four 8-year-old boys stumbling onto an inappropriate Web site could be the cause of this much trouble?

CASE 11: ISSUES FOR ANALYSIS AND REFLECTION

1. Case 11 is related to the INTASC Standard for Communication and Technology and to the following two key indicators for this standard: The teacher (a) models effective communication strategies in conveying ideas and information and when asking questions (e.g., monitoring the effects of messages; restating ideas and drawing connection; using visual, oral, and kinesthetic cues; being sensitive to nonverbal cues both given and received) and (b) uses a variety of media communication tools to enrich learning opportunities. Once you have identified the primary issue, problem, or concern in this case, determine what other content knowledge is needed to ensure positive outcomes.
2. What pedagogical knowledge and skills are needed?
3. What must be done to ensure that desired student learning outcomes are obtained?

Use the DEEPS Method to analyze this case. Keep in mind the INTASC Standard for Communication and Technology and the key indicators listed in item 1.

Determine the primary issue, problem, or concern in this case.

Enumerate the facts that support your belief regarding the primary issue, problem, or concern in the case.

Evaluate the case to find all the possible solutions for resolving the issue, problem, or concern.

Problem solve by thinking critically about each possible solution and accepting or rejecting the solution based on its value in ensuring the professional growth of the teacher in relation to communication and technology.

Summarize your conclusion/solutions and be prepared to present the best possible solution and your rationale to your professor and colleagues.

CASE 11: WHAT THE RESEARCH SAYS

Along with other competencies required for teachers, ethical considerations related to the use of computers and other technologies must now be included. Teachers also bear the responsibility for being sure that instruction which incorporates technology is not frivolous but serves to meet established curricular goals and objectives (Code of Professional Ethics). A number of issues, however, are intertwined when the question of ethical use of technology is considered.

There is mounting evidence that, although *some* use of technology in our classrooms is beneficial, overuse results in decreased learning. A study by Fuchs and Woessmann at the University of Munich, for example, showed that students who "never or rarely use the Internet or computers in the classroom don't do as well as those who make moderate use of them. . . . [But] those same computer-less students outperform peers who *frequently* access the technology" (as cited in Ferguson, 2005). It was found in fact that "once household income and the wealth of a school's resources are taken out of the equation, teens with the greatest access to computers and the Internet at home and school earn the lowest test scores" (p. 28). Fuchs and Woessmann suggest the optimal level for computer and Internet use at schools is relatively low, somewhere between a few times a year and several times a month (Ferguson). Ferguson suggests that one reason for this is the addictive nature of the Internet. Children are inevitably lured into game rooms and chat sites, instant messaging, and pop-up Web sites. This results in a lack of sustained reading and critical thinking. It also takes up hours of time that could be used for study and other forms of active learning. This leads educators to the question of exactly what is the appropriate use of technology in the classroom.

The Alliance for Childhood (2004), an alliance of individuals who came together to promote policies and practices related to children's health and learning, point to other ethical concerns when it comes to incorporating technology into the elementary classroom. "Children need strong personal bonds with caring adults," they write. "Yet powerful technologies are distracting children and adults from each other" (n.p.). The Alliance cautions teachers about what education should do for children.

> Children need time for active, physical play; hands-on lessons of all kinds, especially in the arts; and direct experience of the natural world. Research shows that these are not frills but are essential for healthy child development. Yet many schools have already cut minimal offerings in these areas to shift time and money to expensive, unproven technology. The emphasis on technology is diverting us from the urgent social and educational needs of low-income children. (n.p.)

The Alliance also points to possible negative effects of technology, such as the overuse of drill and practice, trivial games, aggressive advertising, and the possibility of isolating children emotionally and physically from the real world. Overreliance on computers has the possibility of promoting the opposite of "what all children, and especially children at risk, need most—close relationships with caring adults" (Alliance for Childhood, 2004, n.p.). This raises ethical questions as to how funding for education can best be spent. What investments in education are likely to result in the most effective learning opportunities for children?

Armstrong and Casement speak in their 1998 book *The Child and the Machine: Why Computers May Put Our Children's Education at Risk* to yet other ethical concerns related to technology expenditures. Research shows, they tell us, that class size is important if students are to derive the maximum benefits from technology. No more than 20 students per class appears to be the ideal.

The University of Illinois has a Web site dedicated to technology studies in education (http://lrs.ed.uiuc.edu). Its aim is to address the creation and study of technology solutions as they relate to educational problems. A good portion of the Web site is devoted to ethical concerns, such as those just outlined. Also found on the Web site is a Code of Computer Ethics for Teachers (http://lrs.ed.uiuc.edu/students/mickley/ethics.htm). This code suggests that numerous ethical problems can be avoided if schools take into consideration the following nine principles:

1. Identify the social, ethical, legal, and human issues surrounding the use of technology, and apply and model those principles in practice.
2. Identify and employ technology resources that enable and empower learners from diverse backgrounds, characteristics, and abilities.
3. Organize technology environments to help students avoid temptation and to minimize the opportunities for technology misuse in the classroom.
4. Integrate technology throughout the curriculum to support content learning and the acquisition of computing skills while demonstrating ethical principles.
5. Keep abreast of the changes in the world of technology.
6. Support colleagues in their efforts to expand personal and classroom use of available technologies.
7. Ensure the privacy of students while using available technologies. For example, check to see if the school has a policy about disclosing student information.
8. Familiarize students about the commercial nature of Web sites.
9. Involve the community at large to support the ethical use of technology.

These principles are based on the idea that teachers are key to implementing sound technology programs in schools. While these principles won't eliminate ethical issues and concerns, they may contribute to lessening them.

The teacher in this case story was not overly comfortable with the use of technology in her classroom but, like it or not, it appears that technology is here to stay. One of the problems, however, with suddenly making classrooms "technology ready" is that time is often not allotted for teachers to learn the new technologies themselves. A report from the National Center for Educational Statistics (NCES, 2000) related to teacher use of technology in the 21st century states that 82% of teachers said they were not given enough time outside their regular teaching duties to learn, practice, or plan to use computers or other technologies. This, in fact, was perceived as the greatest barrier to using technology in instruction. Another reported barrier was perceived lack of instructional time in the schedule to allow for the use of computers. Coupled with this was lack of sufficient numbers of computers in the classroom to make incorporating them into instruction feasible. Teachers in large urban and rural areas were more likely to report these barriers than were teachers in wealthier suburban districts. As well, teachers in low-income schools with 50% or more minority enrollment were more likely to report outdated and/or unreliable computers and incompatible software as barriers to incorporating technology into their daily planning. As a result, these teachers were far less likely to assign technology into their daily planning. An article in *Leadership Abstracts* sums up all these concerns. The authors of the article, Ayers and Doherty, state that for technology to become a regular part of the educational environment, four things must occur: (a) student and faculty access to computers must be a priority, (b) computer networks must be reliable, (c) school districts must provide multiple opportunities for training and consulting, and (d) schools much establish an ethos that values experimentation and tolerates failure (Ayers & Doherty, 2003). Darlene Ellis, the teacher in this case story, might have benefited from all four of these considerations. Such considerations would also provide a framework for the administrators in the school and district.

Summary of Research

Research indicates that although *some* use of technology in our classrooms is beneficial, overreliance on technology may be harmful and decrease appropriate learning opportunities. The addictive nature of surfing through the many chat rooms, aggressive advertising attractions, and alluring Web sites on the Internet can also result in less time for more hands-on, experiential activity. The constant interruptions necessary for moving from link to link may also result in children failing to develop the capacity for sustained reading and for critical thinking.

The Alliance for Childhood (2004) points to the need for young children to form strong bonds with adults. Frequent use of technology in the classroom may cause physical and emotional isolation, and this is particularly harmful for at-risk youngsters. Considerable research describes the need for ongoing teacher training and support when it comes to incorporating technology into the classroom. Administrators should note that true proficiency in using technology wisely may occur only after about 5 or 6 years of training and classroom experience. In the final analysis, educators must ask themselves how available funding can best be used to provide the best learning opportunities.

CASE 11: TOPICS FOR DISCUSSION

- Younger and less experienced teachers are more likely than older, more experienced teachers to use technology routinely in their classrooms.
- According to the Alliance for Childhood, "Children need strong personal bonds with caring adults, yet powerful technologies are distracting children and adults from each other."
- The optimal level for computer and Internet use at schools is relatively low, somewhere between a few times a year and several times a month.
- There is no sound pedagogical reason to integrate the use of technology into instruction.

CASE 11: EXPLORING THE ISSUES

1. Open your Web browser to http://www.prenhall.com/teacherprep. This will take you to Merrill's Teacher Prep Web site. Once you are logged in, click on *Video Classroom* on the menu on the left side of your screen. When this screen opens, scroll down to *Educational Technology* and click on this. Then, click on *Video 1: Module Inquiry Unit—Part I*. In this very short video, the teacher gives directions to his students about the activities they will complete. After watching the video, go back and script the directions that Mrs. Ellis might have given the four boys in her class so as to avoid the problems that occurred.

2. The communication between the principal, assistant superintendent, and Mrs. Ellis is tense and, at times, hostile. Rewrite the conversation so that the meeting of these three individuals is more productive.

3. Schedule an appointment with the principal or medial specialist in an elementary school in your area. Interview either of these individuals regarding the technology plan that he or she has for the school, the policies and procedures teachers and students are expected to follow, and the policies and procedures for handling infractions related to technology.

4. Work with a small group of your classmates to plan an agenda for a staff development workshop related to the incorporation of technology into instruction.

5. Go back to the staff development agenda you planned with your classmates. Justify each activity or session. Explain why you chose those particular activities, how you knew they were suitable for your audience of teachers, what you hope the outcomes will be, and how you will know if the desired outcomes occurred.

CASE 12: TECHNOLOGY AS ENTERTAINMENT: A CLASS DIVIDED

Thinking Ahead

As you read this case, reflect on the following:

- Why is there such a concern in education with integrating technology into instruction? Haven't there been many other times in our history when schools insisted on the integration of slide rulers, calculators, homemaking classes, career education, and so on? What constitutes *essential* education?
- The film discussed in this case was made about 40 years ago? Can a film made this long ago still have any relevance for 8-year-olds?
- What do you think the goals and objectives of the lesson presented by Claire were? Did she meet her objectives? How will she be able to assess whether or not objectives were met?

Claire Rafferty was feeling good about how much her teaching had improved this year. The move from fifth grade down to third grade was an important factor in her enjoyment of the school year, she mused. "They're still so innocent. And they're so eager to learn everything. Every day is fun." Claire glanced down at the lesson she was preparing for Black History Month. She planned to show a clip from the documentary *A Class Divided*. The documentary had been made nearly 40 years ago but still had a lot of value when it came to generating a discussion about discrimination. Claire had seen the documentary herself during her college years. She hoped her own students would identify with this film the same way she had. She thought of how the teacher in the documentary had divided her Grade 3 students into a brown-eyed group and a blue-eyed group. The blue-eyed students were shown a great deal of favoritism while the brown-eyed students had less access to recess, less access to helpings of food during lunch, and their work and behavior also received frequent negative comments from the teacher. At the end of this experiment, the teacher gathered the class together to discuss the film and helped them express their feelings about what had occurred. The students in the film also generalized about how people must feel when they receive this discriminatory treatment on a daily basis.

Claire considered repeating the experiment in her class so that her own third-grade students would experience it firsthand. "But there's not really enough time," she lamented. "I'll just show a short video clip, and that should be enough for discussion." Claire knew there would be some controversy over showing a section of this documentary, so she first made sure she had her principal's support. She took the extra step of inviting parents to her class one evening to see the film clip before she showed it to her third-grade class. Claire was surprised that only a handful of parents showed up and that they treated the occasion more as a social event than as an opportunity to review this lesson. After seeing the 20-minute clip of the documentary, one parent suggested that she address the use of "the n-word" during the film. "I would never allow my child to talk that way," she said, "I certainly don't want her to learn to say this at school."

Claire reminded the parents of the purpose of showing the film and assured them that at the start of class she would tell her students that the film contained some inappropriate language and behavior and that they should not mimic it. Claire marveled that the parents didn't ask more questions but then quickly reminded herself that this lack of awareness was part of her reason for wanting to show the documentary. "It's pretty much an all-white school," she thought to herself. "It's not that any of us harbor prejudices. It's just that this is the way it is."

Claire read through her lesson plan one more time. She wondered briefly whether or not the 30 minutes she had planned for this lesson was going to be enough. "Twenty minutes for the video clip and ten minutes for focused discussion should be enough," she thought. "These kids are only eight years old," she considered, "so ten minutes is long enough to get them thinking but not so long that the discussion will start going off on tangents." She gave the lesson one last glance and with a small amount of pride in her work pressed the "Submit" button to add her lesson to all the other lesson plans for Black History Month at her school. A second later she clicked on the school's Web site and on "Activities" for Black History Month and began to scroll through the list of lesson and unit plans. She smiled when she came to her own: *Ms. Rafferty's Grade 3: A Class Divided. Ms. Rafferty's students will watch a video clip from this documentary film and discuss how discrimination affects all of us. Wednesday, February 17. 1:30–2:00 p.m.* Claire looked forward to next Wednesday with excitement.

Claire stayed in her classroom during her lunch break and was soon joined by the teacher across the hall, Mary LaGoya. "Hey," Mary said affably as she popped her head in the door. "I saw your Black History lesson plan for next week. Any chance I can come by and watch that film, too?"

"Sure," Clair replied, cheerfully waving her colleague into the room at the same time. "The kids will be happy to see you." Mary taught second grade and many of the children had been in her current class the previous year. She strolled into the room and sat down on one of the third-grade desks. "Risky business," she said, "showing that documentary."

"Just a clip from it—only about twenty minutes," Claire replied. "I think it will be good. I'm really kind of excited about showing it."

"I'm really curious about how the kids will react" her friend replied. "What will you do after the film clip? Do you have some kind of activity or discussion or something?"

"I put aside some time for discussion," Claire answered quickly. "Not too much time because I think they're too young for any deep analysis. Just enough time to let them express their feelings."

"Sounds great," Mary replied. "I'm looking forward to seeing it. Hey, you're welcome to visit my class, too, if you want" she added as an afterthought. We're doing WebQuests about famous black authors. Of course, I have to set it all up ahead of time. I have all the sites bookmarked," she added with a little laugh. "Nothing going on as daring as what you're doing."

After Mary left, Claire wondered why she thought of her activity as daring. "Maybe innovative," she thought. She smiled to herself. "I am bringing this down to their level—and if there are any outstanding concerns, we can discuss them." Claire smiled again. She couldn't help but feel good about this lesson.

On the day of the activity, Claire's third-grade children watched in excitement as she set up the movie screen in front of the room and then walked to the back to set up the projector. Then Claire walked back to the front of the room and explained the activity to her class. "We're going to watch a short film about another classroom and an activity—really an experiment—that the teacher of that class did with her students. Sometimes, some of the children in this class don't use good language, and they call other children names. I don't want to ever hear any of you doing that or saying those words." Claire paused for a minute and glanced around the room. "But you're in third grade now," she said. "I think you're all old enough and responsible enough to know the right way to behave, right?" Some of her children sat up straighter and others nodded in agreement. Claire smiled at their reaction and mused at how young children always like to be told that they behave like adults. "Now guess who is joining us for this film." Claire added. "Ms. LaGoya, your teacher from last year!" The children turned to see Mary LaGoya walk into the room. A few children ran up to greet her. After about 5 minutes, the class was back to order and Claire was ready to begin the film.

Claire watched as her students sat viewing the film. Every now and then one or two students made small exclamations of surprise. Twice, two of the children turned to each other to talk, but Claire gave them a look that said to be quiet. When the film ended and the lights were turned back on, the class sat very quietly, looking at Claire for direction. Clair quickly highlighted some main points of the film.

Tony, a precocious student who was generally well liked by his classmates, timidly raised his hand. "My parents told me that some kids will always be in the slow group," he said, "that it doesn't matter what color their eyes are."

"Yeah, it does. It does matter," Rafael added.

"Why does it matter?" Claire asked gently.

"Cause it does," Rafael muttered. "Tony is stupid." A few other students laughed, and others shook their heads in disagreement. Tony looked painfully embarrassed and hurt.

"Well," Claire said while glancing at the clock. "First of all, we don't call each other names. You must apologize to Tony." Rafael turned to Tony and gave him a reluctant apology. "I can see that this will be a big discussion," Claire continued, "so maybe we will save it for another day when everyone is more ready to have a polite discussion. Right now, I think we better start our reading lesson. Get your books out and get into your groups, please."

As the third-grade children started to get their books out and move around the classroom into their groups, Claire walked down to thank Mary LaGoya for joining them. "How do you think it went?" she whispered as she walked toward the door with her.

Mary hesitated and then answered truthfully. "I think everyone found it interesting. But documentary films are realistic, and I think your class needed some time to discuss it."

"I think they did find it interesting," Claire answered happily. "Did you see how quietly they sat while watching it?"

Mary was surprised at her reaction. "But what did they *think* about it, Claire? You didn't even ask them. They must discuss this. You're using technology to fill time and entertain but not to teach."

Claire looked so hurt that Mary added more softly, "What did you want to teach your students, Claire? Did you have any goals for this lesson?" Then she put her hand on Claire's shoulder and added, "Let's talk later, okay?" Claire nodded and smiled back, but it was easy for Mary to see that she was holding back tears.

CASE 12: ISSUES FOR ANALYSIS AND REFLECTION

1. Case 12 is related to the INTASC Standard for Communication and Technology and to the following two key indicators for this standard: The teacher (a) provides support for learner expression in speaking, writing, and other media and (b) demonstrates that communication is sensitive to gender and cultural differences (e.g., appropriate use of eye contact, interpretation of body language and verbal statements, acknowledgment and responsiveness to different modes of communication and participation. Once you have identified the primary issue, problem, or concern in this case, determine what other content knowledge is needed to ensure positive outcomes.
2. What pedagogical knowledge and skills are needed?
3. What must be done to ensure that desired student learning outcomes are obtained?

Use the DEEPS Method to analyze this case. Keep in mind the INTASC Standard for Communication and Technology and the key indicators listed in item 1.

Determine the primary issue, problem, or concern in this case.

Enumerate the facts that support your belief regarding the primary issue, problem, or concern in the case.

Evaluate the case to find all the possible solutions for resolving the issue, problem, or concern.

Problem solve by thinking critically about each possible solution and accepting or rejecting the solution based on its value in ensuring the professional growth of the teacher in relation to the INTASC Standard for Communication and Technology.

Summarize your conclusion/solutions and be prepared to present the best possible solution and your rationale to your professor and colleagues

CASE 12: WHAT THE RESEARCH SAYS

In this case story there is a discrepancy between the teacher's probable goals in showing the film and what actually transpires throughout the lesson.

Leadership style becomes important when considering the integration of technology into schools. It is generally agreed that technology should be "just one more tool in the toolbox of broadly competent teachers—not just a fix-all or add-on" (McLester, 2002, p. 4). The key to making this happen seems to be teacher training. Teachers have a tendency to replicate their own school experiences and the teaching styles to which they had been exposed while students themselves. This makes it a challenge to transform the culture of schools and incorporate new technologies. In this sense, good leadership must have a shared vision for school improvement and one that empowers and inspires teachers to make positive changes (Barry, 2004). The principal may indeed play a major role in creating an infrastructure that embraces change, but it is the classroom teachers who will implement change and measure the results. It is important, therefore, that teachers become part of the planning process and take on leadership roles that are compatible with their skills and dispositions. This is not to say, however, that it is always easy to identify and enlist the help of the accepted leaders among teachers in a building. The teacher in this case, for example, did begin by consulting with her school principal. While she was encouraged to go ahead with her project, the principal offered no other insights that might have improved this lesson.

Mary Anderson, a school librarian and facilitator for a number of workshops on incorporating technology into instruction, suggests that any technology plan also has to begin with high expectations for how technology should be used. A key ingredient for gaining teacher support is targeting their instructional concerns. When demonstrating any technology, it is likely to gain far more favor if it appeals to the specific curricular area and grade level of teachers in attendance. By the same token, time in which to learn new instructional methods is limited. Either teachers must be given release time to attend technology classes or these classes have to be scheduled at a time that meets the needs of the target audience (Anderson, 2004). Of primary importance is the establishment of a shared vision and the reasons for this vision. In order for teachers to embrace change, there has to be agreement and understanding of how improved learning will occur (Barry, 2004). In this case story, Claire was excited about using a controversial film during Black History Month. The case story, however, gives little insight into her goals for the lesson. It is implied, in fact, that the intention was only to spark interest and controversy and that instructional planning did not extend past this.

Once instructional goals are known, appropriate uses of technology can be determined. The research also shows that school districts are spending considerable amounts of money on technology. It is estimated that in 2004, for example, a little more than $5 million was spent on educational technology. About two thirds of school budgets went to purchase hardware. About 16% went for software purchases, and about 9% went for staff development (Bushweller, 2004, p. 17).

There is a concern, nonetheless, with the quality of technology that schools have, especially in large urban areas. More sophisticated computers can work with large amounts of data and process information at faster speeds. It is unfortunate, however, that about 30% of the nation's schools have not upgraded their computers to high speed processing; many schools still have older models incapable of doing what more sophisticated computers can do. In fact, as recently as the year 2000, about 20% of the nation's school were still using Apple IIs, a computer that is among the oldest in schools today (Meyer, 2001). This concern with equipment itself is heightened in high poverty areas, where repairing problems with hardware of software malfunctioning can be time consuming and costly (Trotter, 2002). All in all, given the lack of time for teachers to learn to use technology effectively, the lack of instructional time in the school day for use of technology, the lack of sufficient numbers of computers in the classroom, and the all-too-frequent presence of outdated and unreliable computers and incompatible software, it is little wonder that resistance is significant when it comes to assigning instructional activities requiring computer and/or Internet access (NCES, 2000).

An interesting view is presented by researchers O'Neill and Simons (2005), who state that one of the considerations when integrating technology into instruction is to ask *what types and forms of information are best manipulated by which technological tools.* Once this is determined, planning should not be left to chance. In regard to using film as an instructional tool, O'Neill and Simons state, students can grasp [issues] if the appropriate technology is integrated into the content of the course. Understanding how to integrate the appropriate technology into a course is only part of the solution. Students also must understand the complexity of the relations between the array of technological tools and the particular questions or concepts raised by the discipline or subject to which the tools are being applied (n.p.). The teacher in this case story began with a brief statement about the film her students were about to see but then failed to raise any questions related to any discipline. The children were left to interpret what they saw on their own. The use of film as a technological tool, in other words, provided entertainment but not necessarily any new *planned* learning.

Summary of Research

A leadership style that empowers and inspires teachers and school staff to embrace change is necessary, not only for the general school climate but also for implementing specific changes, such as the incorporation of technology into curriculum instruction. Technology plans tend to be most successful in schools that have a shared vision for change and agreement as to the reasons for change and how it will occur. Specific teacher needs in terms of subject area and grade level should be targeted in workshops to improve teacher understanding and skills. If at all possible, release time should be provided for training. When this is not possible, workshops should be scheduled at a time that is convenient to the target audience. The already existing knowledge, skills, and dispositions of some teachers to act as change facilitators should not be ignored. The outdated or unreliable technology that many schools have, however, can be a barrier to the use of technology in school. A good technology plan identifies the leaders in the school who can provide guidance and expertise and the resources that will be needed to ensure positive outcomes.

CASE 12: TOPICS FOR DISCUSSION

- About half of all teachers who participated in one study (NCES, 2000) stated that their college experience helped them only to use computers for word processing or Internet searches. They received no other technology training.
- Schools sometimes rely on students to work on and repair school computers (Trotter, 2002). A major concern is that students working on computers must have access to passwords, which also allows them to access student records.
- Knowing how to use computers is one thing; knowing how to use computers to meaningfully and significantly improve instruction is quite another.
- A serious divide separates those students well off enough to be able to afford the latest technology in music, cell phones, and computers and those who cannot afford this technology. This divide is so great that it will impact learning throughout life.

CASE 12: EXPLORING THE ISSUES

1. Go to the Curriculum and Content Area Standards for Technology at http://www.iste.org/AM/Template.cfm?Section=NETS. At the top of the page, click on *NETS for Teachers 2008*. When this page opens, review the technology standards for teachers. How does the teacher in this case story stand up against these standards?
2. Explore using WebQuests in your own instructional planning. Go to the Google search engine and write in "WebQuests" to read more about using this technique. Then plan a lesson that incorporates a WebQuest. Write a short evaluation of your lesson in which you explain what you perceive to be the strengths and drawbacks of using WebQuests in this lesson.
3. Visit three or four classrooms at the grade level that you plan to teach. Observe the methods the classroom teachers use to engage students in mastering the content. How much instructional time incorporates some form of technology? Was this an effective use of time in terms of improving student learning?
4. Review *Parents Guide to the Internet* published by the U.S. Department of Education at http://www.ed.gov/pubs/parents/internet/index.html. How useful is this information for classroom teachers?
5. Open your Web browser to www.prenhall.com/teacherprep. This will take you to Merrill's Teacher Prep Web site. Once you are logged in, click on *Video Classroom*. When this window opens, scroll down and click on *Educational Technology*. Click on *Video 2: Module Inquiry Unit—Part II*. In this video, the teacher has his students use the computer to write their notes regarding a science experiment. How effective is the use of computer technology in this lesson? Could the lesson be just as effective without technology, or is the use of computers an essential component of this lesson?

References

Alliance for Childhood (2004, June). "Fool's gold: A critical look at computers in childhood." Retrieved December 18, 2008, from http://www.allianceforchildhood.net/projects/computers/computers_reports_fools_gold_download.htm.

Anderson, M. A. (2004). "Summer School for Teachers," *School Library Journal, 50*(2), 36–38.

Armstrong, A., & Casement, C. (1998). *The child and the machine.* Excerpt: Computers in education. Retrieved December 18, 2008, from http://www.theparentreport.com/books/display_book.html?book_id=67&show_excerpt=1.

Ayers, C., & Doherty, B. (2003, January). Integrating instructional technology across the campus. *Leadership Abstracts, 16*(1). Retrieved July 15, 2006, from http://www.league.org/publication/abstracts/leadership/lab0103.htm

Barry, B. (2004, November). "Professional Development Quick Tips," *Technology and Professional Development, 25*(4).

Bushweller, K. (2004, November). Technology Spending. *Education Week, 24*(10), 17.

Ferguson, S. (2005, June). "How Computers Make Our Kids Stupid," *Maclean's, 118*(23), 24–31.

McLester, S. (2002, April). "Getting All Our Kids on Board," *Technology & Learning, 22*(9), 4.

Meyer, L. (2001, May). New challenges. *Education Week, 20*(35), 49–55.

National Center for Educational Statistics (NCES). (2000). Teachers' tools for the 21st century: A Report on Teachers' Use of Technology. U.S. Department of Education, Institute of Education Sciences. Retrieved December 18, 2008, from http://nces.ed.gov/pubsearch/pubsinfo.asp?pubid=2000102.

O'Neill, P., & Simons, J. (2005, July 25). Using technology in learning to speak the language of film. Retrieved December 22, 2008, from http://www.academiccommons.org/commons/essay/oneill-simons-film.

Trotter, A. (2002, June 12). Survey finds schools rely on students for help. *Education Week, 21*(40), 12.

7

INTASC Standard 7: Planning

Description of INTASC Standard 7: *The teacher plans instruction based upon knowledge of subject matter, students, the community, and curriculum plans.*

KEY INDICATORS FOR STANDARD 7

The Teacher

- plans lessons and activities to address variations in learning styles and performance modes, multiple development levels of diverse learners, and problem solving and exploration.
- develops plans that are appropriate for curriculum goals and are based on effective instruction.
- adjusts plans to respond to unanticipated sources of input and/or student needs.
- develops short- and long-term plans.

CASE 13: PLANNING AND STANDARDS

Thinking Ahead

As you read this case, reflect on the following:

- Do state and national standards provide an appropriate framework for quality instruction or do standards make lesson planning more difficult?
- If you had to choose one, is it more important for a teacher to be knowledgeable about a subject area or to be enthusiastic?

"Wasn't that exciting?" Matthew was exuberant, even more animated than the 22 first-graders who had just left with Mr. Simmons for their art class.

"Didn't you think their constellations were incredible? Especially Kyle's—and he's usually just bored and disruptive. This activity really kept his interest."

Ms. Robertson sighed. After 4 weeks together, she was certain her student teacher Matthew could not tell that her smile was feigned, intended to buy time while she considered his lesson. In one respect, Matthew was right; the constellation activity *had* kept their interest. However, it had done nothing to help students understand how celestial objects appear to move in patterns, which was the concept that had been the purpose of the lesson. Mentally, she reviewed the lesson plan.

Matthew's written lesson plan had seemed excellent. It was based on one major understanding of the state's core curriculum, specifically the performance indicator, which states that elementary students should understand that "the sun and other stars appear to move in a recognizable pattern both daily and seasonally." Matt had decided to begin by focusing on apparent daily movement, moving into seasonal movement patterns once students demonstrated mastery of the apparent daily patterns. He had incorporated multiple methods for introducing the concept, including having students create human "constellations" that would then "move" in patterns consistent with the motion of Earth's daily rotation and seasonal revolution. Matt had included formative assessments that involved physical movement and whiteboard illustrations, as well as a summative assessment in which students demonstrated their knowledge on paper. The movement of celestial objects was a complicated concept for first-grade students. Jolene Robertson had been impressed by Matthew's eagerness to tackle it and was pleased with his ability to help them make connections to the content.

Thomas Jefferson Elementary School was situated in a relatively rural community. With no skyscrapers, airports, or malls to obstruct their nightly celestial observations, most students were familiar with the stars and the patterns that formed in the night sky. Matthew had capitalized on this background knowledge in his lesson plan by referring to constellations in his anticipatory set and then by having students form "human constellations" in the center of the classroom floor. However, instead of having students move methodically in prescribed patterns, Matthew had been swept away by the students' enthusiasm.

In the midst of his lesson, just as he was supposed to be introducing the concept that stars appear to move in a recognizable daily pattern, Matthew had declared, "Now that we all know what constellations are, let's *create* some!" The children had cheered—actually *cheered*—for this idea, responding in part to the suggestion but primarily to Matthew's zeal. Students chattered about superheroes, animals, and sports team logos as constellation possibilities while Matt pulled out large sheets of black construction paper and lots of "star-making" supplies: glitter pens, handheld hole punches, star-shaped stickers, gold and silver foil, thick and thin markers, and a variety of crayons.

After presenting the materials to the children, Matthew exclaimed, "The stars are your limit!" and told them that they could spend the remaining 50 minutes before art class creating their constellations.

Jolene acknowledged that the first-graders had been extraordinarily engaged in this activity. They plunged into the task, discussing their ideas, developing drafts of their desired shapes, and considering the best media for creating their final products. Even Kyle, who was a reluctant student, worked hard on this project. In honor of his beloved local football team, Kyle had used the hole punch to depict a football, complete with laces. He had begun by drawing a football on his black paper, and then he punched holes along his outline. Next, he had glued yellow construction paper to the black in order to simulate starlight behind his punched holes. Kyle had finished by cutting out a sliver of a moon above his football constellation, painstakingly curving his black paper so as not to crease it, and then gluing gold foil behind it. Kyle, who always rushed through schoolwork, had spent uncharacteristic levels of time and effort on this project. "But," Jolene Robertson wondered to herself, "what did he learn?"

Jolene, still smiling, turned to Matthew, who was practically bouncing with pride as he reviewed the children's work. She was a veteran first-grade teacher in her 21st year at this same school. She was also the first-grade team leader; as such she coordinated curriculum, performed classroom observations of her colleagues, and worked closely with administrators in her building and district. Widely respected in the district and the community, she was one of the most sought-after teachers by knowledgeable parents of prospective first-graders.

Jolene was also an experienced cooperating teacher, one of the few in the district permitted to supervise two student teachers per year. She took this role very seriously, frequently explaining to her colleagues and university liaisons that she perceived cooperating teachers as "gatekeepers for the profession." "*Teaching* student teachers," she would often say, "is only one aspect of being a cooperating teacher. It's also important to ensure that when student teachers leave our classrooms they are ready to assume the duties of professional educators. They must understand the process of teaching and learning—especially planning, setting objectives, and assessing progress. Putting their six weeks in isn't enough. If I wouldn't want them teaching my grandchildren, then I shouldn't allow them to teach anyone else's children either."

Matthew glanced expectantly at Jolene. He was eager to hear her reaction to his lesson. Jolene intentionally adhered to her protocol for critiquing student teachers' lessons, although in this case that meant asking a question she already knew the answer to: "So, Matthew, what did you think of the lesson?"

"Oh, my gosh," he blurted, "it was *so* much better than the written plan! When I realized how interested the students were in constellations, I knew that I had to maximize that connection. I monitored their reaction and adjusted my instruction to it. Did you see how the students were applying background knowledge, making inferences about how to illustrate their interests, and evaluating their own work? There was so much higher order thinking in this activity! And these projects will be perfect to display on Parents' Night, too!"

Jolene took a deep breath. "The projects are stunning, and the students were diligent and engrossed in their work. It's also wonderful that you are so well attuned to their reactions in class. Making connections with students and activating their background knowledge are essential components of good instruction."

Matthew's face fell. Despite Jolene's strategy of beginning her critique with a positive comment, Matthew could sense the impending "but" in her response.

"Let's sit down and review your plan, okay?" she suggested gently.

Matthew slumped into one of the small chairs as Jolene retrieved his lesson plan.

"Matt," she began, "one of the most difficult aspects of teaching is developing objectives, activities, and assessments that align with one another and with the state learning standards. Let's go back to your objective for this lesson. Will you read it aloud please?"

Matt read, "Students will be able to identify and demonstrate how the sun and other stars appear to move in a recognizable daily pattern."

"Matt," Jolene Robertson tilted her head to force him to make eye contact with her, "can you please explain how these projects demonstrate that students have achieved your learning objective?"

Matthew gazed hopefully at the pile of projects to his left. "Well," he ventured, "they do show patterns—the stars are in patterns. . . ."

Jolene waited. Matt was bright, enthusiastic, and cared about students. He displayed a talent for developing creative activities. She didn't want to stifle his strengths, but she needed to help him appreciate the difference between activities that produce and measure progress toward learning objectives and activities that merely relate to the topic at hand.

Matt put his chin on his hand. "I guess they don't. The projects don't really relate to the objective at all, except that they both deal with stars. I suppose I should have stuck with the worksheet I created originally—this one where the students had to fill in stars in a night sky as they appear at 2-hour intervals." He paused and looked at the pile of unused worksheets. "That just seems so *boring*. I guess the only thing that matters in teaching today is meeting the state standards. There's just no room for creativity or what's best for kids."

As Jolene listened to Matt's words, his dejection and self-doubt were palpable. She wondered whether he had the fortitude to continue or whether his desire to depend on his talents would undermine his ability to become an excellent teacher.

CASE 13: ISSUES FOR ANALYSIS AND REFLECTION

1. Case 13 is related to the INTASC Standard for Planning and to the following two key indicators for this standard: The teacher (a) develops plans that are appropriate for curriculum goals and are based on effective instruction and (b) adjusts plans to respond to unanticipated sources of input and/or student needs. Once you have identified the primary issue, problem, or concern in this case, determine what other content knowledge the teacher(s) in this case has to have to ensure positive outcomes.
2. What pedagogical knowledge and skills are needed?
3. What must be done to ensure that desired student learning outcomes are obtained?

Use the DEEPS Method to analyze this case. Keep in mind the INTASC Standard for Planning and the key indicators listed in item 1.

Determine the primary issue, problem, or concern in this case.

Enumerate the facts that support your belief regarding the primary issue, problem, or concern in the case.

Evaluate the case to find all the possible solutions for resolving the issue, problem, or concern.

Problem solve by thinking critically about each possible solution and accepting or rejecting the solution based on its value in ensuring the professional growth of the teacher in relation to planning.

Summarize your conclusion/solutions and be prepared to present the best possible solution and your rationale to your professor and colleagues.

CASE 13: WHAT THE RESEARCH SAYS

In this case story, we have the classic story of the teacher who mistakes student interest and enjoyment for meaningful learning. In his book *A Resource Guide for Teaching K–12*, Kellough (2007) emphasizes the depth of responsibility to plan lessons so that they are significant in content and meaningful to the learner. Kellough writes,

> As a classroom teacher, your instructional task is two-fold: (1) to plan hands-on experiences, providing the materials and the supportive environment necessary for students' meaningful exploration and discovery, and (2) to facilitate the most meaningful and longest-lasting learning possible once the learner's mind has been engaged by the hands-on learning including, although not necessarily limited to student learning of any curriculum that may be mandated by your state and local school district. To accomplish this requires your knowledge about curriculum, and competence in the use of varied and developmentally appropriate methods of instruction." (p. 137)

Kellough could have been talking directly to Matthew, the preservice teacher in this story. Although Matthew did engage the interest of his students with a hands-on activity, the activity was only tangentially related to the understanding that the sun and other stars appear to move in a recognizable pattern both daily and seasonally. The only relationship at all, in fact, was that his art project had to do with making colorful stars. Matthew had planned a more comprehensive lesson and one more related to his objective, but at the first opportunity he abandoned his lesson plan (and his role as teacher) and succumbed to a childlike desire to "just have fun." The result of this is that no meaningful learning took place. To quote Kellough (2007) again, teachers sometimes "fail to focus on what the learning objectives in these activities truly are—that is, what the students will be able to do (performance) as a result of the instructional activity" (p. 217). Eby, Herrell, and Jordan (2006) reiterate this concern. They refer to the National Board for Professional Teaching Standards (NBPTS) and the five propositions believed to be fundamental requirements for effective teaching. Matthew, the student teacher in this case story, ignored at least propositions 2 and 3. The following are the five propositions:

1. Teachers are committed to students and their learning.
2. Teachers know the subject matter they teach and how to teach those subjects to students.
3. Teachers are responsible for managing and monitoring student learning.
4. Teachers think systematically about their practice and learn from experience.
5. Teachers are members of learning communities. (p. 17)

In Matthew's favor, he is an eager and dedicated individual who is truly concerned with his students' learning, but as a teacher he is still immature. It is important, for example, that his planning have as a primary focus state and professional standards. In fact, Matthew might begin future planning with a standards-based planning process. One researcher describes this as the ability to identify outcomes and assessment criteria and plan communications so they align with desired learning outcomes (Rutherford, 2006, p. 22). For such planning to occur, several variables are important. Among them, two pertain particularly to planning (pp. 25–26).

1. Recognizing standards-referenced versus standards-based planning, instruction, and assessment. The lesson that Matthew conducted was a *standards-referenced* lesson. That is, there was reference to the standards and it was clear that some understanding of something related to stars was desired. *Standards-based* lessons, on the other hand, focus on essential understandings related to the topic. Meeting the objective of Matthew's lesson is far more complicated that cutting out and coloring paper stars. To obtain the desired learning outcome, students must first comprehend the meaning of the objective. The use of the word *appear* (appear to move in recognizable patterns), for example, is critical and leads the student to the understanding that stars and constellations are not moving at all. They *appear* to move because of the rotation of Earth on its axis. Students also should be able to make connections to other recognizable patterns in nature (e.g., growth of plants, seasonal weather, seasonal appearance of various constellations, etc.). Of course, students should reach understandings regarding what patterns are authentic (e.g., growth in plants) and that only appear to be authentic (e.g., the sun rising and falling). In this sense, Matthew's lesson failed miserably.

2. Being knowledgeable about key concepts and big ideas in all disciplines. It is impossible for the teacher to help students make connections between and among disciplines if the teacher lacks knowledge of the connections.

Baxendell (2003) suggests that one method of planning that helps to make these connections and ultimately benefits both the teacher and the students is using graphic organizers to illustrate key concepts. Basically, a graphic organizer is nothing more than a visual representation of key concepts. If used purposefully and with knowledge of key concepts, however, it is a powerful tool in developing understandings. Baxendell believes effective graphic organizers have three characteristics: They should be consistent, coherent, and creative (p. 46). Consistency refers to ensuring that a routine for using graphic organizers is in place. Providing labels or arrows showing the relationship between ideas leads to coherency. Finally, teachers must model creativity in the use of graphic organizers. Ideally, they will be used in a variety of ways to reinforce learning, throughout both planning and implementation of instruction and independently by large and small groups of students (Baxendell).

The interactive nature of the learning process also has to be kept in mind when planning instruction. Not only the teacher but also students influence instruction. Just as an individual's health relies on both the doctor's prescription for good health and the patient's compliance and follow-through with the doctor's advice, so does teaching rely on the interaction of teacher and students. "Although effective teaching is fundamental to teaching and learning, overemphasis on the importance of teaching methodology in the process of learning implies that we should ignore the dynamic learning process in which students are the significant players, not just teachers" (Ding & Sherman, 2006, p. 45). Teachers and students are equally accountable for learning. In the preceding case story, both teacher and students, overcome by the excitement of other activities, abandoned the planned lesson. To plan and implement lessons effectively, teachers must keep learning objectives in the forefront, know the characteristics of individual students, and be aware of the context in which teaching and learning take place (Ding & Sherman). The student teacher in the case story is still developing this awareness.

When it comes to student teachers who are still developing their skills, some of the responsibility belongs to the cooperating teacher. There is, for example, research that shows that the quality of feedback given to novice teachers is an essential ingredient in their later growth and success as teachers. Essential elements of feedback designed specifically to promote professional growth include the following:

1. Feedback should be based on descriptive, observable data. Asking the student teacher how he or she met program goals may lead to a concrete criticism, but it does not lead to improved understanding. Discussing observable events in the implementation of the student teacher's lesson is more likely to lead to self-reflection and growth.
2. Feedback should be compared against characteristics of effective teaching. It is not enough for novice teachers to know what went wrong. They also must know best practices.
3. Feedback should promote effective inquiry and self-directedness to foster improvement in teaching. If feedback was effective, then improvement should occur and be observable. (Feeney, 2007, p. 191)

Unfortunately, feedback is often too shallow to make a discernible difference in teacher behaviors.

Borich (2004) sums up the essential ingredients of good planning, stating that a system approach is needed, one in which the relationship among individual lessons is considered. In other words, new lessons should be designed to build on the outcomes of previous lessons and also provide a foundation for future learning. With this criterion in mind, effective planning, implementation, and evaluation of those plans requires that teachers be knowledgeable in five interrelated areas: knowledge of aims and goals; knowledge of learners; knowledge of subject-matter content and organization; knowledge of teaching methods; and tacit knowledge acquired from day-to-day experiences and feedback in the classroom (pp. 126–127). While seemingly a simple formula, effectively implementing lesson plans based on this system approach requires enormous understanding and self-reflection on the part of teachers. To quote two experienced writers, researchers, and teachers, "effective teaching doesn't just happen; it must be planned for and designed in a systematic way" (Kauchak & Eggen, 2008, p. 380).

Summary of Research

Effective teaching is the result of careful planning on the part of the teacher. Instructional plans should begin with clear learning objectives and clear expectations for student learning outcomes. According to Borich (2004), this requires that teachers have knowledge in several areas: knowledge of aims and goals; knowledge of learners; knowledge of subject-matter content and organization; knowledge of teaching methods; and tacit knowledge acquired from day-to-day experiences and feedback in the classroom. Instructional planning is most effective when the instruction is meaningful to the learner, connects to past learning, and lays a foundation for future learning.

CASE 13: TOPICS FOR DISCUSSION

- Instructional planning should have as a primary focus state and professional standards.
- Too little emphasis is put on the accountability of students in the teaching/learning process. Students are the ones who have to take primary responsibility for their own learning.
- Teachers are often told that new lessons should be connected to prior learning. Yet it is next to impossible to know what another individual does and does not know, much less to know what each child in an entire class knows and does not know.
- Learning does not have to be fun for the student to gain knowledge and skills.

CASE 13: EXPLORING THE ISSUES

1. Look up the standards for science in your state. Write a lesson plan to meet one of the standards. Use the Lesson Plan Builder on Merrill's TeacherPrep Web site. Go to http://www.prenhall.com/teacherprep. Once you are logged in, click on *Lesson Plan Builder* on the menu on the left. Then, click on *Lesson Plan Guidelines.* Follow these nine steps in planning your own lesson.

2. While still on Merrill's TeacherPrep Web site, click on *Video Classroom.* Then click on *Foundations/Introduction to Teaching.* When this window opens, click on *Module 6: Curriculum and Instruction.* Then, click on *Video 5: PowerPoint Guides and Prompts Teaching.* In this video, the benefits of incorporating PowerPoint into instructional planning are explained. After watching this video, recall a class you recently attended in which PowerPoint was used. Write a reflection paper in which you discuss your perceptions of how the use of PowerPoint contributed to instructional planning and desired student learning outcomes and/or how it detracted from desired student learning outcomes.

3. The elementary teacher in this case story has not taken many courses in science and math and deliberately avoids teaching these subjects when she can. Do some research on your own by using peer-reviewed articles to see what has been done to encourage elementary teachers to become more qualified to teach mathematics and science. Create an annotated list of at least five innovative practices that can be used in any discipline, including science and math. Discuss the one in which you would be most likely to participate. Explain why this venture appeals to you.

4. Assume that you are chair of your elementary school's science and mathematics department. Write a proposal in which you propose a staff development workshop (or series of workshops) designed specifically to help teachers to improve instructional planning in science and mathematics. Keep in mind that teachers have to have knowledge of the subject matter and of facts, principles, and concepts related to the subject matter. They also have to have the pedagogical skills to ensure that students learn.

5. Write a two- to four-page essay titled "Instructional Planning in the Second Half of the 21st Century." In this essay, include your predictions as to how technology will influence instructional planning, teaching, and learning in all disciplines in the second half of this century.

CASE 14: PLANNING AND KNOWLEDGE OF SUBJECT MATTER

Thinking Ahead

As you read this case, reflect on the following:

- Does a teacher have to be genuinely knowledgeable in the subject matter he or she is teaching, or is it enough to stay a few steps ahead of the students?
- How do you prepare to teach subjects for which your subject matter knowledge is limited, especially if there is an expectation to make connections among disciplines?
- In other professions such as medicine and law, practitioners are expected to know the subject matter for the area in which they are working. Why don't we have this expectation for teachers?

Erica Fournier walked into the main office and offered a tired but friendly smile to Maryann, the principal's secretary. "I'm so glad it's Friday!" Erica announced, reaching for the sheaf of papers in her office mailbox.

Maryann nodded in agreement. "It sure has been a busy week! Oh—you have a phone message here. I didn't have a chance to put it in your box." She reached over and handed Erica a square slip of pink paper. "I wouldn't wait until Monday to return *that* call," Maryann advised.

Erica glanced at the name on the memo. *Mrs. Harrison.* It was probably Melissa Harrison's mother. Melissa was a terrific student. Why would Mrs. Harrison want to speak with her? Erica's palms began to sweat.

It was only Erica's second year of teaching, and she was unfamiliar with the nuances of parent power in this well-off suburban district. Plus, it was October 17, just 7 weeks into the school year. Midterm reports had not come out, and parent conferences weren't scheduled for another 2 weeks. Erica hadn't spoken with the parents of any of her 23 fifth-grade students yet.

Erica turned back to Maryann. "What do you mean?" she asked. "Did Mrs. Harrison say anything?"

As a 35-year veteran of the school, Maryann took it upon herself to help new teachers as much as she could. Often, what they needed most was assistance understanding the culture of the school, understanding where the *real* sources of power and information were. Potentially powerful stakeholders included not just administrators and colleagues but also parents, support staff, and board members. New teachers needed to learn how to navigate these relationships. Maryann knew that a few well-chosen words could frequently preempt serious problems.

"Don't worry," Maryann responded. "Mrs. Harrison is really very nice and easy to get along with. She has high expectations. That's all." Maryann smiled warmly at Erica, hoping to alleviate her anxiety.

"Isn't she a professor at the university or something?" Erica asked.

"Chemistry professor," Maryann replied. "Her son Daniel went here a few years ago in fact and was accepted into the science magnet for high school—a program for gifted and talented kids. Mrs. Harrison was so proud when that happened."

Erica nodded to acknowledge this information. She glanced down at the message again. It had both home and work numbers listed, conveying a sense of urgency. "Why do you think she wants me to call?" Erica asked.

Maryann shrugged her shoulders. "You have her daughter Melissa, right? She seems like a good kid."

"She's a terrific kid," Erica replied, "a great student and a great personality. Maybe her mom just wants to know how she's doing."

Erica wished Maryann a happy weekend and left the office. She was pretty sure she knew why Mrs. Harrison had called. This call was shaping up to be Erica's worse nightmare. "A science professor whose kid ends up with a teacher who doesn't know anything about science!" Erica thought.

Throughout her years of schooling, Erica had been an excellent student. She worked hard, selected challenging upper-level courses, and earned exceptional grades in all her subjects—with one notable exception: science. Erica had vivid memories of her science classes that went all the way back to her own elementary school days. She remembered bringing home a test with a barely passing grade. The test was on classifying animals, and the look of disappointment on her mother's face when she showed her the test was still in her memory. She managed to avoid showing her mother other tests in science as she went through high school. Despite earning grades of A in her two required introductory college math courses, Erica found taking anything more advanced too frustrating. She had vowed to avoid taking science altogether but was required to take at least one course in college.

Erica met her science requirement by taking two 1.5 credit electives: Global Warming and Health and Nutrition. As the titles indicated, each course focused on a particular current topic and coursework involved reading, discussing, and writing about issues and personal experiences. Erica was thrilled to discover science courses that didn't cause any anxiety, but she was just as thrilled when the courses were behind her. "Never again!" she said to herself. "I'll never have to think about science again!"

Until now. Mrs. Harrison's message still had to be answered. Erica knew that one of her teaching responsibilities was to cover the science in her fifth-grade curriculum. She had no illusions about her weaknesses in this area. She tried to compensate for her weak science instruction by providing excellent instruction in other areas. Her colleagues often complimented her on her creative approaches to teaching social studies or English/Language Arts. She got no such compliments for her science and math lessons.

For science and math, Erica relied heavily on the textbook, often having one student read sections aloud while the others followed along. She used tests that came with the textbook series, but she usually completed them orally in class rather than administering them as assessment. She relied heavily on using the key that came with the tests. Erica scheduled science for the end of the day and sometimes other activities ran over. Assessing students on material she hadn't really covered didn't seem fair, but by reading the test question out loud, she at least let students know what they were expected to know.

Now she had to return Mrs. Harrison's call. What could she possibly say about science to someone like Mrs. Harrison?

CASE 14: ISSUES FOR ANALYSIS AND REFLECTION

1. Case 14 is related to the INTASC Standard for Planning and to the following two key indicators for this standard: The teacher (a) plans lessons and activities to address variations in learning styles and performance modes, multiple development levels of diverse learners, and problem solving and exploration and (b) develops short- and long-term plans. Once you have identified the primary issue, problem, or concern in this case, determine what other content knowledge is needed to ensure positive outcomes.
2. What pedagogical knowledge and skills are needed?
3. What must be done to ensure that desired student learning outcomes are obtained?

Use the DEEPS Method to analyze this case. Keep in mind the INTASC Standard for Planning and the key indicators listed in item 1.

Determine the primary issue, problem, or concern in this case.

Enumerate the facts that support your belief regarding the primary issue, problem, or concern in the case.

Evaluate the case to find all the possible solutions for resolving the issue, problem, or concern.

Problem solve by thinking critically about each possible solution and accepting or rejecting the solution based on its value in ensuring the professional growth of the teacher in relation to the use of planning.

Summarize your conclusion/solutions and be prepared to present the best possible solution and your rationale to your professor and colleagues.

CASE 14: WHAT THE RESEARCH SAYS

We live in a society dependent on science and technology. States and districts are struggling to graduate students who are skilled in these disciplines and who can meet the increasing need for expertise in these areas. At the elementary level, stakeholders are trying to ensure teacher content knowledge when it comes to science instruction and develop strong curricula with strong assessment components. As stated by Stamp and O'Brien (2005), "sufficient quality and quantity of science education at the elementary school level is the key to developing science literacy and inspiring students about the potential careers in science" (p. 70). The United States, however, is not producing scientists and engineers needed for the rapid economic growth in this area. According to another researcher (Payne, 2004), a push toward greater science literacy needs to begin as early as kindergarten when the stage can be easily set for further science learning. The primary grades are the time and place in which it is easy to get children involved in discovery learning through hands-on activities, critical thinking, and problem solving (Payne).

Unfortunately, the preceding case story relays a familiar scenario: the elementary-level teacher who has taken little or no science coursework during college or university studies. Erica, the sixth-grade teacher in the case story, avoided science courses during her college studies and focused only on those courses in which she excelled.

A warning from the Greek philosopher Aristotle might have been helpful to her. In a discussion about the training of athletes, Aristotle states that if parents allowed their children to devote themselves only to athletics, the children would later be useful to the state in that one quality only. Sadly, the same seems to be true of the elementary-level teacher. Elementary-level teachers who have devoted themselves only to the humanities are not particularly helpful to the school and its students when it comes to math and science.

In an article on science education reform, Wheeler (2006) cites studies (Chaney, 1995; Darling-Hammond, 2000; Druva & Anderson, 1983) that show a positive correlation between teacher knowledge and student achievement. A significant number of teachers, Wheeler states, lack degrees or coursework in science, and this is especially true at the elementary level (p. 30). This concern is reinforced by the low performance of so many elementary students on the National Assessment of Educational Performance (NAEP). According to Cavanaugh, low scores have to lead to the conclusion that students are simply poorly prepared to do better. This may be due to the way in which science is taught. Cavanaugh states that "many experts say U.S. schools are hampered by the absence of a national curriculum in math and science, with students being taught a mishmash of topics in different states and schools" (Cavanaugh, 2006, p. 16). This is not necessarily solved by establishing a national curriculum for math and science but it does require districts to ensure that expectations are in place for what should be taught at different grade levels and that this sequence of studies be logical and sequential (Cavanaugh). Another study by Wenglinsky and Silverstein (2006/2007) reports that the quality of classroom instruction in science is directly related to the quality of teacher knowledge and the ability to deliver content. In fact, the same researchers state that "the best predictor of student achievement is teacher course-taking patterns: The more science courses teachers had taken in college, the better their students performed" (p. 30).

Teachers themselves have voiced their own concerns about their lack of confidence when it comes to teaching science. In a 2004 survey title *Making Sense of Science* (as reported in Payne, 2004), science was the only subject for which new teachers consistently stated they lacked confidence and ability to teach. Newly hired teachers were quoted as stating that they wished science had been emphasized more in their teacher preparation programs; that they teach other core subjects every day but choose not to teach science; that they do not feel qualified to teach science; and, according to 30% of the respondents, that they rated their school's science program as poor (p. 34). There is an obvious need to raise the science content knowledge of elementary teachers. As this case story implies, a teacher may be skilled at planning but, when it comes to instruction and assessment, teachers cannot teach what they do not know.

Wenglinsky and Silberstein (2006/2007) believe that teacher training programs have to ensure that preservice elementary teachers develop critical skills in four areas:

1. *Laboratory skills*   Teachers who are trained in this area are far more likely to help students make connections between laboratory experiences and underlying scientific concepts.
2. *Hands-on learning*   Research shows that students who have had early, meaningful hands-on investigative experiences in science tend to perform better on science tests and show greater interest in science.

3. *Instructional technology* Teachers skilled in both science and instructional technology were able to create firsthand, virtual experiences for their students (e.g., a volcano erupting).

4. *Frequent formative assessment* Formative assessment that is directed at ways to improve learning has been shown to be a highly effective means of increasing desired student learning outcomes. (p. 30)

What actually happens in teacher preparation programs and in professional development programs, however, is that a series of isolated science experiments or science activities are presented. The underlying science concepts are given far less emphasis than the activity itself (Wheeler, 2006/2007).

Fortunately, all the research regarding teaching science in the elementary school is not bleak. Recently, focus has been on teaching investigative science skills to teachers early in their career. Doing so will help teachers to develop content pedagogy that resembles authentic science. The idea here is that scientists *do* science; they don't just talk about it. The fear, according to at least one researcher (McNally, 2006), is that investigation can often be trivial and not at all scientific. The example is given of a lesson on pollution. The children were told to color a spoon "like a fish" and put it in a jar of water. Then, polluted matter was poured into the jar. The concept the teacher wanted to establish was that the more pollution that is added to the water, the more the habitat is destroyed (as evidenced by inability to see the "fish" once the water became cloudy). This simply does not translate into a worthwhile science activity. First of all, the conclusion is faulty. Second, the children are not investigating at all; they are merely being led to a predetermined conclusion. The results are already known and the teacher is simply looking for agreement (McNally).

Another promising practice is an interdisciplinary approach in which skills acquired in one area are transferred to other disciplines. In reading, for example, children are taught not only phonics and comprehension but also to look for main ideas and themes and to draw inferences and conclusions. These same skills are needed in science learning. It has been shown, in fact, that exemplary science teachers and exemplary reading teachers both have a good grasp on the relationship between content and pedagogy and use a variety of purposeful methods to ensure learning. Among these methods are appropriate scaffolding, use of discovery learning and problem solving, experimentation, prediction, emphasizing key concepts, and making learning relevant (Ediger, 2005).

There is a need for teacher preparation programs to focus more on science learning. Bybee (2005) suggests that colleges should design college-level science courses specifically for elementary teachers. These courses should be designed to deepen conceptual understandings related to science and also to provide laboratory experiences that reinforce understandings. It is important, however, that these courses ensure that preservice teachers are supported not only in the learning of subject matter related to science but also that they understand "best practices" for delivery of content (Parker, 2004). One of the most effective methods of planning science lessons has been to focus on what has become known as the 5 Es. The 5 Es refer to engaging, exploring, explaining, elaborating, and evaluating. Of necessity, this is based on an inquiry and investigative approach, much in keeping with constructivist approaches (Lloyd, 2007). Planning with the 5 Es in mind is enhanced when the planning itself is organized and sequential. Rettig, McCullough, Santos, and Watson (2003) suggest three strategies to improve planning:

1. *Develop pacing guides*   Ideally, this is done together with all teachers teaching the same unit. The pacing guide becomes the framework for planning the lesson itself. That is, the time available to cover any subject is limited. Effective teaching requires an awareness of that time and how to best use it. For example, in a discussion of how to find the mass of an object, is it best to begin to explain the idea of comparison, or is it best to begin by actually making the comparison? How much time should be given to either approach? What is the sequence of the rest of the activity?

2. *Become skilled in making formative assessments*   Formative assessment lets the teacher know the students' prior learning, questions that arise, and where instruction has and has not been successful. Formative assessment may take place "on the fly" through careful observation of and attention to learners, or it may be the result of judicial review throughout a lesson or at the beginning or end of a lesson.

3. *Participate in regularly scheduled staff meetings*   The purpose of these meetings is to discuss student progress, analyze formative assessments, and generate ideas to improve science instruction. Such meetings also provide peer support for teachers. Research shows that when departments have held regularly scheduled staff meetings, all teachers gained new knowledge and confidence, which resulted in more effective academic interventions for students and a more effectively differentiated curriculum (pp. 71–72).

Finally, as one author points out, there is a decades-old debate about the origins of good teachers. Some claim that good teachers have natural ability that cannot be taught in any program. Others state that good teachers are the result of good teacher training programs. Still others claim that good teaching comes from a good education, time, persistence, and energy (Rust, 2006). The debate will no doubt continue for many more decades. What does seem to be true, however, is that colleges must take the lead in developing strong teacher training programs with a far greater emphasis on science knowledge and pedagogy and, in fact, instructional planning in general. As Payne (2004) states, when it comes to creating a healthy science curriculum with well-prepared and highly qualified teachers, "colleges and university teacher training programs are where it all begins" (p. 36).

Summary of Research

Districts and states are struggling with the demand to graduate students talented in science, math, and technology. At precisely the time when careers in science and math are so much in demand, there are not sufficient numbers of individuals to fill positions in these fields. Some researchers suggest that authentic training in science must begin as early as kindergarten to instill the interest to continue studies in this area.

A body of research indicates that teachers, particularly those at the elementary level, are not well trained in science. Some have avoided taking courses altogether in this area, and others have taken only the bare minimum of courses. The results of this are poor instructional planning related to science and little meaningful feedback to young learners that might enhance further learning. Colleges and universities with teacher preparation programs have begun to recognize the need for stronger science programs and have made revisions to existing programs to better develop the skills of prospective teachers in this area.

CASE 14: TOPICS FOR DISCUSSION

- Elementary-level teachers who have taken mostly humanities courses are not particularly helpful to the school and its students when it comes to teaching math and science.
- "Many experts say U.S. schools are hampered by the absence of a national curriculum in math and science, with students being taught a mishmash of topics in different states and schools" (Cavanaugh, 2006, p. 16). A national curriculum is needed in the United States.
- At the elementary level, economic stakeholders are trying to ensure teacher content knowledge when it comes to science instruction to meet the needs for a 21st-century workforce skilled in science and technology. It is not, however, the job of schools to produce a workforce.
- The best predictor of student achievement is teacher content knowledge in the subject area. The more science course teachers had taken in college, the better their students will perform on tests of science.

CASE 14: EXPLORING THE ISSUES

1. Divide into small groups and rewrite Matthew's lesson plan on constellations. With the rest of the group acting as the first-grade students, one member of the group should act as the teacher and teach the lesson you just designed. After the lesson is completed, critique the lesson for its strengths and weaknesses. How well did the person acting as the teacher help you to understand that "the sun and other stars appear to move in a recognizable pattern both daily and seasonally"? Did your group manage to engage the "students" to the same extent that Matthew did but also to cover the required content?
2. Discuss Matthew as a teacher. What are his strong and weak points? If you were his teaching supervisor or his college professor, what would you do to help him improve his skills when it comes to planning and instruction?
3. Go back to the lesson plan you just developed. Assume that your first grade consists of 20 students. Twelve of your students have English as their first language. Four students speak Spanish at home but are fluent in English, although they often use the vernacular. One student recently emigrated from Yemen and speaks only Arabic. Two other students, a brother and sister, arrived in this country 4 months ago from Russia and are just beginning to be able to converse comfortably in English. One student is from East Africa, and although he speaks three languages in his own country, he does not yet know enough English to carry on a conversation in English. Revise your lesson plan to meet the needs of all students in your class. Make sure to include the assessment measures you will use to know that students have met the objectives for this lesson.

4. Open your Web browser to http://www.prenhall.com/teacherprep. Once you are logged in, click on *Video Classroom*. Once there, click on *Science Methods*. When this window opens, click on *Module 6: Lesson Modules* and then open *Video 1: The Learning Cycles*. After you watch this video, answer the questions that relate to the teaching module and the interaction between students and teachers. Does having a model to follow make instructional planning easier or more complex?

5. Read the following article: Darling-Hammond, L. (2006, November). Highly qualified teachers for all. *Educational Leadership, 64*(30), 14–20. In this article, Darling-Hammond writes about the need for all students to have equitable access to highly qualified teachers. The quality of instructional planning, Darling-Hammond believes, is directly related to the competency of the teacher doing the planning. Darling-Hammond proposes some solutions to ensure equitable access to qualified teachers. Discuss the worth of her proposal and whether or not you agree with it as it relates to teaching in all disciplines.

References

Baxendell, B. W. (2003, January/February). Consistent, coherent, creative: The 3 Cs of graphic organizers. *Teaching Exceptional Children, 35*(3), 46–53.

Borich, G. (2004). *Effective Teaching Methods*. Upper Saddle River, NJ: Pearson/Merrill/Prentice Hall.

Bybee, R. W. (2005, Winter). Science education. *Issues in Science & Technology, 21*(2), 17–18.

Cavanaugh, S. (2006, June 7). NAEP scores show few budding scientists. *Education, 25*(39), 15–16.

Chaney, B. (1995). Student outcomes and the professional preparation of 8th grade teachers in science and mathematics. Unpublished manuscript. Prepared for NSF grant RED 9255255. Rockville, MD: Westat.

Darling-Hammond, L. (2000, January). Teacher quality and student achievement: A review of state policy evidence. *Education Policy Analysis Archives, 8*(1). Retrieved January 6, 2009, from http://epaa.asu.edu/epaa/v8n1.

Darling-Hammond, L., & Berry, B. (2006, November). Highly qualified teachers for all. *Educational Leadership, 64*(30), 14–20.

Ding, C., & Sherman, H. (2006, June). Teaching effectiveness and student achievement: Examining the relationship. *Educational Research Quarterly, 29*(4), 39–49.

Druva, C. A., & Anderson, R. (1983). Science teacher characteristics by teacher behavior and by student outcome: A meta-analysis of research. *Journal of Research in Science Teaching, 20*(5), 467–479.

Eby, J., Herrell, A., & Jordan, M. (2006). *Teaching in K–12 schools: A reflective action approach*. Upper Saddle River, NJ: Pearson/Merrill/ Prentice Hall.

Ediger, M. (2004, March). Addressing reading in the science curriculum. *College Student Journal, 39*(1), 26–30.

Feeney, E. G. (2007, March). Quality feedback: The essential ingredient for teacher success. *Clearing House, 80*(4), 191–198.

Kauchak, D., & Eggan, P. (2008). *Introduction to teaching: Becoming a professional*. Upper Saddle River, NJ: Pearson/Merrill/Prentice Hall.

Kellough, R. D. (2007). *A resource guide for teaching K–12*. Upper Saddle River, NJ: Pearson/ Merrill/Prentice Hall.

Lloyd, M. (2007, Spring). Can you teach an old dog new tricks? A teacher's perspective on changing pedagogy using primary connections. *The Journal of the Australian Science Teachers Association, 53*(3), 27–29.

McNally, J. (2006, March 18). Confidence and loose opportunism in the science classroom: Towards a pedagogy of investigative science for beginning teachers. *International Journal of Science Education, 24*(4), 423–428.

Parker, J. (2004, December). The synthesis of subject and pedagogy for effective learning and teaching in primary science education. *British Educational Research Journal, 30*(6), 820–840.

Payne, J. (2004, Fall). Pre-college science teachers need better training. *Science & Technology, 21*(1), 33–36.

Rettig, M., McCullough, L. L., Santos, K., & Watson, C. (2003, November). A blueprint for increasing student achievement. *Educational Leadership, 61*(3), 71–76.

Rust, F. O. (2006, June). Editorial. *Teachers & Teaching: Theory & Practice, 12*(3), 261–263.

Rutherford, P. (2006, September/October). Leading the learning. *Leadership, 36*(1), 22–26.

Stamp, N., & O'Brien, T. (2005, January). K–12 partnership: A model to advance change in science education. *Bioscience, 55*(1), 70–77.

Wenglinsky, H., & Silverstein, S. C. (2006, December/2007, January). The science training teachers need. *Educational Leadership, 65*(4), 24–29.

Wheeler, G. (2006, December/2007, January). Strategies for science education reforms. *Educational Leadership, 64*(4), 30–34.

8

INTASC Standard 8: Assessment

Description of INTASC Standard 8: *The teacher understands and uses assessment strategies to evaluate and ensure the continuous intellectual, social, and physical development of the learner.*

KEY INDICATORS FOR STANDARD 8

The Teacher

- selects, constructs, and uses assessment strategies appropriate to the learning outcomes.
- uses a variety of informal and formal strategies to inform choices about student progress and to adjust instruction (e.g., standardized test data, peer and student self-assessment, informal assessments such as observation, surveys, interview, student work, performance tasks, portfolio, and teacher-made tests).
- uses assessment strategies to involve learners in self-assessment activities to help them become aware of their strengths and needs, and to encourage them to set personal goals for learning.
- evaluates the effects of class activities on individuals and on groups through observation of classroom interaction, questioning and analysis of student work.
- maintains useful records of student work and performance and can communicate student progress knowledgeably and responsibly.
- solicits information about students' experiences, learning behavior, needs, and progress from parents, other colleagues, and students.

CASE 15: ASSESSMENT AND DIVERSITY

Thinking Ahead

As you read this case, reflect on the following:

- Is there a one-size-fits-all assessment method, or does assessment always have to be individualized?

- Even though the student in this case is fluent in English, he still has cultural and linguistic characteristics that differ from the mainstream. What impact does this have on assessment?
- How important is it for teachers to understand the culture of their students?
- How important is it for teachers to be familiar with leading research in the field as it relates to assessment and diversity?

It was a cool, crisp October morning, and the students in Jay Robbins' sixth-grade class were eagerly awaiting the return of their graded social studies projects. The projects, which focused on "World Explorers," had been completed over a 1-week period and included library research time and word processing in the school's new computer lab.

Mr. Robbins had designed the project specifically to be done during class time. He wanted to see how his students would perform independently without the often intrusive assistance of parents. He had seen more than his share of brilliantly completed homework essays and projects that he knew were really the work of overly helpful parents. In his class, students would be evaluated on what *they* could do—not on the academic capital of their parents.

The students were particularly excited because Mr. Robbins had presented the entire project to them as a "research paper" and had successfully convinced them that they were doing "middle school work." They were quite proud of themselves.

His students had embraced the project and, to the best of their abilities, each produced a paper of three to five pages in length. The subjects of their projects varied: Mario wrote about Christopher Columbus, Jared chose to research Magellan, Nikolette selected Vasco da Gama, Gabrielle chose John Cabot, and so on.

"Listen up, everybody," said Mr. Robbins. "I have the graded projects here, and I'll be passing them back to you individually. In the meantime, I want you to open your math books to page ninety-eight and do problems one through twenty. Okay, are you with me?"

For the next 2 minutes or so, predictable sounds of the classroom emerged: Math books were located and opened, paper was retrieved from notebooks, and pencils were extracted from pencil cases, while Mr. Robbins heard the usual array of questions and comments:

"What page was that?"

"I left my notebook at home."

"Can I borrow some paper?"

"May I sharpen my pencil?"

"Is it okay if we use a pen?"

Mr. Robbins responded to all these questions and comments with infinite patience and humor.

Soon the students settled into their math activity, and Mr. Robbins was moving from seat to seat, handing back the "World Explorers" papers and offering final comments that consisted primarily of words of encouragement and praise, coupled with occasional minor critiques, such as "Jenny, next time be sure to include the proper heading" and "Devon, always use the spell check. It's a tool to help you." However, as Mr. Robbins moved closer to Ahmed, the tension became palpable—for both the teacher and the student.

Ahmed Mhamed, whose family had come from Morocco a year ago to this midwestern town, had become a challenge for Mr. Robbins. As a veteran of 12 years in the elementary classroom, Mr. Robbins had dealt successfully with many types of students. The building principal often assigned the most difficult students—both academically and behaviorally—to Mr. Robbins. His classroom management and good-natured kidding with the students usually yielded positive results. "Ahmed," Mr. Robbins found himself thinking, "seems bright enough and his English is fluent, but he can be argumentative. It's no surprise the principal assigned Ahmed to my class. Mrs. Collins next door would be at a loss with what to do with Ahmed."

From the outset, things had not gone well between Mr. Robbins and Ahmed. This social studies project was a microcosm of the problem. When introducing the project, Mr. Robbins gave his students a list of 30 world explorers from whom to choose. Ahmed reviewed the list and informed Mr. Robbins that he wished to do research on Ibn Battuta, a North African explorer who lived during the 14th century but was not on the list. Mr. Robbins, who was well versed in the content standards of the state's social studies curriculum (as well as the requirements of the state social studies test for sixth-graders) commended Ahmed for "thinking outside the box" but insisted that he select from the prescribed list of explorers. In planning the project, Mr. Robbins had worked extensively with the school librarian to develop a database related to his list of world explorers.

Ahmed had heard stories of the great explorer Ibn Battuta from his father, and he wanted to learn more about this fascinating man. Ahmed was angry and hurt when Mr. Robbins refused to let him report on Battuta. Ahmed had never heard of the other explorers and could not understand why he was not allowed to do his report on an explorer of his choice.

Still, Ahmed reluctantly respected his teacher's authority and decided to do research on Henry Hudson. While Ahmed and his class were in the school library, he read three short articles about the explorer, checked several related Web sites, and took notes on the readings. At the end of the library period, Mr. Robbins, as was his practice, collected all written work. This was in keeping with one of the lesson's objectives: that students would learn to work independently within a prescribed time frame. It also provided a measure of accountability.

Ahmed, at first, would not share his notes with Mr. Robbins. Then he asked if he could take his notes home to continue his project outside of class. Mr. Robbins, growing a bit exasperated, again insisted that Ahmed follow the project rules and turn in all notes.

Ahmed's efforts to understand Henry Hudson's importance as a world explorer had used up some of his allotted time in the library. This bothered Ahmed, and he wanted to make up the time by revising his work at home. When Mr. Robbins took all his notes, Ahmed was pretty sure he wouldn't be able to finish the project on time. Ahmed shared his frustration with his parents and older siblings and told them he probably wouldn't do as well as he wanted to do on this assignment. Ahmed's father seemed surprised but just told his son to do his best. After his father had left the room, Ahmed's older brother told him that just because things were difficult it was not a reason not to do well.

On the fourth day of the in-class project, Mr. Robbins reviewed each student's work and offered oral and written feedback. Ahmed recalled his interaction with Mr. Robbins vividly. Mr. Robbins began by noting that Ahmed "had better hurry up" because he was behind the rest of the class in finishing the paper. When Ahmed asked (again) if he could finish at home, Mr. Robbins said something to the effect that Ahmed had to "git 'er done" in the classroom. Ahmed wasn't sure what Mr. Robbins meant, but he was certain that he could not take the work home. When Ahmed reviewed the written feedback on the draft, he was hurt by the comments made by Mr. Robbins. Next to the opening paragraph, Mr. Robbins had drawn a line under one sentence and put a question mark next to it. In the right margin of the fifth paragraph, Mr. Robbins had written, "Think before you write." At the bottom of the second page, Mr. Robbins had written, "Add biographical details." At the end of the draft, Mr. Robbins had written, "Add transitional phrases."

Ahmed agreed to add transitional phrases, as Mr. Robbins recommended, but he questioned his teacher's request to "add biographical details" on Henry Hudson. The discussion erupted into an unpleasant exchange.

"Why do you wish me to add more biographical data?" Ahmed asked.

"That's an important part of the assignment," Mr. Robbins added, without further explanation.

"Aren't Henry Hudson's explorations more important?" Ahmed asked. "Don't you want to know more about what he accomplished?"

Mr. Robbins answered curtly, "It's part of the assignment to add the biographical details, Ahmed. Stop arguing about it."

Ahmed sat in silence. He wanted to express his disagreement further but could tell that he had somehow angered his teacher with his questions.

Interpreting Ahmed's silence as acquiescence, Mr. Robbins concluded the conversation by simply saying, "Listen, Ahmed, just follow the directions, okay?"

Ahmed took pride in his schoolwork, and he always thought about what he wrote. At home in Morocco, he was often praised for his written work. "Who cares where Henry Hudson was born and where he went to school?" Ahmed thought, thoroughly annoyed with the whole project. "How could Mr. Robbins care so little about what Hudson accomplished?" But Ahmed remembered his brother's words and worked hard on the assignment. He went back and added biographical details and tried to add the other details his teacher had suggested on the draft, but he had no confidence that Mr. Robbins would like his final paper. He waited nervously as Mr. Robbins walked around the class returning papers to his classmates.

Mr. Robbins was finally at Ahmed's desk. "You received a grade of C−, Ahmed. I expected you to do better. I'm disappointed," Mr. Robbins said as he handed the paper to Ahmed. Ahmed stared incredulously at the grade scrawled with red ink at the top of his paper.

Ahmed was overwhelmed with frustration. He wanted to like Mr. Robbins—he really did—but there was something about the man that frustrated him. Ahmed loved school and had been an excellent student in Morocco, but no matter how hard he tried in Mr. Robbins' class, he seemed to disappoint his teacher.

"I know you're probably disappointed with your grade," said Mr. Robbins, "but I'm disappointed, too. I'm disappointed in your minimal efforts to improve your paper." Mr. Robbins spoke quietly but definitively. Earlier today, he had promised himself that he would not argue with Ahmed.

Ahmed did not see discussing his work as an argument. He always discussed ideas at home with his family. With barely concealed frustration, Ahmed looked up at Mr. Robbins and said, "I did what you asked. I worked very hard to do what you asked."

"Perhaps you did," said Mr. Robbins, "but let's look at the overall quality of your final paper."

Mr. Robbins pointed to some awkward sentence structures and to the lack of sufficient biographical information. Ahmed was not listening. He felt like crying, but he knew that was unacceptable. He kept his eyes glued to the C−. Mr. Robbins stared at the top of Ahmed's head, keenly aware of the emotions running through the boy.

"Listen, Ahmed," said Mr. Robbins, "let's talk about this after school today, okay?"

Ahmed said nothing. Moving on to the next desk, Mr. Robbins wondered whether he would ever be able to forge a connection with Ahmed. Ahmed thought about how much he longed to return to Morocco where his work was respected by his teachers.

CASE 15: ISSUES FOR ANALYSIS AND REFLECTION

1. Case 15 is related to the INTASC Standard for Assessment and to the following three key indicators for this standard: The teacher (a) selects, constructs, and uses assessment strategies appropriate to the learning outcomes, (b) evaluates the effects of class activities on individuals and on groups through observation of classroom interaction, questioning, and analysis of student work, and (c) solicits information about students' experiences, learning behavior, needs, and progress from parents, other colleagues, and students. Once you have identified the primary issue, problem, or concern in this case, determine what other content knowledge is needed to ensure positive outcomes.
2. What pedagogical knowledge and skills are needed?
3. What must be done to ensure that desired student learning outcomes are obtained?

Use the DEEPS Method to analyze this case. Keep in mind the INTASC Standard for Assessment and the key indicators listed in item 1.

Determine the primary issue, problem, or concern in this case.

Enumerate the facts that support your belief regarding the primary issue, problem, or concern in the case.

Evaluate the case to find all the possible solutions for resolving the issue, problem, or concern.

Problem solve by thinking critically about each possible solution and accepting or rejecting the solution based on its value in ensuring the professional growth of the teacher in relation to assessment.

Summarize your conclusion/solutions and be prepared to present the best possible solution and your rationale to your professor and colleagues.

CASE 15: WHAT THE RESEARCH SAYS

This case story about the tensions between a student and his teacher and its impact on assessment raises very real questions about the human element of assessment practice. Three issues are related to this case: (a) the impact of culture on fair assessment practices, (b) the role of teacher preparation programs in preparing graduates who are skilled in fair assessment practices, and (c) effective assessment techniques.

We know from the case review that Ahmed, a sixth-grade student, has moved to a midwestern town from Morocco, North Africa, just over a year ago. He is fluent in English, a serious and responsible student, and a young man who values education. The teacher in Ahmed's new U.S. school, on the other hand, views Ahmed as unusually argumentative and as a student who had been assigned to his class because he was viewed by the principal as one of "the most difficult students—both academically and behaviorally." From the outset, we learn, things had not gone well between Ahmed and his teacher, Mr. Robbins. Given recent immigration statistics, the problem in this case is likely to be repeated over and over again in schools across the nation.

In an article on the importance of recognizing cultural and linguistic differences in learners, Chamberlain (2005) states that there is danger in failing to see how assessment practices can lead to underestimating a student's abilities and the subsequent stereotyping of some cultural groups as low performing or as presenting behavioral challenges. It is important to note as well that more than just culture and ethnicity can contribute to differences. For example, a disruptive home life, poverty, limited prior schooling, educational attainment of parents, poor instruction, size of household, family commitments, and such can all influence learning outcomes. Misconceptions about behaviors and abilities, however, are often due to "cultural clashes" between the culture and values of the student and the culture and values of the teacher (p. 195). Mr. Robbins, for example, probably views his direct manner as honest and helpful when he told Ahmed that he needed to think before he wrote or "to just follow directions." In Arab culture, however, politeness is conveyed by indirect speech. The use of a question or a proverb or a reminder of family expectations is more acceptable (and powerful) than a direct complaint about progress. As one writer explains, "In Arabic . . . directness is frequently understood as rudeness and is condemned, whereas in English, for example, it is regarded as a tool for true communication and is appreciated" (Aballasan, n.d.). As well, in parts of the Middle East and North Africa eye contact is expected and is held longer than in European culture. It is used to punctuate important points in a conversation and is a sign of being open and honest (Eyring, 2006). In European culture, if a student maintains eye contact with a teacher, it is often interpreted as defiance. A simple but poignant concept to keep in mind in this regard is that when schools talk about cultural and linguistic differences, in effect they mean "different from the mainstream culture and language, a culture that reflects European values and content (Chamberlain, 2005, p. 197). In the cultural clash between Mr. Robbins and Ahmed, Mr. Robbins views himself as making honest efforts to deal fairly with a young man who is aggressive and bordering on poor academic performance. Ahmed, on the other hand, is frustrated by his efforts to behave politely and responsibly toward an authority figure, an authority figure he perceives as continually treating him rudely. It does seem that "the recent trend toward the growing mobility of instructors and students underscores the importance of understanding the role played by national culture in judgments of fairness" (Tata, 2005, p. 402). One way to better ensure that teachers are prepared for using assessment methods in equitable ways with all populations of students is for teacher preparation programs to address issues of fair assessment in college coursework.

A teacher preparation program at one university attempted to find solutions to the concern with being culturally responsive to learner diversity and simultaneously ensuring that state and national standards are met. A major goal in this teacher preparation program was finding ways to provide graduates of the university's program with the necessary knowledge and skills for effective assessment practice (Bernhard, Diaz, & Allgood, 2005). A promising practice turned out to be encouraging preservice teachers to rely heavily on current research related to testing and assessment practices. By requiring preservice teachers to validate responses with findings from research, the teacher candidates quickly built an understanding of best practices when it comes to assessment. They were empowered to judge the merits of assessment practice and to clarify their own pedagogy. Using research in assessment as a basis for discussion also decreased tensions that might have otherwise arisen between discussants. All individuals in the discussions shared a common base of understanding when it came to evaluating culturally and linguistically different students (Bernhard et al.).

Researchers Salend and Taylor (2002) suggest that teachers must become skilled in defining behaviors in ways that are not judgmental or accusatory. Reporting behaviors objectively as contributing to further learning or diminishing opportunities for further learning is something that requires skill, and this skill comes with practice. In an article that is predominantly concerned with the over-referral to special education of students who are culturally and linguistically different, the research states that teachers not only must use instruments that accurately measure behaviors that appear to impede learning, teachers must also have knowledge of a student's "cultural perspective and experiential and learning background [to determine] whether the student's behavior has a sociocultural explanation" (p. 106). This knowledge of cultural perspective is equally important in communicating assessment results to the student and/or the student's family.

Finally Eby, Herrell, and Jordan (2006) suggest that preservice teachers must practice aligning planning, instruction, and assessment. If both students and teacher know what skills the student is expected to demonstrate as a result of an assignment, the likelihood for success is much higher. Assessment procedures are also made easier by aligning assessment with objectives to determine whether or not students have acquired the expected skills (p. 265). In Ahmed's case, for example, a rubric clearly describing the characteristics of a "good" paper would have helped in later discussion of the paper. There is, in fact, no indication that researching the life and explorations of Ibn Battuta would have interfered with meeting social studies standards for Ahmed's grade level. Even allowing Ahmed to make comparisons between Hudson's and Ibn Battuta's explorations might have gone a long way toward ensuring the assignment had relevance for him but simultaneously did not compromise meeting social studies standards. The tension between Mr. Robbins and Ahmed appears to be largely related to individual perceptions of authority and respect and has less connection to evaluating outcomes related to social studies content.

Darling-Hammond, a professor of education at Stanford University, founder of the Stanford Leadership Institute, and author of over 200 publications on teacher practice, states that students sometimes fail simply because they don't know what is expected of them and how their work will be evaluated by their teachers. Darling-Hammond suggests that good assessment is likely to follow when teachers begin by assigning work that is worth the effort and is authentic and engaging. The work should also be doable. The teacher has to consider whether or not completing assignments will require assistance and whether or not this assistance is available. Darling-Hammond also suggests that there be opportunities for collaboration and for making student work public. This allows students to see exemplars of acceptable and very good work and to also critique their own work (Darling-Hammond & Hill-Lynch, 2006).

The role of formative assessment in improving outcomes is another assessment method that is too often overlooked or trivialized. Formative assessment is an ongoing assessment process intended to give students feedback on their learning progress and to give teachers an indication of what students have mastered and where they are having difficulty. It allows the teacher to make adjustments in instruction, fill in gaps in prior knowledge, and give feedback related to learning as the lesson progresses. But, like all assessment methods, formative assessment has to be used appropriately. In a review of over 250 articles related to formative assessment, for example, it was found that formative assessment often has a negative impact, especially when feedback is given to students who are considered to be low ability students by their teachers (Black, Harrison, Lee, Marshall, & William, 2004). The focus of formative assessment should not be to praise a student or to bring the student's abilities into question. The purpose of formative assessment, as with any assessment, is to promote student learning. Again, in the case of Ahmed, assessment feedback was used negatively, simply to tell him which directions he did not follow and that he was not completing the assignment in the time frame established by the teacher. Hearing that he was not doing well in school was a new experience for Ahmed, a young man who had always been considered a good student. This type of feedback did nothing to promote further learning. Instead it led to feelings of confusion and failure.

To make formative assessment more effective, Mr. Robbins would have to begin with dialogue that engages the student (Black et al., 2004). This might involve questions such as *Did you find any similarities between Ibn Battuta and Hudson*? or *What is it about explorers that interests you?* This line of questioning, according to the research, might have extended Ahmed's thinking about this project. Effective dialogue might also have put more focus on listening to the student's explanations of his work and then giving concrete feedback at appropriate intervals to better guide progression through the assignment (Black et al.).

Formative assessment also takes place when grades are attached to student work. In this regard, comments should be designed to improve future work. Ideally, such comments "should identify what has been done well and what still needs improvement, and give guidance on how to make that improvement" (Black et al., 2004, p. 14). Finally, students should have planned opportunities to respond to comments. Any attempt made by Ahmed to respond to his teacher's criticism was interpreted by the teacher as argumentative behavior. A planned opportunity for response, however, would have made Ahmed a collaborator in the assessment process and overall would provide opportunities for him to better understand expectations for performance. As one writer states, "when teachers know how students are progressing and where they are having trouble, they can use this information to make necessary instructional adjustments, such as re-teaching, trying alternative instructional approaches, and offering more opportunities for practice. These activities can lead to improved student success" (Boston, 2002). This is an opportunity that Mr. Robbins missed in evaluating the work of his young student.

Summary of Research

Effective assessment requires knowledge of the learner and skill in ensuring that assessment leads to improved further learning. It is important for teachers and other professionals involved in evaluating any student to make sure that assessment procedures are culturally appropriate. Teacher preparation programs can do more to assist preservice teachers in developing knowledge and skill in assessment. Putting more emphasis on current research related to "best practices" in assessment and providing opportunities for preservice teachers to practice formal and informal assessment techniques may be helpful. Formative assessment, when used appropriately, has been shown to be one method of assessment that leads to improved student learning outcomes.

CASE 15: TOPICS FOR DISCUSSION

- The eurocentric curricular approach that many U.S. schools follow sets up children of color and children with language and cultural differences for failure.
- The expectation for all teachers, not just preservice teachers, should be to validate responses with findings from research. This would decrease the possibility of teachers imposing their own value system on students.
- Effective assessment requires knowledge of the curriculum more than it requires knowledge of the learner.
- Every teacher brings his or her physical appearance, culture, and values into the classroom. The extent to which these differ from the physical, cultural, and intellectual backgrounds of the students in the class will have a profound effect on teacher–student interactions and learning.

CASE 15: EXPLORING THE ISSUES

1. Open your Web browser to http://www.prenhall.com/teacherprep. This will take you to Merrill's Teacher Prep Web site. Once you have logged in, click on *Video Classroom* on the menu on the left. When this opens, click on *General Methods* and then click on *Module 10: Learner Assessment*. When this window opens, click on *Video 1: Assessing Higher Order Thinking*. The lesson you will watch takes place in a high school but could easily be adapted to a K–6 setting. The teacher is asking the students to find similarities and differences among states on a U.S. map. Her objective is to engage the students in higher order thinking skills. After watching the lesson, discuss whether or not higher order thinking did occur and how the teacher might assess and report student achievement on this assignment.

2. A March 2007 blog recounted the following incident in West Virginia:

> The parents of a high school student are suing the girl's teacher and the board of education over a failing grade on a late assignment. On the day the assignment was due the student was away on a school-approved student council trip. According to the school's attorney, however, "the class had ample notice that late submissions would not be accepted. Part of going to school is learning there are rules, learning there are deadlines. Unfortunately, this is a pretty good student. But sometimes you just have to learn from your mistakes." The attorney hired by the girl's family, on the other hand is suing for damages for "emotional stress, loss of enjoyment of life, loss of scholarship potential."
>
> Interview three teachers at three different grade levels to get their reaction to this incident. Ask what they believe should be done to resolve this high profile assessment case. Report back to your peers to see how similar or different responses were. Attempt to reach majority consensus in your classroom as to what the appropriate action should be in this incident.

3. Reflect on your own schooling and a time when you believed you were graded unfairly because the teacher did not understand your work or your behavior. As someone soon to be a teacher yourself, how would you now interpret that incident?

4. Read the following article: Ahmad, I., & Szpara, M. Y. (2003, October). Muslim children in urban America: The NY city schools experience. *Journal of Muslim Minority Affairs, 23*(2), 295–301. In this article Muslim youth discuss their experiences in the public school system in New York City. After reading the article, discuss what teachers could do in schools to create a better understanding and respect for not only Muslim immigrants but also for immigrants from all backgrounds.

5. Choose an academic subject area at the K–6 level. Describe when you believe traditional assessment in the form of traditional, teacher-made tests is appropriate. Describe when you believe authentic forms of assessment are more appropriate. Explain how outcomes from each form of evaluation might differ in the circumstances you describe.

CASE 16: ASSESSMENT AND STANDARDIZED TESTING

Thinking Ahead

As you read this case, reflect on the following:

- Why is it that so much is written about the disadvantages of standardized testing but so little is written about the advantages?
- If someone does poorly on a standardized test, is it a reasonable conclusion that the individual, for whatever reasons, didn't know the correct answers on that test?
- Aren't teacher-made tests just as much high stakes tests as are standardized tests? Wouldn't a child who failed every teacher-made test face unpleasant consequences?

At the end of another busy school day at Walken Park Elementary School, the slightly shabby and aging school building was quiet once again. As is typical in many older cities, Walken Park and its neighborhood had seen more prosperous days. The neighborhood was filled with old Victorian homes that were now mostly divided into rental apartments. Any single-family homes were owned by working-class families who would not be able to buy in more established neighborhoods. Most of the teachers enjoyed the vibrant and diverse neighborhood and its bright engaging students.

On his way home Samuel Wilson walked past Abby Forster's third-grade classroom. Sam had served as a mentor to Abby since she was hired a few years earlier and liked to check in on his younger colleague at the end of the school day. Sam, the senior third-grade teacher who has been at the school for 10 years, noticed that Abby was staring intently at something on her desk. The two teachers shared a congenial work relationship, and Abby, who was just finishing her third year of teaching, enjoyed her end-of-the-day visits with Sam. Sam had been tempted to just wave his greetings and hurry home, but then he noticed that his friend looked upset. He gave a perfunctory knock on the door and walked in.

"Hi, Abby. What are you still doing here? It is five o'clock, and your bags aren't even packed yet."

"Oh hi, Sam," Abby replied halfheartedly. "I didn't hear you passing by. I thought that I was the only one still here." The frown on Abby's face stood in sharp contrast to the bright and lively tone of Abby's classroom. The walls were covered with student artwork and assignments. The desks were set up in small stations where the students faced each other, making it easier for them to work cooperatively. The reading nook Abby had built herself was full of well-worn furniture and well-loved books. The room, in fact, reflected Abby's welcoming and earnest personality.

"So what's up, Abby? You look pretty upset," Sam asked.

"I just got my student's reading and language arts exam results back, and it is not all good news," Abby said with a sigh. "Oh, Sam, I am starting to dread these standardized test results more and more every year."

"Aren't you being a bit dramatic, Ab?" Sam chuckled.

"I wish I were. I just feel like those tests are working against our students, and I resent it!"

"Come on, Abby, how bad were your kids' results?"

"Not all bad," she replied. "But some were. And Wynford Lewis is in the lowest stanines. He's below the cutoff point for promotion."

"Really?" Sam said with genuine surprise. Wyn Lewis? He always seems to be doing well in school, and he is such a bright kid. Is he the only one who did poorly?"

"No, there were a couple of other low scores," Abby said. "But Wyn's score surprised me the most. I guess I knew Cody and Ashley would struggle because they have been working below grade level all year. Those scores are disappointing, too, but at least I was prepared for the possibility that they might do poorly."

"So you never expected Wynford might fail?" Sam inquired. "Well, you know, Abby, these kids are still young. They don't take these tests too seriously yet. Maybe Wyn just rushed through it to get it over with. He could be a bad test taker."

"I think it's more than that," Abby replied ruefully.

"What do you mean?"

"For three years now I have watched a good percentage of my non-white students fail those exams after doing well and working hard all year. I am really starting to think those tests are culturally biased against the minority kids." Abby watched Sam's face as she said this, hoping to get some confirmation from him.

"Abby, what are you talking about?" Sam responded immediately. "These kids are all from the same neighborhood and all about the same in terms of family circumstances. They may be different colors, but they all come from the same background." Sam paused for a minute to let this sink in. Then he added, "I'm worried about that comment, Ab. You might be the one that's biased here. You're expecting some kids to automatically find the tests more difficult than others—and only because of their skin color. One of your favorites fails, and all of a sudden there's a conspiracy going on?"

This, thought Abby, was typical Sam. There was nothing he loved more than playing devil's advocate. It was part of the reason he had been such a good mentor: He always forced Abby to see more than one side of an issue. Abby, however, was not in the mood to debate just for the fun of it.

"Sam, don't oversimplify this. You know as well as I do that cultural bias is always a danger when it comes to standardized tests. That's why so many parents and teachers resent these high stakes tests."

"That is true," Sam replied, "but you read that test while your students were taking it. Did you find any racial stereotyping or cultural bias? I certainly didn't. Besides I am sure that the test's creators are much more familiar with the standards of educational and psychological testing than we are. I have to believe that they have looked into issues of fairness in testing. Did you even read the manual, by the way? Do you know how the test was standardized?"

Abby thought for a moment before replying. "Okay, no," she replied. "I didn't read the manual all the way through, so I don't know how the test was standardized. You got me there." She paused for a second and added, "I remember noticing that the test creators did a good job of mixing boys' and girls' names into the test questions, and they also sprinkled in a fair number of ethnic-sounding names, but test bias is much more sophisticated than that."

Sam opened his mouth to respond, but Abby continued.

"Those tests are written for an average testing audience, and average generally means white and middle class. You've read Alfie Kohn! You know that social factors like race and class greatly influence student test scores. Look around you, Sam. How many middle-class kids do you see in this neighborhood?"

Sam knew this was a rhetorical question but chose to respond just the same. "Abby, it is true that our kids are all working class and that there is a good balance of white and non-white students. If you took the time to read how the test was standardized, you would know that it was standardized on a population just like the kids in our school. Anyway, you can't say that test discriminated against your favorite student but was okay for the other students. A whole lot of students in this school pass those tests, both white and non-white kids! Besides, this is the way school works! It's our job to help our kids to improve themselves so that they can fit into the larger culture! A test is not the worst thing they will ever face. And, you know, maybe you should be preparing your students more directly for the test?"

"Prepare?" exclaimed Abby. "Of course I prepare them. Sam, what are you suggesting?"

"Well," replied Sam "do you remember that big poetry unit you did about two months ago where you incorporated songs and music? I could hear your kids all the way down the hall."

"Yes," Abby replied cautiously, she did not like what she thought Sam was getting at.

Sam continued. "While you were doing that I was quizzing my kids on grammar and multiplication. We did drills and activities every day."

"Sam, you complimented me on that unit! It helped my students learn to write and read poems. They learned about meter and rhyme and improved their comprehension. By the end of the unit they were reading and enjoying works by Langston Hughes and doing their own writing. They learned not to be afraid of poetry. It was so exciting! Do you remember that poem Wynford wrote? It was fantastic. He got it published in the local paper."

"Okay, Abby" Sam responded a bit patronizingly, "that is very nice, but writing that poem did not do Wynford much good when it came to passing that test or even knowing the stuff he needs to know to succeed in the world."

Sam realized that his comment was a bit harsh and softened his tone. "All I am saying is that focusing a bit more on the content related to the year-end tests won't hurt. There's material that just has to be covered, no matter what else you want to do. All the other activities really are great, but we do have a curriculum to cover. And these kids deserve the same instruction they would get if they lived across town and went to one of those suburban schools. After all we should be preparing our kids to compete in the real world."

"Honestly, Sam, sometimes you can be pretty obtuse," Abby retorted. "What world do you think they live in now? I'm not saying that we should teach our kids to use slang and Ebonics. I am simply saying that those test writers are probably not from neighborhoods like this one. They think giving reading samples about summer camp and setting up lemonade stands are relatable for all kids! For once I would like to see a test that reflects the realities that our kids face. How about a word problem about a child like Tommy Wu? He spends a couple of hours after school every day working in his parents' store. Do you know he translates business transactions into English for his parents and deals with all the deliveries they receive? Or what about Graciela Vargas? She cooks dinner for her family after school because her mom works the second shift and her dad works the third shift. Why isn't their real world reflected in those tests?"

"Abby, I know most of our students have stories like those," Sam sighed. "It is true that those tests are not written about the Tommy Wu's of the world. But if Tommy can do business transactions in his father's store, he should be able to do them on a paper-and-pencil test. That's not a big leap."

Abby's frustration continued to grow. "We both work hard all year to find materials for class that our students relate to because we believe that it keeps them more engaged. Then what happens? We turn around at the end of the year and test them using materials that negate their experiences! How does that make any sense?"

Sam smiled despite himself. One of the things that made Abby such a good teacher was her passion, and she was really showing it now—plus, she had him cornered. They did spend a lot of time talking about finding books to which their kids could relate. He really liked his students and their families, and he could not imagine cutting their experiences out of his curriculum.

Sam held up his hands in mock surrender. "Okay, okay, Abby. You've got me there. We do spend time making the materials relevant. I don't remember you being such a good debater three years ago when you started this job."

Abby laughed. "I have a very stubborn mentor to thank for that," she said.

Smiling, Sam added, "It's my night to cook dinner at home so I had better get moving. Do you want to join us? At this rate it looks like a pizza night."

"Thanks, Sam, but I can't," replied Abby grimly. "I'm waiting to have a meeting with Wynford's mother after she gets off work at six. I need to break the bad news that, thanks to those tests, her son will be repeating third grade. She is going to be devastated."

"Well," replied Sam, "just remember that, pass or fail, Wynford is lucky to have a teacher like you fighting for him. And hey, Abby, take at look at that test manual before you meet with Wyn's mother, okay? It will tell you something about how those tests were standardized."

"Why do I want to know that?" Abby asked listlessly.

"Because," Sam said seriously, "maybe it's not the tests that are at fault. Maybe it's how our school uses those test scores to promote or retain kids. I'm guessing the test makers didn't write this test as a way to decide who does and does not get promoted. That's the issue you and Wyn's mom might want to discuss."

Abby smiled. "Always the mentor," she said warmly. "Goodnight, Sam."

"'G'night, Abby," Sam said as he threw his book bag over his shoulder.

CASE 16: ISSUES FOR ANALYSIS AND REFLECTION

1. Case 16 is related to the INTASC Standard for Assessment and to the following three indicators for this standard: The teacher (a) uses a variety of informal and formal strategies to inform choices about student progress and to adjust instruction (e.g., standardized test data, peer and student self-assessment, informal assessments such as observation, surveys, interview, student work, performance tasks, portfolio, and teacher-made tests), (b) uses assessment strategies to involve learners in self-assessment activities to help them become aware of their strengths and needs and to encourage them to set personal goals for learning, and (c) maintains useful records of student work and performance and can communicate student progress knowledgeably and responsibly. Once you have identified the primary issue, problem, or concern in this case, determine what other content knowledge is needed by the teacher(s) to ensure positive outcomes.

2. What pedagogical knowledge and skills are needed?

3. What must be done to ensure that desired learning outcomes are obtained?

Use the DEEPS Method to analyze this case. Keep in mind the INTASC Standard for Assessment and the key indicators listed in item 1.

Determine the primary issue, problem, or concern in this case.

Enumerate the facts that support your belief regarding the primary issue, problem, or concern in the case.

Evaluate the case to find all the possible solutions for resolving the issue, problem, or concern.

Problem solve by thinking critically about each possible solution and accepting or rejecting the solution based on its value in ensuring the professional growth of the teacher in relation to assessment.

Summarize your conclusion/solutions and be prepared to present the best possible solution and your rationale to your professor and colleagues.

CASE 16: WHAT THE RESEARCH SAYS

Few conversations about assessment evoke more passion than a conversation about standardized testing. To begin, the sheer amount of testing that occurs annually in our schools is staggering. Assessing students in reading and math, as mandated under No Child Let Behind (NCLB), for example, requires 45 million standardized tests annually. Another 11 million will be added to this when new science testing begins (Scherer, 2006). Some research indicates that teacher acceptance of annual standardized testing has varied from state to state and from teacher to teacher. Results of studies in Virginia, Washington, and Massachusetts, for example, reveal that "teachers who have been teaching only a year or two seem to embrace testing, at least initially, while more experienced teachers tend to eschew it . . . [for new teachers] tests give both purpose to their teaching and foster a sense of unity and collaboration" (Gorman, 2001, pp. 29–35). Other results indicate far less satisfaction with standardized testing. In a nationwide poll of 5,600 teachers in kindergarten through Grade 12, 42% stated they do not believe that standardized testing does anything to improve teaching or student performance. Only 1% of the teachers in the survey responded that standardized testing was a legitimate means to assess the quality of schools (Greifner, 2007). The 39th Annual PDK/Gallup Poll of the Public's Attitudes Towards the Public Schools (Lowell & Gallup, 2007) had the following to say about standardized testing (although not all would agree with the veracity of this statement):

> What the data say to us is that the public is growing disenchanted with the increasing reliance on standardized testing. It seems likely that there is no coincidence in the fact that the criticism of standardized testing has developed since standardized testing became the principal strategy in implementing NCLB. (Lowell & Gallup, 2007, p. 37)

The question of why standardized tests are needed and what purpose they serve is one that drives both teachers' reactions in the preceding case story. Abby is dismayed that one of her students, who she perceives to be intelligent and creative, has received low scores on the annual standardized tests. To her dismay, her colleague suggests that she must pay more attention in instructional planning to meeting the State standards. She insists that the instruction in her class is engaging and relevant and, if standardized tests were not biased against some populations, the results of her instruction would be more apparent. Research in this area is not conclusive; it supports either side of this debate.

Among the benefits of standardized testing are that it provides a means to track student achievement across a number of grades and across school districts. Parents also are able to evaluate how well individual schools are doing in meeting state standards. As well, intervention services in the form of new programming, new personnel, increased funding, or other resources can be more easily directed to schools that have been shown to be low performing (Samuelson, 2001). An online Web site related to national education and disability resources states in one of its publications that the two major advantages of standardized tests are that they are psychometrically valid and reliable with results that can be generalized and replicated. Results of the tests can also be aggregated. While any one individual score may not provide useful information, the aggregated scores of a school, district, or state are valid indicators of how well the school system is doing (K–12 Academics, n.d.).

However, fresh concerns about the validity and reliability of standardized tests were raised in a *New York Times* article (Winerip, 2006). In the article, Thomas Toch, a co-director of a research group called EducationSector, describes the testing industry as overextended and underregulated. Toch states that standardized test questions require students to merely recall and restate facts, rather than requiring more demanding tasks like applying or evaluating information. In fact, the author of the article reports that Margaret Spellings, Secretary of Education at the time, even suggested to the State of Connecticut that it move from an essay format on its annual tests to multiple choice questions because it is more cost efficient (Winerip). In other words, although the demand is great to use standardized tests to ensure accountability, by the same token there is a willingness to "dumb down" the tests to preserve time and money. According to Toch, "The scale of N.C.L.B. testing requirements, competitive pressures in the testing industry, a shortage of testing experts, insufficient state resources, tight regulatory deadlines and a lack of meaningful oversight of the sprawling N.C.L.B. testing enterprise are undermining N.C.L.B.'s pursuit of higher academic standards" (as cited in Winerip, 2006).

Along these same lines, Michelle Fine, a distinguished professor of psychology at the City University of New York, voices concerns similar to those of Abby Forster, the third-grade teacher in this case story. Abby was concerned about the impact of standardized test results on minority students in her class. In a paper on the impact of the requirement for all students in New York State to pass Regents Examinations to graduate, Fine expresses concern over the impact of this mandate on minority and low-income students (Fine, 2005). Fine describes a high school in New York in which low performing students were discharged rather than taking the chance that they would lower test scores for the school. According to Fine, 50% or approximately 1,600 of its students are discharged each year to boost student scores and graduation rates (p. 25). A citizen's class action suit has been filed against the school. Fine also states that poor and minority children begin with a disadvantage because they are most likely to be educated by "less qualified teachers, such as those failing the general knowledge certification exam. . . . These same students are less likely to complete a rigorous curriculum or to receive any encouragement to do so" (p. 25). This effects tests scores. Another researcher (Sturgeon, 2006) states that standardized tests can be helpful in providing needed information regarding who is and is not meeting standards. Standardized tests, however, must be balanced with other curriculum assessments that can give more immediate results. It can sometimes take 6 months to a year to get the results of standardized testing, and this expanse of time is of no use to teachers for whom the very nature of their jobs requires them to make minute-to-minute decisions about student learning (Sturgeon). Further research concludes that the biggest instructional payoffs occur when "short cycle assessments" are used.

That is, teachers must continuously use formative assessments to provide feedback to students regarding their learning. It is very important, however, not to make the faulty assumption that all standardized tests are bad and all teacher-made assessments are good. "Teacher-tests are sometimes poorly made and not aligned with learning objectives, and provide little information to improve further learning" (Popham, 2006, pp. 86–87). By the same token, there is no guarantee that all teachers are equally well versed in using alternative assessments.

There may be some validity to the comment made by Abby's colleague when he suggests to her that she should pay more attention to meeting standards and to the quality and content of instruction. A 3-year study of teaching and learning took place in 19 different schools and over 400 elementary classrooms and involved approximately 5,000 students in Chicago, Illinois. The researchers in this study concluded that "assignments calling for more authentic intellectual work actually improve scores on conventional tests" (Newman, Bryk, & Nagaoka, 2001, p. 2). They add that "if teachers, administrators, policy-makers, and the public-at-large place more emphasis on authentic intellectual work in classrooms, yearly gains in standardized tests [in Chicago] will surpass national norms" (p. 2). The quality of teaching, in other words, has an impact on the quality of student learning outcomes, and this translates to performance on standardized tests.

The researchers in this study emphasize that they are not advocating one teaching approach over another. They state emphatically that the intellectual demands embedded in classroom tasks are more likely to influence student engagement than using a particular strategy or teaching approach. By the same token, they stress that effective teaching does matter and, for it to occur, teachers need opportunities for professional growth in this area. According to this group of researchers, "The mere appearance of more challenging assignments is classrooms is not enough. To use these materials well in their classrooms, many teachers will have to learn new teaching methods and acquire more subject matter knowledge as well. They will need support and assistance in integrating more challenging assignments with instruction targeted at basic skills, in evaluating the students' answers to show more complex interpretation than conventional recitation questions, and, most of all teaching their student to succeed in the more demanding assignments" (Newman et al., 2001, pp. 31–32). The payoff, however, is that when higher level assignments requiring critical thinking and analysis are used appropriately, even in urban areas with large populations of disadvantaged youngsters, improved gains in standardized tests results have occurred.

It is possible that Abby's colleague is passing on valuable advice to her. The quality of instruction is a critical component leading to desired student learning outcomes. For assessment of any type to be effective, at least four elements have to be in place:

1. Teachers have to have mastered state and national standards so that they can incorporate them into learning objectives.
2. Teachers have to be able to deconstruct standards into lessons and provide meaningful assistance to help students fill in gaps in their learning.
3. Teachers have to be proficient in assessing student learning outcomes, whether through performance criteria in simulations, presentations, and so on, or through multiple-choice tests and essays.

4. Students themselves must understand learning objectives and their own performance and strengths and weaknesses in relation to the learning objectives (Sturgeon, 2006, p. 60). Unfortunately, "the irony is that historically teachers have not been trained to create dependable assessments" (p. 60).

The lack of intensive training in assessment strategies in teacher preparation programs leads to what has been termed the "deskilling of teachers" or reducing teachers to mere technicians who carry out tasks determined by someone else. The teacher's role is essentially that of a middle-level manager or controller, and this shift in power is one that, not surprisingly, accompanies the nationwide increase in standardized testing (Ricci, 2004, p. 342).

The debate over standardized testing as a means of assessment is neatly summed up in a comment by Allan Olson, director of the Northwest Evaluation Association (NWEA), a nonprofit organization for educators in Portland, Oregon. Olson states, "I am often asked by directors of curriculum, 'If we use your test, will student learning improve?' And I say 'no.' If you use our tests and teachers and administrators and counselors use the data to change what they do, then learning will improve" (Sturgeon, 2006, p. 63). Any assessment instrument or method, in other words, depends on the knowledge and skills of the person using it.

Summary of Research

Standardized testing is a hotly debated topic. On one side, researchers and educators point to advantages such as the ability to evaluate how well schools are doing. On the opposite side are those who are concerned with negative impacts on low income and minority children, school dropout rates, and the high stakes decisions that are made as a result of test results (for example, decisions related to promotion and retention).

There is also concern that the testing industry is overextended and underregulated. A balance must be sought between standardized testing and curriculum-based assessments that can provide more immediate results that allow teachers to adjust instruction to meet the needs of individual learners. For any assessment to be effective, however, teachers must clearly understand state and national standards and be able to integrate them into instruction. They also must continue to develop knowledge and skills related to assessing student learning outcomes. The objective of any assessment technique should be to improve further learning.

CASE 16: TOPICS FOR DISCUSSION

- When it comes to standardized testing, poor and minority children begin with a disadvantage because they are most likely to be educated by less qualified teachers, such as those failing the general knowledge certification exam. This makes it more likely that they will do poorly on standardized tests.
- Standardized tests do little to improve teaching or student performance.
- A significant advantage of standardized tests is that they allow parents to evaluate how well schools are doing.
- The problem with standardized tests is not the test themselves but the misuse of the tests by school districts. For example, some districts use results of the test to make decisions about promotion and retention.

CASE 16: EXPLORING THE ISSUES

1. Open your Web browser to http://www.prenhall.com/teacherprep. This will take you to Merrill's Teacher Prep Web site. Once you have logged in, click on *Video Classroom* on the menu on the left. When this window opens, click on *General Methods.* Then go to *Module 10: Learner Assessment.* When this window opens, click on *Video 2: Performance Assessment.* You will watch a discussion of portfolio assessments and other forms of authentic assessment. After watching the video, answer the questions at the bottom of the page. Then write a one-page reflection in which you discuss reasons that you either agree or disagree with the content of this video.

2. Read the following article: Lattimore, R. (2001, March). The wrath of high stakes tests. *The Urban Review, 33*(1), 57–67. In this article, the writer tells the story of three minority youngsters' preparations for a standardized test. After this, he critiques standardized tests in general. After reading Lattimore's article, write your own article in which you support standardized testing. (Note that it is not important that you agree with either point of view. It is important, however, for you to understand both sides of the debate on standardized testing.)

3. Pretend that you are the teacher who must meet with Wynford's mother and explain to her that her 8-year-old son failed the standardized test and must repeat the third grade. Have different people with different points of view play the role of Wynford's mother (a mother who rightly or wrongly supports the teacher, a mother who is outraged, a mother who asks challenging but appropriate questions, etc.).

4. Schedule a meeting with three teachers and three parents (from three separate families). Interview each to determine whether or not they believe academic grades should receive added points for effort, attendance, and participation. Compare your results with those of your peers.

5. In groups of four or five discuss the placement and assessment of students with mild cognitive disabilities in the inclusive classroom. Come to agreement with your group on how to fairly assess individuals with cognitive disabilities and still hold the individual to district, state, and national standards.

References

Aballasan, A. (n.d.). Politeness strategies in the speech of characters in Mafouz's *The False Dawn.* Retrieved October 1, 2007, from http:// www.nord.helsinki.fi/clpg/CLPG/ Alham% 20Albassam.pdf.

Bernhard, J. K., Diaz, C. F., & Allgood, I. (2005, August). Research-based teacher education for multicultural contexts. *Intercultural Education, 16*(3), 263–277.

Black, P., Harrison, C., Lee, C., Marshall, B., & William, D. (2004, September). Working inside the black box: Assessment for learning in the classroom. *Phi Delta Kappan, 86*(1), 9–21.

Boston, C. (2002). The concept of formative assessment. *Practical Assessment, Research & Evaluation, 8*(9). Retrieved October 2, 2007, from http:// pareonline.net/getvn.asp?v=8&n=9.

Chamberlain, S. P. (2005, March). Recognizing and responding to cultural differences in the education of culturally and linguistically diverse learners. *Intervention in School & Clinic, 49*(4), 195–211.

Darling-Hammond, L., & Hill-Lynch, O. (2006, February). If only they'd do their work. *Educational Leadership, 63*(5), 8–13.

Eby, J., Herrell, A., & Jordan, M. (2006). *Teaching in K–12 Schools*. Upper Saddle River, NJ: Pearson/Merrill/Prentice Hall.

Eyring, P. (2006, July). Broadening global awareness. *T & D, 60*(7), 69–70.

Fine, M. (2005, Summer). High stakes testing and lost opportunities: The New York State Regents Exam. *Encounter, 18*(2), 24–29.

Gorman, S. (2001, September 22). Teachers begin to accept standardized tests. *National Journal, 33*(38), 2935.

Greifner, L. (2007, April). Report roundup: Standardized testing. Article courtesy of *Education Week*. Retrieved January 5, 2009, from http://www.teachersnetwork.org/aboutus/edweek041807/index.htm.

K–12 Academics. (n.d.) Standardized testing: Advantages. Retrieved January 6, 2009, from http://www.k12academics.com/standardized_testing_advantages.htm.

Lowell, C. R., & Gallup, A. M. (2007, September). The 39th Annual Phi Delta Kappan/Gallup Poll of the public's attitudes toward the public schools. *Phi Delta Kappan, 89*(1), 33–45.

Newmann, F. M., Bryk, A. S., & Nagaoka, J. K. (2001, January). Authentic intellectual work & standardized tests: Conflict or coexistence? Chicago: Consortium on Chicago School Research. Retrieved December 23, 2008, from http://ccsr.uchicago.edu/publications/p0a02.pdf.

Popham, J. W. (2006, November). Phony formative assessments: Buyer beware! *Educational Leadership, 64*(3), 86–87.

Ricci, C. (2004, October–December). The case against standardized testing and the call for a revitalization of democracy. *Review of Education, Pedagogy, & Cultural Studies, 26*(4), 339–361.

Salend, S. J., & Taylor, L. S. (2002, November). Cultural perspectives: Missing pieces of the functional assessment process. *Intervention in School & Clinic, 38*(2), 104–113.

Samuelson, S. (2001, September). Standardized testing: The stakes are rising. *State Legislature, 27*(87), 30–34.

Scherer, M. (2006, November). The NCLB Issue. *Educational Leadership, 64*(3), 7.

Sturgeon, J. (2006, August). A new kind of testing. *District Administrator, 42*(8), 59–63.

Tata, J. (2005, September). The influence of national culture on the perceived fairness of grading procedures: A comparison of the United States and China. *Journal of Psychology, 139*(5), 401–412.

Winerip, M. (2006, March 22). Standardized tests face a crisis over standards. *New York Times*. Retrieved August 22, 2007, from http://www.nytimes.com/2006/03/22/education/22education.html.

9

INTASC Standard 9: Reflective Practice/ Professional Development

Description of INTASC Standard 9: *The teacher is a reflective practitioner who continually evaluates the effects of his or her choices on others and who actively seeks out opportunities to grow professionally.*

KEY INDICATORS FOR STANDARD 9

The Teacher

- uses classroom observation, information about students, and research as sources for evaluating the outcomes of teaching and learning and as a basis for experimenting with, reflecting on, and revising practice.
- uses professional literature, colleagues, and other resources to support self-development as a learner and as a teacher.
- consults with professional colleagues within the school and other professional arenas as support for reflection, problem solving, and new ideas, actively sharing experiences, and seeking and giving feedback.

CASE 17: REFLECTION, RESEARCH, AND RETENTION

Thinking Ahead

As you read this case, reflect on the following:

- What does the research say about the impact on achievement if a child is retained?
- What should come of reflection? Is it just thinking, or is it thinking that should lead to action?
- How does one learn "to reflect" in a manner that leads to further learning? Is reflection a lifelong habit, or is it something that can be taught?

John Grimaldi was completing his 10th year of teaching as an elementary teacher at the Charlotte Avenue School. During that period, he had taught second grade for 3 years and had spent the last 7 years as a fourth-grade teacher. After what seemed to be years of steady growth and increasing confidence, John was beginning to see conflicts and contradictions in an array of professional practices and school policies.

John had developed and executed hundreds of unit plans and literally thousands of lessons. He had accumulated a treasure chest full of materials and supplies. He communicated effectively with parents and was even considered the de facto leader of his grade level. "Things had seemed so easy just a few years ago," John thought. But today he was faced with yet another difficult decision. As he prepared his final grades for submission, he had to decide what he should do with Alexis. Alexis was a quiet, industrious child who, unfortunately, was working below her peers in every subject area. "I could retain her," John said out loud to no one in particular. "But maybe not," he added, still mumbling aloud. "Maybe she will get an understanding teacher next year." The issue was complicated because, although she lagged behind her peers, Alexis was a hard worker. In addition, John had learned from the guidance counselor that enrollment in summer school was out of the question as far as his student's family was concerned because Alexis's parents were intent on sending her to New Jersey to spend the summer with her aunt for a summer vacation that had been planned for the last 2 years.

In his career, John had retained a total of about five students, but in each of those cases problems with attendance, coupled with profoundly low academic achievement, made his decision a lot easier. "And besides," he thought now, "I didn't think quite so much about it then. The more I learn, the harder it is to make good decisions." John chuckled out loud at this conclusion.

Right then, John's friend and colleague Roger walked into the room. "Talking to yourself?" his friend asked. "Always happens after the first few years I'm afraid."

John laughed appreciatively. Roger had been teaching for nearly 20 years and was the "father figure" of the building. His word and advice were taken on practically any topic from school politics to pro football. He and Roger had developed a close friendship over the years.

"I've been debating what to do with Alexis Rhyner," John said. "Remember when I spoke to you about her a few weeks ago."

"I remember," Roger said. "Are you still thinking about retaining her?

"I'm not sure what to do," John answered. "This is the first time I've had a student who worked so hard but had so little in the way of positive results. What would you do?"

"I'd probably retain her," Roger replied without hesitation. "I know those teachers over at the middle school. They'll eat that kid alive. Another year here wouldn't hurt her. She has the same teacher here all day, except for phys ed and art, of course. They change classes at the middle school, and I think she will have six different teachers. You're not doing her any favors to pass her on."

John listened thoughtfully to his colleague and remembered how slowly and methodically Alexis worked and how he had to regularly extend the time for her to finish the simplest of assignments. He had completed a referral for testing, but the report came back saying there was no evidence of a disability. Alexis just worked slowly.

John was more conflicted than ever. He had been thinking of promoting Alexis, but Roger's advice made him reconsider. The thought of Alexis trying to maneuver her way around the middle school was chilling. Yet, at some point she had to move ahead. The question was, Should it be now or a year from now? A horrifying image of Alexis popped into John's mind—an image of her lost in the building, trying to find her way to her next class, and ending up in the principal's office trying to explain why she seemed to be skipping class.

Roger read the worry on John's face and laughed out loud. "I see you're getting my point," he said. "Trust yourself. You'll do the right thing. Are you heading out soon?

"Not for a bit," John answered. "I've got to finish this up first." John said goodbye to his colleague and went back to his papers and his concerns about Alexis. It occurred to him to talk to Karen, the school librarian. He got up again and took a brisk walk down the hall to the school library.

Karen, the librarian, was a relative newcomer to the school staff. Though in her mid-thirties, this was only her 3rd year as a teacher. John had heard that she had waited till her two children were in school before she went back to school herself to get her certification. John found Karen in her office, where she was completing an inventory.

"Karen," said John, "I hate to bother you while you're in the middle of this, but do you have a minute or two?"

Karen had two seemingly contradictory characteristics: She was always busy, and she always had time for people. Karen invited John into her office, and John spent a few minutes sharing the details of Alexis's academic abilities and personal attributes, as well as his conflict over whether or not to retain her in fourth grade. He also relayed Roger's perception of the middle school and the impact it would have on Alexis. Though it felt odd to be conferring with a colleague with so much less experience, Karen's good listening skills and her professional demeanor impressed everyone.

When John had finished, Karen said, "Okay. Now I have a couple of questions."

"Sure," said John. "Anything at all."

"You painted a picture of high effort and low achievement, "Karen began, "but since Alexis is in your classroom all day, it's easy to blur the lines of ability. In what areas is she the strongest?"

John thought for a moment. "Well, I suppose writing," he said after a moment. "At least her ideas are creative. Her sentence structure is not bad really."

"Anything else?" Karen asked.

"She's plays the viola and she did join the school orchestra. I've never heard her play, so I don't know how good she is."

Karen smiled and encouraged John to go on.

"Alexis did a great job in the few science experiments we conducted. I have to admit I haven't taught too much science this year, but Karen seems to have enjoyed what little we did.

"And what about her weaknesses?" Karen asked.

"That's an easy one," John answered quickly. "Reading and math." John thought for a moment. "Well, at least if we are going by the basal reader tests—you know, those end-of-the-unit mastery tests. Alexis fails those miserably. They're timed tests, though. She has lots of trouble working within time limits."

"One of the things you've got to consider," Karen said, "is that this is a kid who has been lagging behind her classmates for a few years. You can't expect her to catch up in one school year. How is Alexis doing compared to Alexis?"

This was a new thought for John. "What do you mean?" he asked.

Karen smiled. "I mean how does she do over time. What kind of growth have you seen this year in reading and math and even in finishing her work on time? Instead of comparing her to her peers, compare her to herself."

John was quiet for a minute. "But she still has to be able to do grade-level work," he said hesitantly. "She might be making progress, but she is still way behind her peers."

"Well, just think about it," Karen replied. "Think about the rate at which she's learning and whether or not another year in fourth grade will help or hurt her."

"Okay," John said, "you've given me lots to think about, as usual." He thanked Karen and walked back slowly to his room. He remembered reading about portfolio assessment and wished he had required his students to maintain some kind of portfolio. Portfolios of Alexis's work in reading and math and other subject areas would give him some good evidence of her progress right now. But all John had was a bunch of low grades in his record book.

CASE 17: ISSUES FOR ANALYSIS AND REFLECTION

1. Case 17 is related to the INTASC Standard for Reflective Practice/Professional Development and to the following two key indicators for this standard: The teacher (a) uses classroom observation, information about students, and research as sources for evaluating the outcomes of teaching and learning and as a basis for experimenting with, reflecting on and revising practice and (b) consults with professional colleagues within the school and other professional arenas as support for reflection, problem solving and new ideas, actively sharing experiences and seeking and giving feedback. Once you have identified the primary issue, problem, or concern in this case, determine what other content knowledge is needed to ensure positive outcomes.

2. What pedagogical knowledge and skills are needed?

3. What must be done to ensure that desired learning outcomes are obtained?

Use the DEEPS Method to analyze this case. Keep in mind the INTASC Standard for Reflective Practice/Professional Development and the key indicators listed in item 1.

Determine the primary issue, problem, or concern in this case.

Enumerate the facts that support your belief regarding the primary issue, problem, or concern in the case.

Evaluate the case to find all the possible solutions for resolving the issue, problem, or concern.

Problem solve by thinking critically about each possible solution and accepting or rejecting the solution based on its value in ensuring the professional growth of the teacher in relation to reflective practice/professional development.

Summarize your conclusion/solutions and be prepared to present the best possible solution and your rationale to your professor and colleagues.

CASE 17: WHAT THE RESEARCH SAYS

In the preceding case story, a veteran teacher struggles with whether or not to retain a student who appears to be behind her peers when it comes to academic achievement. The teacher, John Grimaldi, knows that his decision will have a lifelong impact on his young student, and he wants to make sure his decision has more positive effects than negative ones. The research on grade retention is interesting in itself, and the teacher in this case story might have benefited from being more familiar with the research literature. Part of what is needed in reflection is the ability to step back and objectively look at what has occurred and, in the process, to understand how one's own assumptions and beliefs can influence decision making (Rodgers, 2006).

Retaining a student (or grade repetition) generally occurs for one of four reasons: (a) a belief that an extra year of schooling will result in better achievement for the individual; (b) the child is perceived to be behind his or her peers in terms of social and emotional maturity, and it is believed that an extra year of schooling will help the child to mature; (c) the child does not meet academic criteria for promotion to the next grade; or (d) for a variety of reasons, there were too many unexcused absences or accumulated days of non-attendance (Bowman, 2005, p. 42). According to Darling-Hammond, however, decades of research show no evidence of any of these reasons being valid (as cited in Black, 2005). Darling-Hammond states that retention

- Fails to improve low achievement in reading, math, and other subjects.
- Fails to inspire students to "work harder."
- Fails to develop social adjustment skills or self-concept.
- Shows no evidence of long-term benefits for the child. (p. 40)

On the other hand, there is considerable evidence that grade retention in any year is likely to contribute to lowered self-esteem, feelings of inadequacy, and dropping out of school before completing high school. As well, although there may be immediate academic gains for the child, these gains are temporary and generally do not carry through over subsequent years of schooling (Black, 2005; Bowman, 2005; Rodgers, 2006).

If grade retention is considered at all for a child, it should be only after all other alternatives have been exhausted. We don't have any evidence from the case story that the child's teacher kept a running record of any academic interventions or specific learning outcomes for the child in question. Although the teacher reports that his student "appears to like to write," "plays the viola in the orchestra," and "did a great job in the few science experiments in class," the teacher seems to have no idea what the student knows and does not know. All he knows about this student is that she has not done well on graded assignments in comparison to her peers and that she will be required to work more independently in middle school. He is right, however, to worry about teacher reactions to promoting the child. One researcher notes that a teacher sometimes retains a child to avoid criticism from teachers in the next grade. This concern might be lessened, the researcher writes, if decisions about promotion and retention were made by a school team rather than by just one individual alone (Black, 2005).

There are promising strategies that lead to enhanced reflective practice and professional development when it comes to critical decision making. First and foremost, formative assessment in the hands of a skilled practitioner is invaluable in helping the teacher to know and respond to learner needs. Yet, "after more than a hundred years of exhortations and a significant body of research on the topic, the idea that assessment and teaching are reciprocal activities is still not firmly rooted in the practice of educators" (Heritage, 2007, p. 140). Teacher preparation programs spend a lot of time teaching preservice teachers how to conduct lively and engaging lessons but relatively little time teaching these same individuals how to assess student learning to "ensure that the student receives appropriate support so that the new learning is incrementally internalized and ultimately becomes part of the student's independent achievement" (p. 145). Formative assessment used frequently and effectively might have given John Grimaldi the insights necessary to assist his student in filling in learning gaps throughout the year so he could avoid being faced with such critical decisions at the end of the year.

Some teacher preparation programs have recently begun to pay more attention to reflective practice and professional growth in structured and dramatic ways. As one writer states, the whole point of teacher preparation programs is to help preservice teachers gain insights into the teaching–learning process and enhance skills related to reflection (Alger, 2006). One method to do this has been to require students to write cases as part of coursework. Preservice teachers are required to identify a problem, incident, or issue during their field experience and write cases that identify the complexities of the problem solving that must occur. The cases are shared with their professors, cooperating teachers, and other preservice teachers. The result of this practice has been that preservice teachers become increasingly aware of how their own assumptions and beliefs affect their decision making, and this awareness causes them to reflect on problems more objectively (Alger). Ironically, what happens in teacher education programs is that preservice teachers enter the program with more than 10,000 hours of classroom observation, if all the years of being a student from kindergarten through college are counted. No one comes to teacher preparation programs without a significant amount of experience in schools. It is important, however, for instructors to make good use of this experience because "this long apprenticeship exerts a tremendous influence upon students' often unexamined perceptions of teaching and learning. If left unexamined, memories can serve as a de facto guide for teachers as they approach what they do in the classroom" (Bailey, 1997, p. 5). This view is supported by more recent research that found that prior knowledge and experiences influence reflective practice—that is, the "knowledge and beliefs about learning, teaching, students, and content pre-service teachers bring to their teacher education and placement classes matter. Their understandings and beliefs function as interpretive lenses through which beginning teachers make sense of their experiences" (Alger, 2006, p. 288). A number of attempts by teacher preparation programs to improve reflective practice take this into account.

Similar to having preservice teachers write cases, another program incorporates reflective journal writing. This is part of the candidates' field experiences, and the intent is to get the preservice teacher in the habit of authentic problem solving. After each visit by the placement supervisor/field instructor, preservice teachers write about their lesson and reflect on the strengths and weaknesses of the lesson in terms of whether or not instruction resulted in desired student learning outcomes. The instructors respond to each student in writing and offer encouragement and suggestions (Harrington & McGlamery, 2007). The critical role of reflection during field experiences cannot be overestimated. The very nature of field experiences provide the preservice teacher with authentic opportunities to move beyond simple anecdotal information and judgments. Field experiences provide a meaningful context in which preservice teachers are able to engage in self-dialogue and critically question their values and judgments. It is also a critical time to build a network of teachers and instructors who can serve as mentors and advisors throughout their careers, thus increasing the possibilities of effective reflective practice and professional development (Grushka, McLeod, & Reynolds, 2005).

Perhaps one of the most valuable practices leading to the development of reflective practitioners is one known as descriptive inquiry reports. Although this strategy is also highly effective in field experiences, it can be used at any point in a teacher's career, from preservice onward. This method was used in a longitudinal study designed specifically to access the impact of the inquiry process in helping to overcome bias and to make preservice teachers more mindful of the basis of their professional judgments (Kesson, Traugh, & Perez, 2006). The descriptive inquiry assignment requires preservice teachers to begin by observing one child and writing a full description of the child, including physical presence, temperament, relationships with others, and what the preservice teacher perceives as the student's modes of thinking. This is discussed in class to uncover prejudices, biases, and judgments and to reinforce positive insights. When the preservice teachers begin field experiences, they use the skills mastered in their descriptive inquiry assignments to analyze their own teaching practices. They continue to work with their instructors to tease out biases and refine their own practice so that they become more mindful of learning needs of individual children (Kesson et al.).

Another practitioner (Wagner, 2006) applied this method to what she termed a 360 Degree Evaluation. She began her descriptive inquiry/evaluation by asking herself what she already knew and did well. From there, she asked what she needed to learn to be more effective in her job. With these questions in mind, she set about writing her own self-evaluation or description of her strengths and weaknesses and "gathering input from colleagues, parents, students, and administrators" (p. 30). According to Wagner, this process can make one acutely aware of strengths and weaknesses and open the door for serious reflection on what to do better. The major benefit of this type of reflective practice is that it "leads to innovative practice through the continuous process of setting and attaining goals" (p. 32).

In regard to the preceding case story, the real question to be asked is, What alternatives did the teacher have to retaining a student who is not doing well academically in relation to grade-level standards? The response requires reflection. As John Dewey, U.S. philosopher and educator, remarked over a hundred years earlier, "We speak, legitimately enough, about the method of thinking, but the important thing to bear in mind about method is that thinking is method, the method of intelligent experience" (Dewey, 1916; 1944, p. 153). Broader reflection on the part of the teacher in this case story might have led him to consider alternatives such as mandatory summer school, increasing his own repertoire of skills to assist students falling behind their peers, promotion with academic interventions targeted at learning gaps, before- and after-school tutoring, and careful matching of this learner's needs with the teachers with whom she will be placed in the next school year (Bowman, 2005). As one researcher suggests, the question of whether or not to retain a child is essentially the wrong question. What should be asked is, What is the best way to help the student succeed? As has often been stated, teacher quality is a strong predictor of student success, and for all students what is needed is "a combination of prevention, targeted intervention, and sustained support" (District Administrator, 2005, p. 76).

Summary of Research

Research related to student retention gives little evidence of long-term benefits for students. Any critical decision making, such as that related to promotion or retention, require thoughtful reflection on the part of the teacher. Some methods shown to enhance reflection that leads to better decision making include writing and analyzing case stories, reflective journal writing with feedback from experienced practitioners, descriptive inquiry or critical incident reports with feedback from cooperating teachers and college instructors, and self-evaluations supported by feedback from parents, students, administrators, and colleagues.

CASE 17: TOPICS FOR DISCUSSION

- There is no evidence to show that retaining a child for one or more grades has any long-term positive effects on reading, math, or other subjects.
- A teacher sometimes retains a child to avoid criticism from teachers in the next grade. This concern might be lessened if decisions about promotion and retention were made by a school team rather than by just one individual alone (Black, 2005).
- Teacher quality is the strongest predictor of student success.
- Retaining a child who is not academically and/or physically ready for the next school year is a common practice in U.S. schools. On the other hand, teachers are very hesitant to accelerate a student by letting him or her skip one or more grades.

CASE 17: EXPLORING THE ISSUES

1. Design a rubric that evaluates an instructional period under the categories *excellent, good,* or *poor teaching.* Be sure to precisely describe the criteria for what constitutes excellent, good, or poor teaching. With two of your peers, observe a lesson in a classroom and, using your rubric, evaluate the quality of teaching. After the lesson, see if your two colleagues agreed with your evaluation.
2. Write a one-page essay in which you write your personal goals for becoming a teacher who reflects on theory and practice. In your essay, include *how* you will meet these goals.
3. Do some research on what the literature describes as the qualities of an effective teacher. Design a checklist in which you list each quality as *not observable, somewhat obvious, obvious.* Visit a classroom at the K–6 level for at least an hour (or view a teaching video). Rate the teacher in each of the categories for effective teaching that you have on your checklist (e.g., uses multiple and varied instructional techniques).
4. Read the position statement on acceleration (grade skipping) written by the National Association for Gifted Association. It can be found at http://

www.nagc.org/index.aspx?id=383. Reflect on whether you agree or disagree with this position statement and whether you would apply the same rationale for retaining a child.

5. Open your Web browser to http://www.prenhall.com/teacherprep. This will take you to Merrill's Teacher Prep Web site. Once you log in, click on *Video Classroom*. When this opens, click on special education and then on *Module 1: Knowing Teachers and Professionals in Special Education*. Click on *Video 1; Meet the Teacher—Mrs. Maheady*. In this video, a teacher takes you on a virtual tour of her classroom and explains the rationale for each activity area in the classroom. You are asked to reflect on how classroom design influences student learning, motivation, and behavior. After watching the video, discuss the questions at the bottom of the page with your classmates. Then reflect on how you might design your own classroom.

CASE 18: RESPONSIBILITY AND REFLECTION

Thinking Ahead

As you read this case, reflect on the following:

- Generally speaking, teachers are reluctant to accept changes. What are the reasons for this?
- What are some ways to ensure effective communication when new programs are introduced?
- Schools are constantly bombarded with new programs that claim to make learning easier and fun. These new programs, however, seem to come and go quickly. Why is this?

Standing outside the principal's office, Sandra recalled how energized she had felt in September, when the Higher Order Thinking Skills (HOTS) initiative had begun. For the first time in her 10 years teaching at her school, it had seemed like the faculty was poised for professional growth. As chairperson of the school's Professional Development Team (PDT), Sandra had worked closely with the principal to implement an initiative focused on HOTS. The initiative had emerged from the Student Achievement Committee, a group of teacher volunteers who had met regularly with the principal during the previous year. Since the HOTS proposal had begun with the concerns and ideas of teachers, Sandra, the principal, and the committee members had high hopes for its success.

"Sandy! C'mon in!" The principal, Jeff Torrance, smiled broadly and gestured for Sandra to be seated. "What's going on?"

"I just wanted to review our progress on HOTS," Sandra replied. She set the manila folder and the three-ring binder labeled "HOTS" on Jeff's desk in front of her. "How do *you* think things are going?"

Jeff stood, walked behind Sandra, and closed his office door. Settling back in his chair, he placed his palms on the edge of his desk and tapped his index finger twice.

"Well, I know there are some very unhappy teachers in our building. But I don't think we can back down now."

Sandra nodded slowly and glanced out the window toward the parking lot. "You know I stay out of the faculty room," she said, "but there is a lot of dissension. It seems like everyone is complaining, even new teachers. Everyone hates doing those lesson plans. Writing them is bad enough, but *submitting* them to the committee—! There's a lot of resistance. And resentment." She pushed the manila folder toward Jeff. "Here are the lesson plans for this month. Fifty-five teachers turned in lessons. We're waiting for sixteen others, the same ones who are usually late."

While Jeff reviewed the contents of the folder, Sandra considered the evolution of the HOTS implementation plan. Once the Student Achievement Committee (of which Sandra had been a member) had selected HOTS as an initiative, a subcommittee of teachers had agreed to work with the principal on it. Sandra volunteered to chair the PDT subcommittee, which had secured district funds to hire a consultant to spend a year facilitating the implementation of HOTS with the faculty. PDT members had met with the consultant numerous times over the summer to plan and prepare for this year.

Sandra had been instrumental in the process. She had arranged meetings, managed communication, distributed documents, and assembled the in-service calendar. Since all teachers had been trained in the fundamentals of using HOTS in the classroom, this year's plan focused on implementation. The goal for this year was for all teachers to explicitly foster higher order thinking in their classrooms.

With the principal's encouragement, members of the PDT considered two challenges: first, how to provide support for teachers as they explored and employed HOTS strategies, and second, how to ensure that teachers were implementing HOTS in their daily lessons.

To provide support for teachers, the committee hired a consultant to be on site once a week to assist with lesson planning. To ensure that HOTS lessons were, in fact, being developed and implemented, the committee decided to have teachers submit one lesson plan a month that used a HOTS strategy. In an effort to model principles of effective education, the committee, along with the principal, agreed to provide feedback on the lessons.

Although the committee had discussed the likelihood of teacher resentment and resistance, the faculty's reaction to the requirement to submit lesson plans had been unexpectedly negative. Because tenured teachers at Sandra's elementary school were not otherwise expected to turn in lessons, the union president had threatened to file a grievance about the one-lesson-per-month HOTS mandate, stating that it represented a change in working conditions.

Sandra, the principal, and the committee had discussed all these developments and, for the most part, felt that the faculty was moving in the right direction. Most teachers were submitting lesson plans, and most of the plans demonstrated effective applications of higher order thinking skills.

"These look pretty good, Sandy," Jeff looked over his glasses at Sandy and gestured toward the stack of lessons. "I agree with the concerns you've identified, too."

"Actually, Jeff, that's what we must talk about," Sandra began. "Take a look at Alan's lesson—the one about his class play." Alan Maxwell was a 38-year veteran teacher and chairperson of the upper grades. Besides being a district icon, known for staging superb annual drama productions, Alan was acknowledged as one of the pedagogical leaders in the building. Jeff pulled Alan's lesson from the pile. A square yellow note was stuck to the first page of the lesson.

"The lesson, of course, is excellent," Sandy said. "But he really didn't use any of the HOTS strategies—not explicitly, anyway."

Jeff nodded. "Right. I see what you mean. I suppose *this* section," he pointed to one of the lessons procedures, "could be related to the idea of 'Making Inferences,' but the lesson doesn't indicate that."

"Exactly!" Sandra exhaled in relief. "That's what I thought, too." She took a deep breath and looked straight at Jeff. "That's why I talked to Alan—you know, because we agreed to provide feedback on the lessons that were submitted. We didn't want teachers to think no one was looking at them, right?"

Jeff was watching Sandra carefully. "That's right, Sandy. Teachers need feedback on the lessons they submit. So, what happened?"

"Well, he's the chairperson for the upper grades—that's my department—so our rooms are next door to each other. I stopped in at the end of the day yesterday and asked if he had a few minutes to talk about the HOTS lesson. I sat down next to his desk, but when he saw the note I wrote on the top, he stood up right away."

Jeff looked at the note, which read, "HOTS not explicit. Revise and resubmit." He tried to imagine a time when Alan had been critiqued on any aspect of his professional expertise.

Sandra continued. "I could tell he was really upset, so I told him that the lesson was terrific and that it seemed like 'Making Inferences' was in there, but it hadn't been made explicit for the students—which is an important part of what we're trying to do." Sandra swallowed hard, trying to maintain her composure. "And then he asked me whether I thought I understood the meaning of 'professionalism.' He told me that he had seen dozens of professional development initiatives come and go and that this one was going to be gone by next year anyway. He said I had no right to evaluate him or his lessons, and that I was way, *way* out of line in doing so. Alan said he's going to report me to the union president. And then he told me to leave his room."

Clasping her hands in her lap, Sandra looked up at Jeff. "I'm sorry, Jeff. I just don't think I can continue with this committee. Alan's not the only one who is angry at me. Helen, who I talked to last week about improving her lesson, started to cry during our meeting. She said that she is just too old to change. She's a great teacher, like Alan, and it just doesn't seem right."

Jeff interrupted. "Sandy, all you did was ask her to add the HOTS strategy to her objectives. It was hardly an indictment of her teaching—or even of that lesson! Please, Sandy, calm down. Try to think of this is a positive sign, a sign that things are moving forward. Real learning is difficult, and change is hard. If this were going smoothly, it probably wouldn't be effective."

Jeff persisted. "Sandy, consider all the benefits this program is having and could have in the future. Most of these lessons are terrific. Our students are not just being exposed to higher order thinking—they are being *taught* how to apply these skills."

"Yes, but Alan is the chairperson of my section. He creates my schedule. And Helen and I work together on the Honors Celebration. I'm sorry, Jeff. I feel terrible. *Really* terrible. But I just don't think I can do this anymore."

"Sandy, just think it over. Please. If you withdraw, the program may die. Without strong teacher leadership from people like you we can't sustain programs like this. We need you. Our students need you." Jeff put his hand down on the stack of lessons and pressed his lips together. "You know how important this is. You believe in this strategy. You have to trust the process of change. Please reconsider, Sandy. Please."

For the first time since she had been a teacher in this school, Sandra wished she were somewhere else.

CASE 18: ISSUES FOR ANALYSIS AND REFLECTION

1. Case 19 is related to the INTASC Standard for Responsibility and Reflection and to the following key indicator for this standard: The teacher uses professional literature, colleagues and other resources to support self-development as a learner and as a teacher. Once you have identified the primary issue, problem, or concern in this case, determine what other content knowledge is needed to ensure positive outcomes.
2. What pedagogical knowledge and skills are needed?
3. What must be done to ensure that desired student learning outcomes are obtained?

Use the DEEPS Method to analyze this case. Keep in mind the INTASC Standard for Responsibility and Reflection and the key indicator listed in item 1.

Determine the primary issue, problem, or concern in this case.

Enumerate the facts that support your belief regarding the primary issue, problem, or concern in the case.

Evaluate the case to find all the possible solutions for resolving the issue, problem, or concern.

Problem solve by thinking critically about each possible solution and accepting or rejecting the solution based on its value in ensuring the professional growth of the teacher in relation to responsibility and reflection.

Summarize your conclusion/solutions and be prepared to present the best possible solution and your rationale to your professor and colleagues.

CASE 18: WHAT THE RESEARCH SAYS

This case story begins with a teacher's frustration in trying to assist with professional development activities in her school. The Higher Order Thinking Skills (HOTS) Curriculum (North Central Regional Educational Laboratory, 1987) described in this case story has been described as "a computer-based thinking program for at-risk students in grades 4 through 7. It was designed by Stanley Pogrow of the University of Arizona and includes a network of more than 1,300 schools across the United States" (North Central Regional Educational Laboratory, 1995). The program is designed to improve skills "in metacognition, inference from context, decontextualization, and information synthesis." The HOTS program is intended to be conducted in a computer lab with small groups of 10 to 14 students. It is a pullout program, but when used with the whole class the recommendation is to have a HOTS specialist work with one half of the class while the classroom teacher conducts HOTS activities with the other half of the class. This information is important because it immediately brings into question why the HOTS program is being used with an entire class and without the added benefit of the accompanying computer software. The preceding case story illustrates a very real school-based scenario in which attempts at improving school achievement may be eclectic. That is, for a number of reasons that include limited budgets and an already overworked staff, good practices are often "borrowed" from various programs and adapted to meet the perceived needs of a school. In this particular case, it is difficult to tell if the frustration of Sandra, the program coordinator, and her colleagues is due to the adaptations they made in the HOTS program or if there is real resistance from faculty to attempts at professional development.

One of the concerns with professional development in any school is finding the time for activities. Teachers already have busy schedules, and there generally is no release time during the day for "extra" activities. It has been suggested, in fact, that schools must "create a culture in which continuous professional improvement is an expected, intentional part of the fabric of teachers' work that is supported through time and money" (Rooney, 2007, p. 87). Some research suggests that as much as 20% to 50% of work time should be dedicated to professional development (North Central Regional Educational Laboratory, 1997). A related issue is the number of competing areas needing exploration and time for reflection and professional development. One writer, for example, notes that professional development activities have to take into consideration the current climate of educational reform. The reforms themselves may present professional development conflicts, and this writer suggests that at least five competing reform movements must be considered (Little, 1994):

- *Reforms in subject-matter teaching* These reforms take into consideration questions of standards, curriculum, and pedagogy and include the need for professional development in areas such as HOTS, character education, authentic performances, new math curricula, science instruction, etc.
- *Reforms centered on problems of equity among diverse populations* Staff development is needed for both new and experienced teachers to develop knowledge and skills related to making teaching and learning more equitable for all students.
- *Reforms in the nature, extent, and uses of student assessment* There are multiple related issues here, including standardized testing, authentic assessment, test construction, fair grading, alternative assessment practices, and so on.
- *Reforms in the social organization of schooling* Professional development in this area focuses on school leadership, partnership and collaboration, questions related to extended school days and/or an extended school year, grade structure (e.g., looping, split grades, transitional grades, etc.).
- *Reforms in the professionalism of teaching* Again, a number of associated topics are related to this area. Included are statewide tests for certification of teachers, standards-based training, collaborative decision making, career opportunities in teaching, and so on.

Although professions such as medicine and law have long considered the need for professional development as a serious responsibility, teachers all too often find themselves overwhelmed with working conditions where much of their time is spent on non-teaching duties such as completing forms, managing disruptive students, spending time on lunch or bus duty, or generally organizing a chaotic teaching environment. Little time is provided for instructional planning, let alone professional development. Teachers might be eager for more professional development opportunities, but there is little time allotted for them.

Considering the complexities of professional development, some researchers suggest that awareness of the need for professional development and an induction into professional development activities should begin in teacher preparation programs. Campbell and Brummett (2007), for example, state that teachers first begin to develop their identity as a teacher while still in their preparation programs, which makes teacher training the ideal time to deliberate on dilemmas related to classroom practice, question assumptions and values, observe and discuss teaching-learning environments, and even to assume personal responsibility for seeking out professional development activities. Taking advantage of these opportunities requires that institutions establish an atmosphere of open communication and collaboration among college professors, cooperating teachers, administrators, and school staff (Campbell & Brummett). This same open attitude and critical awareness of the need for professional development has to carry over from the teacher preparation program to employment as a teacher. So dire is this need for professional development that Northwest Central Regional Educational Laboratory (1997) has written that "instead of being devoted exclusively to discrete in-service days, [professional development] must be part of virtually every school day and must be closely linked to the day-to-day demands of teaching (e.g., collaborative lesson planning, assessment of student work). Schools must create time for professional development as an integral part of teachers' professional life."

Several promising practices related to professional development can be easily adapted, given time and resources, to any school. One such practice originated as a common method of teacher preparation for elementary and middle schools in Japan. This type of lesson planning is called *jugyou kenkyuu* or "lesson study" (Alvine, Judoor, Schein, & Yosida, 2007, p. 109). Lesson study is a "process in which teachers collaboratively plan, execute, observe, and discuss lessons in the classroom" (p. 109). The general format of "lesson study" is for one person to present the lesson while others observe. The lesson is then discussed among the group and strengths and weaknesses are analyzed. Ideally, debate about the lesson is intense, with in-depth discussion of instructional choices, learning issues that might arise, and best practices to deliver content. Decisions are sometimes made to revise the lesson based on group feedback. In this instance, the lesson is then taught a second time, perhaps to a larger group of peers to obtain more feedback. A great value of this approach is that "novice teachers can gain an idea of what to expect before they step before the students" (p. 110). This activity provides multiple opportunities for teachers to explore curricular goals, explore various points of view, improve content, and observe the efficacy of various instructional strategies. It is equally as valuable a method during teacher preparation programs as during future employment as a teacher (Alvine et al.).

At one school the principal put the responsibility for professional development in the hands of the teachers. A budget was put in place, and teachers at each level determined the activities that would take place. The benefits of giving teachers control of professional development and control of the budget for professional development were numerous. When there is an in-house approach to professional development, for example, faculty members learn from one another, and this helps to build collegiality and makes faculty aware of individual areas of expertise. The content of professional development activities can be geared directly to the specific needs of the school. Dialogue tends to be more focused and relevant because common goals are shared among the faculty, who already know each other well enough to "jump right in" to discussion (Hoerr, 2007). In another school this same approach was followed. The principal of that school made budgeting for professional development a priority. Teachers formed a committee and developed activities such as "brown bag lunches" to share successes and challenges. The middle school teachers used their funding to bring in guest speakers. Often the guest speakers were the specialists in that school, such as the counselor or the reading specialist. Positive outcomes of this were that teachers developed new areas of interest and expertise, paid more attention to the research literature, and increased the amount of differentiated instruction in the classroom, thus responding more effectively to individual student learning needs (Rooney, 2007).

Finally, it is important for schools to recognize the correlation between opportunities for meaningful professional development and teacher efficacy. Teacher efficacy has been described as "a teacher's expectation that he or she will be able to bring about student learning" (p. 50). The value of teachers' beliefs regarding self-efficacy is that "teachers who believe they will be successful set higher goals for themselves and their students, try harder to achieve their goals, and persist through obstacles more than do teachers who are not sure of their success" (Ross & Brva, 2007, p. 50). Professional development influences self-efficacy beliefs, which in turn enhance the teacher-learning environment.

Summary of Research

Although teachers recognize the need for ongoing professional development, little time is allotted to this in schools. Some researchers suggest that as much as 20% to 50% of work time should be devoted to professional development. With limited time and limited budgets, however, it is difficult to know which professional development activities should be emphasized. Some promising practices are to begin professional development in teacher preparation programs using activities such as lesson study. Some schools have devoted part of their annual budget to professional development and, with good results, have turned responsibility for activities over to teachers. Research (Ross & Brva, 2007) indicates that meaningful professional development activities influence teachers' self-efficacy, which in turn enhances the teaching-learning environment.

CASE 18: TOPICS FOR DISCUSSION

- Schools must "create a culture in which continuous professional improvement is an expected, intentional part of the fabric of teachers' work that is supported through time and money" (Rooney, 2007, p. 87). Some research suggests that as much as 20% to 50% of work time should be dedicated to professional development (North Central Regional Educational Laboratory, 1997).
- Teachers all too often find themselves overwhelmed with working conditions where much of their time is spent on such non-teaching duties as completing forms, managing disruptive students, spending time on lunch or bus duty, or

generally organizing a chaotic teaching environment. Little time is provided for instructional planning, let alone professional development.

- The elimination of the time it takes to prepare students for standardized tests and the elimination of seriously disruptive students in the classroom would leave ample time for professional development activities.
- Teachers currently in the system have had no more or no less opportunity for professional development than teachers about to enter the field. Professional development is one area where both novice teachers and experienced teachers are on a level playing field. Teacher preparation programs must do far more to induct preservice teachers into professional development activities.

CASE 18: EXPLORING THE ISSUES

1. Charlotte Danielson, author of *Enhancing Professional Practice: A Framework of Teaching* (Alexandria, VA: Association for Supervision and Curriculum Development, 1996, 2007), divides the activity of teaching into four domains. These are Planning and Preparation, The Classroom Environment, Instruction, and Professional Responsibilities. Reflect on these categories and make your own list of what the components clustered under each domain might be. Read the book and see how closely your components match those of the author. Reflect on the reasons for differences.

2. In most professions, such as medicine, law, and criminology, the novice has a long internship before he or she assumes full responsibilities within the profession. The novice teacher, however, is immediately expected to carry out every activity with the same level of thoroughness and effectiveness as the teacher of 20 years. Reflect again on the four domains that Danielson lists and reflect on your own knowledge and skills at this point. Where might you be in need of assistance? How can you obtain that assistance? What will happen if you do not receive the assistance that you need?

3. In an article on reflective practice, Altherton writes that it can be argued that "reflective practice needs another person as mentor or professional supervisor, who can ask appropriate questions to ensure that the reflection goes somewhere, and does not get bogged down in self-justification, self-indulgence or self-pity!" (Altherton, 2005). Think about times in your own life when you have served as a mentor for others. What did you do so that "reflection goes somewhere" with the individual you were mentoring?

4. Open your Web browser to http://www.prenhall.com/teacherprep. This will take you to Merrill's Teacher Prep Web site. Once you have logged in, click on *Video Classroom*. When this window opens, click on *Special Education* and then *Module 1: Knowing Teachers and Professionals in Special Education*. Then click on *Video 2: Meet the Teacher—Ms. Trask-Tyler*. This teacher explains the purposes of her very well thought out organizational system for her classroom. After watching the video, answer the questions at the bottom of the screen. Reflect on whether or not this organizational system would be just as effective in the general education classroom.

5. INTASC Standard 9 states that "the teacher is a reflective practitioner who continually evaluates the effects of his or her choices and who actively seeks out

opportunities to grow professionally. Reflect on your own experiences as a student in a program leading to teacher certification. Recall a time when reflecting on choices you had made caused you to grow professionally. Write about this incident in a one- or two-page paper.

References

Alger, C. (2006, August). What went well, what didn't go so well: Growth of reflection in preservice teachers. *Reflective Practice, 7*(3), 287–301.

Altherton, J. S. (2005.) Learning and teaching: Reflection and reflective practice. Retrieved December 1, 2007, from http://www.learningandteaching.info/learning/reflecti.htm.

Alvine, A., Judoor, T. W., Schein, M., & Yosida, T. (2007, Summer). What graduate students and the rest of us can learn from lesson study. *College Teaching, 55*(3), 109–113.

Bailey, K. M. (1997). Reflective teaching: Situating our stories. *Asian Journal of English Language Teaching, 7*, 1–9.

Black, S. (2005, February). Second time around. *American School Board Journal, 19*(11), 40–42.

Bowman, L. J. (2005, Spring). Grade retention. Is it a help or hindrance to school academic success? *Preventing School Failure, 49*(3), 42–46.

Campbell, M. R., & Brummett, V. M. (2007, January). Mentoring preservice teachers for development and growth of professional knowledge. *Music Educators Journal, 93*(3), 50–55.

Dewey, J. (1916; 1944). *Democracy and Education.* New York: Macmillan.

District Administration. (2005, February). Retention or promotion? Wrong question. *District Administration, 41*(2), 76. Retrieved November 3, 2007, from http://www.thefreelibrary.com/Retention+or+promotion%3f+Wrong+question.-a0128784377.

Grushka, K., McLeod, J. H., & Reynolds, R. (2005, May). Reflecting upon reflection: Theory and practice in one Australian university teacher education program. *Reflective Practice, 6*(2), 239–246.

Harrington, J., and McGlamery, S. (2007, Spring). Developing reflective practice: The importance of field experience. *Delta Kappa Gamma Bulletin, 73*(3), 33–36, 45.

Heritage, M. (2007, October). Formative assessment: What do teachers need to know and do? *Phi Delta Kappa, 89*(2), 140–145.

Hoerr, T. R. (2007, March). How I spent my summer vacation. *Educational Leadership, 64*(8), 85–86.

Kesson, K., Traugh, C. & Perez, F. (2006, September). Descriptive inquiry as reflective practice. *Teachers College Record, 108*(9), 1862–1880.

Little, J. (1994). Teachers' professional development in a climate of educational reform [Electronic version]. Retrieved September 3, 2007, from http://www.ed.gov/pubs/EdReformStudies/SysReforms/little1.html.

North Central Regional Educational Laboratory. (1987). HOTS Curriculum. Retrieved December 23, 2008, from http://www.ncrel.org/sdrs/areas/issues/students/atrisk/at7lk20.htm.

———. (1995). Higher Order Thinking Skills (HOTS) Program. Retrieved December 23, 2008, from http://www.ncrel.org/sdrs/areas/issues/students/atrisk/at7lk53.htm.

———. (1997). Critical issue: Finding time for professional development. Retrieved December 23, 2008, from http://www.ncrel.org/sdrs/areas/issues/educatrs/profdevl/pd300.htm.

Rodgers, C. R. (2006, Summer). Attending to voice: The impact of descriptive feedback in learning and teaching. *Curriculum Inquiry, 36*(2), 209–237.

Rooney, J. (2007, April). Who owns teacher growth? *Educational Leadership, 64*(7), 87–88.

Ross, J., & Brva, C. (2007, September/October). Professional development effects on teacher efficacy: Results of randomized field trial. *Journal of Educational Research, 10*(1), 50–60.

Wagner, K. (2006, November/December). Benefits of reflective practice. *Leadership, 36*(2), 30–32.

10

INTASC Standard 10: School and Community Involvement

Description of INTASC Standard 10: *The teacher fosters relationships with school colleagues, parents, and agencies in the larger community to support students' learning and well-being.*

KEY INDICATORS FOR STANDARD 10

The Teacher

- participates in collegial activities designed to make the entire school a productive learning environment.
- links with counselors, teachers of other classes and activities within the school, professionals in community agencies, and others in the community to support students' learning and well-being.
- seeks to establish cooperative partnerships with parents/guardians to support student learning.
- advocates for students.

CASE 19: PARENT INVOLVEMENT

Thinking Ahead

As you read this case, reflect on the following:

- Is it possible for parents and teachers to be equal partners in a child's education?
- Should parents be involved only in extracurricular activities, or should they be involved throughout the school day, too?
- What if a child doesn't want his or her parents to be involved in the school? Does this feeling help or hinder learning?

"And *here*," with a flourish, Nadine unrolled a bright yellow sheet of poster board, "is the *Countdown Calendar!*" Beaming, she looked expectantly at Rochelle Brown, her cooperating teacher.

Reviewing the array of materials Nadine had set before her, Rochelle could not help but return Nadine's grin. Nadine was only in her second week with Rochelle's first-grade class at Southside Elementary, but she had already made an excellent impression.

Nadine was intelligent, having earned straight A's at the local university's prestigious teacher preparation program, and a professional. She was charming and enthusiastic as well, always presenting a professional demeanor. She was certainly hard working, a trait proven by the assortment of materials related to her current project: Community Connections.

Community Connections represented a collaborative endeavor between Southside Elementary and the university where Nadine was enrolled. For this portion of their student teaching experience, preservice teachers were required to plan a project that integrated the classroom and the community. To fulfill this requirement, student teachers typically added information to the school's Web page or volunteered to assist at a community-sponsored event. Naturally, Nadine's project was ambitious.

Gesturing toward the calendar, Nadine said, "This way, students can check off the dates until the big day! I left the dates blank, though, because I knew we'd need to discuss the specifics together." Nadine had spent the weekend planning and preparing materials for a third-grade Career Day exhibition.

Rochelle nodded. "Good idea," she said. "We *will* need to discuss some aspects of your project."

"Oh, I know *that!*" Nadine replied. "I almost called you about a dozen times over the weekend with questions about this project, but I thought that would be rushing things a bit."

Rochelle perused the extensive assortment of materials Nadine had developed— an overview of the Career Day plan, a formal proposal to the principal, sign-up sheets for parents, promotional materials, and supplementary lessons with rubrics for assessment. It was a well-planned event and an exciting prospect for integrating the classroom and the community.

"Wow!" Rochelle began. "It's a terrific idea. Before we examine these documents more carefully, why don't you give me a quick overview of your plan?"

"Okay." Nadine smoothed her skirt and adjusted her headband. "Well, this project actually addresses two standards: community involvement *and* the section of the first-grade social studies curriculum that deals with occupations and community helpers. It also involves the parents by inviting them into the classroom to be active participants in their children's construction of knowledge. First, the class will develop an interview protocol about careers, and then each child will use the protocol to interview a parent. The children will bring the answers to the interview questions to class and create posters presenting the key information about their parents' careers. Then—this is the best part—for Career Day, parents will be invited in to discuss their careers with the class while the child displays the poster. That's what the calendar is for, so students can count down to the big day!"

Nadine looked at Rochelle and waited. Mature and poised, Nadine had always accepted criticism well. She knew she had a lot to learn. Once, a professor had described her as a sponge, soaking up every bit of information and feedback that was offered to her.

"Before we fill in the calendar, I have a couple of questions, Nadine," Rochelle tapped her lips with her index finger. "First, how do you plan to include the parents who don't have careers?"

"Oh, if they're retired, you mean? That shouldn't be a problem at all. My father retired a few years ago, and he gives talks about his work all the time, all over the country! Same thing if they own their own businesses. My aunt has her own business, and she *loves* to talk about it. Parents could talk about whatever they do." Nadine smiled. "I would never discriminate about something like *that!*"

"No, Nadine, I mean if they don't work at all," Rochelle studied Nadine's face.

"Well, my mother never had a paying job, but she had a master's degree in art history and was on the board of the museum, so she could have presented that kind of information." Nadine was talking too fast. She could tell by Rochelle's expression that something was wrong. "What do you mean," she asked, "if they don't work at all?'

Rochelle walked over to one of the round tables in the classroom and pulled out two chairs. She sat down and motioned for Nadine to follow suit. Nadine noticed that Rochelle's face was uncharacteristically solemn.

"Nadine, part of the purpose of this project is for you to get to know our community. What do you know about this community?"

"Well," Nadine began, "Southside is a suburban community. It has a big mall, and the population is mostly white . . ." she faltered.

"What types of employment are available in Southside? Where do most of the parents of our children work?" Rochelle pressed further. "What kinds of jobs do they have?"

"Of course, I don't know all the particulars," Nadine spoke slowly, "but I would imagine there would have to be doctors, lawyers, accountants, engineers, police officers, and teachers in *any* community. Right?"

"Not exactly, Nadine." Rochelle removed her glasses and set them on the table. "As a student dorming at the university, you may not be aware of the dynamics of this region. Southside has always been a working-class suburb of the city of Freeport. A few years ago, Southside suffered a major economic setback. The local industrial plant relocated to Mexico, where operating costs—especially labor—were much lower."

Nadine tilted her head, listening intently. The private university she had chosen was far from her home, so she was relatively unfamiliar with the region.

"That plant employed more than three quarters of the parents whose children go to Southside schools. Most of those parents are still out of work. There was no severance package. They have no health insurance. And their unemployment benefits, if they received them, ran out some time ago." Rochelle let the information sink in.

She continued, "At Southside, Nadine, I have never taught the child of a doctor, a lawyer, or an engineer. In fact, the professionals who live in this community send their children to private schools. They don't go here."

Nadine shook her head in disbelief, unwilling to absorb this new information. "But," she asked, "what will we do on Career Day?"

CASE 19: ISSUES FOR ANALYSIS AND REFLECTION

1. Case 19 is related to the INTASC Standard for School and Community Involvement and to the following two key indicators for this standard: The teacher (a) participates in collegial activities designed to make the entire school a productive learning environment and (b) seeks to establish cooperative partnerships with parents/guardians to support student learning. Once you have identified the primary issue, problem, or concern in this case, determine what other content knowledge is needed to ensure positive outcomes.
2. What pedagogical knowledge and skills are needed?
3. What must be done to ensure that desired student learning outcomes are obtained?

Use the DEEPS Method to analyze this case. Keep in mind the INTASC Standard for School and Community Involvement and the key indicators listed in item 1.

Determine the primary issue, problem, or concern in this case.

Enumerate the facts that support your belief regarding the primary issue, problem, or concern in the case.

Evaluate the case to find all the possible solutions for resolving the issue, problem, or concern.

Problem solve by thinking critically about each possible solution and accepting or rejecting the solution based on its value in ensuring the professional growth of the teacher in relation to school and community involvement.

Summarize your conclusion/solutions and be prepared to present the best possible solution and your rationale to your professor and colleagues.

CASE 19: WHAT THE RESEARCH SAYS

This case story focuses on parent involvement in schools. Considerable research points to the benefits of parental involvement. According to Ferrara and Ferrara (2005) for example, parental involvement promotes better school attendance and fewer behavior problems. In urban studies it has been show to decrease school dropout rates and improve graduation rates. With the passage of the No Child Left Behind Act (NCLB), efforts to ensure parent involvement in schools is now mandated. In a parents guide related to NCLB, the need to involve parents in local and district activities is clearly spelled out. This document (U.S. Department of Education, 2003) states, "No Child Left Behind supports parent involvement because research overwhelmingly demonstrates the positive effect that parent involvement has on their child's achievement." The document then enumerates the ways in which parents can and should be involved in schools. These ways include "parent-teacher meetings or special meetings to address academic problems at the school; volunteering to serve as needed; encouraging other parents to become involved; and training about the schools' special challenges, community resources, and the No Child Left Behind Act" (p. 10). Parents are encouraged to talk regularly with teachers, principals, and school board members and to take part in curriculum planning and programming, especially as it relates to improving the achievement of low performing students, but the burden is not just on the parents to approach the schools and volunteer their services. Schools are obligated to document efforts to involve parents in "overall planning at the district and school levels; written policies in parent involvement at both levels; annual meetings; training; coordinating parent involvement strategies about federal education programs (e.g., Head Start and Reading First); and evaluating those strategies and revising them if needed" (pp. 10–11).

Given the extent of this federal mandate for parent involvement in schools, it is surprising that many preservice teachers appear to receive very little formal training to work effectively with parents. Yet such preparation is important. Novice teachers have just made the transition from being students themselves. They bring with them the attitudes they have shaped over a lifetime as members of families and communities. It is very likely that they may have ideological differences with parents who differ from themselves in terms of racial, ethnic, or social class. Recent graduates of teacher preparation programs may also have well-formed expectations for teacher–parent relationships (Grane, 2005). Much of this has to do with identity formation throughout one's life. "Prospective teachers are subject to multicultural forces as they begin to construct a professional identity. They use the tools of [their own] background to form standards of practice for parents and teachers and this is a recipe for culture clash when they work across cultural differences" (p. 180). This reality, unfortunately, is rarely addressed in teacher preparation programs. As other researchers state, teachers often worry about teacher–parent relationships and the ways in which they will have to "avoid and resolve conflict, cope with critically judgmental parents, and work with parents that may be harming their children" (Brown & McMurray-Schwarz, 2004, p. 58). Teachers generally feel bothered or threatened by the idea of parent involvement, principals are resentful when it comes to involving parents in decision making, and parents themselves are distrustful of a system that traditionally has not welcomed them (Webster, 2004). Other barriers to greater involvement of parents in schools may include the parents' negative memories of their own school experiences, fear of lawsuits on the part of the school, and teachers' lack of knowledge of effective strategies for working with parents, as well as feelings of inadequacy for dealing with culture and language barriers (Witmer, 2005).

One researcher interviewed preservice teachers about their readiness to involve parents as partners in their child's education. Although these prospective teachers saw clear communication and an attitude of caring as essential, they tended to value teacher knowledge over parent knowledge. Much of the discussion regarding parents revolved around ways in which the teachers could communicate their needs to the parents (e.g., come to class prepared, check on homework, etc.). There was little discussion about what parents would contribute to the process. Communication and caring, in other words, were teacher driven and focused on sending information from school to home. The parents' only role in this "partnership" was to support the teachers' agenda (Grane, 2005, p. 178).

Schools and faculty in teacher preparation programs all recognize the need for parent involvement in schools, but teachers enter their careers with little experience working with parents. Nadine, the young student teacher in this case story, is a prime example of this. She is well organized and well prepared and enthusiastic and dedicated to her profession. Content knowledge and pedagogical skills appear to be assets she brings with her to her teaching internship. Knowledge that she lacks, however, is how to establish cooperative partnerships with parents to support student learning. The parent involvement project Nadine planned with her elementary school and her university took everything into consideration except the parents themselves. As stated, teacher knowledge is often valued more than parent knowledge. The student teacher in this case story is more concerned with completing a "teacher project" than she is with forming a partnership with parents where both parties have valuable contributions to make. Some researchers and educators, as is the case in this case story, have taken steps to increase the amount and quality of parent involvement in schools.

One middle school with a large number of immigrant parents formed a community involvement task force to identify "individuals who speak a variety of languages to personally invite parents to serve on district required boards such as the School Advisory Council and the School Improvement Team. The teachers [also] reinforce involvement by inviting parents to attend school events such as PTA meetings, a family math night, and an annual multicultural fair. All the school's communication with parents and partners is translated into relevant languages" (Larocque, 2007, p. 159). This type of planning requires that schools have a framework for planning and evaluating their efforts. Such a framework begins with ensuring that the school has the capacity for parent involvement (e.g., funding, space, time for involvement, etc.). Staff training is also required so that teachers are made aware of the benefits of parent involvement and of the research that provides examples of exemplary initial planning to increase the role of parents in schools. Finally, options have to be considered in relation to involving parents from diverse groups in meaningful ways. Often the agenda for parents is predetermined by the school. Careful planning, however, provides an opportunity for both parties to learn about lifestyle and cultural expectations. An opportunity is also present for systematic monitoring and evaluation of this interaction so that future planning is based on empirical evidence (Webster, 2004).

There has been very little research, in fact, about what does cause some parents but not others to be involved in their child's school. In one study by Anderson and Minke (2007) surveys were sent to parents in an urban district. The key finding from the study was that parental perception of being invited and welcomed by teachers was the greatest factor leading to parent involvement. According to these researchers, "for parents, two thirds of whom were African-American, the ways in which their beliefs about involvement (role construction) affected their involvement behaviors at home and at school varied according to their perceptions of being invited specifically to participate" (p. 319). The researchers conclude that preservice teachers, however, receive little training for working with parents and with developing strategies to welcome and include them in meaningful ways.

In a 1997 survey of 257 preservice teachers, the prospective teachers reported that they received little training in course work for working with parents. Most of their experience came from their own volunteer work or from employment as teacher aides or camp counselors. Once they entered their field experiences, they reported they found themselves in need of more instruction in effective communication with parents, strategies for responding to parents' points of view and concerns, diversity training, and theory and research related to parent involvement (Tichenor, 1997). Now, a decade later, the same concerns are still found in the research. One educator writes about teachers' lack of training and parents lack of political clout to overcome the poor conditions of some schools. We all need better training in terms of teaching, writing, and coursework to "not only provide the best practice in the field of teaching and learning . . . but also to provide future teachers with methods and forums to study and discuss the relationship between the most vexing problems of our time—racism, poverty, sexism, violence, prejudice—and the routines of the institutional schooling that historically have hidden and perpetuated these injustices" (Jones, 2007, p. 600). Such a reform in schools requires the collaboration of parents and community.

One innovative district in Ontario, Canada, sought to make dramatic changes in involving parents meaningfully in their schools. They began by running an after-school program for children ages five to thirteen. The schools these children attended were in urban settings, and the population was ethnically diverse. The program had three goals: (a) to raise the achievement level of their language minority students through activities directed specifically at language and literacy learning, (b) to familiarize parents with the school system and educational expectations (for both the school and the parents), and (c) to promote a culturally sensitive climate in which diversity is valued. The program involved parents, administrators, teachers, student volunteers from upper grades, and parents. Throughout the program, children spent blocks of time working with parents and teachers on literacy. While children worked independently or with student volunteers, parents, teachers, and administrators spent time in discussions about school and community-related topics. A follow-up survey showed increases in student achievement, student attendance, and parental involvement (Schecter, Ippoito, & Rashkovsky, 2007). Another school had as its goal a curriculum that nurtures a sense of community. The school established a home visitation program in which teams of teachers visited homes to answer questions, talk about school policies, and start to understand language and culture differences so as to plan for them in instruction. The school also established a teacher advisement program in which teachers met once or twice a month with students. This allowed teachers to get to know their students better and also to better understand family and community (Witmer, 2005).

The need to train teachers to build effective home–school partnerships is summed up well in an article on home–school collaboration. The writers of this article state that the barriers to home–school collaboration are numerous. They include invalid assumptions on the part of both teachers and parents regarding each other, parents own history of experiences with schools, general distrust of institutions, cultural and language differences, lack of familiarity with the bureaucracy of schools, and sufficient time to be involved. All home–school collaborations have to begin with the following: (a) being proactive rather than reactive; it is important for teachers to learn how to be welcoming to all parents and community members and not just those who share the same cultural background and values as they have; (b) an attitude of sensitivity to and respect for the cultural backgrounds of students and their families; (c) recognition of and value for the important contributions parents have to make to the educational process; and (d) powerful, meaningful two-way communication based on mutual respect and trust. (Raffaele & Knoff, 1999). These skills and attitudes should be introduced in teacher training programs and linked to staff development training throughout the individual teacher's career.

The student teacher in the preceding case story is fortunate to be exposed to working with parents in the school where she is completing her practicum. She would have benefited, however, from early training in her teacher preparation program.

Summary of Research

The INTASC Standard for School and Community Involvement has as a key indicator the need for teachers to establish cooperative partnerships with parents/guardians to support student learning. Research indicates that parent involvement in school increases attendance and school achievement. It is considered such an important variable in student success that mandates for ensuring parent involvement in their child's education are a part of the No Child Left Behind Act.

Until recently, teacher preparation programs have put little emphasis on parent–teacher communication. Prospective teachers gained experience working with parents through volunteer and work experience and sometimes through experiences in their student teaching. Generally, however, training in communication strategies was not part of the teacher preparation program. Some schools and higher education institutions have begun to place more emphasis on home–school partnerships.

CASE 19: TOPICS FOR DISCUSSION

- The No Child Left Behind Act mandates that schools document efforts to involve parents in overall planning at the district and school levels, written policies in parent involvement at both levels, annual meetings, training, coordinating parent involvement strategies about federal education programs, and evaluating outcomes. However, this federal act does not provide the funds with which to carry out its mandates.
- All written communications with parents should be carefully proofread to ensure that they contain no errors in spelling, grammar, or punctuation. Teacher education programs, however, sometimes graduate individuals who lack good written communication skills.
- Some parents object to kindergarten children being given grades for their work.
- Many teachers complain that homework handed in is too often obviously done by parents, particularly project homework.

CASE 19: EXPLORING THE ISSUES

1. Interview five parents (from different families) about the factors that influence them to be involved in their child's school or not. Interview five teachers to determine their feelings about parent involvement in their school. Compare and contrast findings.
2. Open your Web browser to http://www.prenhall.com/teacherprep. This will take you to Merrill's Teacher Prep Web site. Once you are logged in, click on *Video Classroom* and then click on *General Methods*. When this window opens, click on *Module 2: Student Learning in Diverse Classrooms*. Then click on *Video 1: Incorporating the Home Experiences of Culturally Diverse Students*. In this video, some parents talk about their experiences as being culturally and linguistically

different from their public school peers. After watching this video, divide into groups of four or five and write a plan for welcoming and encouraging the involvement of these particular parents in your school and classroom.

3. Write an imaginary conversation between yourself as a teacher, the school principal, and the gentleman in the video whose father insisted that he speak only Greek at home. Assume that the school policy is to encourage all students to speak English at home so they can become proficient in the English language. You fully understand the father's position and support it, but you also are expected to follow school policy and encourage the speaking of English at home.

4. Script an imaginary parent–teacher conference in which you are meeting with a parent to inform her that her child is performing above her peers in reading and math. You are considering having this first-grade child go to the second-grade class for these two subject areas. The parent rightfully asks what will happen to her daughter when she is in second grade.

5. Script another guardian–teacher conference. This time the first-grade child is in a foster home (her fourth since birth). The circumstances are still the same: You are meeting with the foster parent to inform her that her child is performing above her peers in reading and math. You are considering having this first-grade child go to the second-grade class for these two subject areas. The foster parent, however, tells you that the child is a problem at home and will not do anything she is told, and she intends to call the social worker and return the child to state care. In an angry voice, the foster parent tells you that the child— a child who has always been polite and well behaved in your class—recently hit the family dog with a stick and then kicked and punched another younger foster child in her home.

CASE 20: BANKING ON A PARTNERSHIP

Thinking Ahead

As you read this case, reflect on the following:

- Teachers and students received training related to this project. Why did things still go wrong?
- How does a school decide which business partnerships to accept and which to refuse?
- What kinds of additional training do teachers need so they can work effectively with community members?

Alan looked at the partnership report before him and frowned. "How did I ever get myself into this," he thought. He remembered that middle school faculty meeting last August where Brett Holloway, the school principal, had announced the potential partnership with a local bank. Alan's head spun at the possibilities back then. He thought mostly about how he could integrate his mathematics instruction and make it seem practical and meaningful to his sixth-grade students. After the meeting, Alan had rushed up to Brett and volunteered to help with the new math curriculum and related projects for this partnership with Welton Bank. The principal went a step further and on the spot made Alan the school liaison for the partnership. "You'll have to make sure these bank officials understand that we have national and state standards." Brett told Alan. "And the middle school faculty have to come together on this, too. It's going to require compromises all around."

Alan nodded, already feeling some anxiety. "Just make sure we stick to the state standards, okay," Brett added. He shook hands with Alan, and put a hand on his shoulder. "I'm counting on you, Al. You're the point man on this one!"

At first, it all worked better than could be imagined. Alan had set up four meetings with the bank officials and the school faculty. After a lot of discussion, everyone agreed that the best use of the partnership would be to establish a bank within the school. Middle school students would be selected on a rotating basis to serve as bank employees. A few teachers would volunteer to supervise the project. Alan's school also agreed to find a secure place for the student bank to operate, to set up a schedule of operation, to advertise the services offered, and to provide support and encouragement for the participation of students from "at risk" or disadvantaged homes. For the first few weeks, the whole school was literally buzzing with excitement over having a student-run bank in the building. Even the primary-age children were eager to be part of the project in some way, and simple jobs like emptying the waste baskets or making sure there were deposit and withdrawal slips available were assigned to them.

The bank also provided much needed resources for the school. Eleven new computers were provided for the middle school classrooms, and three additional computers were donated to the student bank. All the teachers who had volunteered for the project were given laptop computers. The bank also sent three of its own employees to spend a week at the school to train student employees and teacher-supervisors. One of the bank vice presidents even spent a morning interviewing students for their "jobs" at the bank. Students were delighted with the entire process, and the waiting list of those applying for the bank jobs grew longer and longer. Teachers quickly saw how this bank could help meet state learning standards for math, English, social sciences, computer technology, and careers. At every grade level a newfound excitement about teaching was felt.

"Unfortunately," Alan thought now, "none of the excitement lasted too long." At the end of October, the school found itself out of space for other projects. Brett Holloway made a decision to have the itinerant speech therapist share a space in the formerly secure room that was set aside for banking activities. This meant that the lunchtime banking hours were canceled, and banking took place only before and after school. Then one of the teachers who was supposed to have been supervising bank operations reported that one hundred dollars were missing from the bank drawer. About half the students who had opened savings accounts withdrew their money. As one of the students explained, "We must make sure our money is safe. Man! Can't trust the banks." To make matters worse, the end-of-semester report showed that the school had not done any advertising and had not made any effort to encourage students from disadvantaged homes to participate in the bank partnership. Students in special education classes were ignored altogether. In short, regardless of the training and other resources Welton Bank had provided, the school had failed miserably to do its part.

Alan glanced up at the clock above the door. In 30 minutes he was meeting with one of the bank vice presidents and with the school principal to discuss how they could showcase this partnership project in the community. "What will they think," Alan wondered, "when they find out our school didn't fulfill any part of its agreement with the bank? Will we still have a partnership? Will I have to take the blame for everything that went wrong?"

CASE 20: ISSUES FOR ANALYSIS AND REFLECTION

1. Case 20 is related to the INTASC Standard for School and Community Involvement and to the following two key indicators for this standard: The teacher (a) participates in collegial activities designed to make the entire school a productive learning environment and (b) links with counselors, teachers of other classes and activities within the school, professionals in community agencies, and others in the community to support students' learning and well-being. Once you have identified the primary issue, problem, or concern in this case, determine what other content knowledge is needed to ensure positive outcomes.
2. What pedagogical knowledge and skills are needed?
3. What must be done to ensure that desired student learning outcomes are obtained?

Use the DEEPS Method to analyze this case. Keep in mind the INTASC Standard for School and Community Involvement and the key indicators listed in item 1.

Determine the primary issue, problem, or concern in this case.

Enumerate the facts that support your belief regarding the primary issue, problem, or concern in the case.

Evaluate the case to find all the possible solutions for resolving the issue, problem, or concern.

Problem solve by thinking critically about each possible solution and accepting or rejecting the solution based on its value in ensuring the professional growth of the teacher in relation to school and community involvement.

Summarize your conclusion/solutions and be prepared to present the best possible solution and your rationale to your professor and colleagues.

CASE 20: WHAT THE RESEARCH SAYS

In this case story, a seemingly accomplished and well-meaning teacher is faced with a unique problem. A local bank is eager to form a partnership with the school and to provide training and resources for an in-school bank. The bank keeps its end of the bargain, but the school fails miserably at adhering to its part of the agreement.

As important as community involvement in the schools is, when it comes to business partnerships schools may find themselves faced with value-laden concerns. John Abbarno, past president of the International Society for Value Inquiry and a professor of philosophy, writes that corporate-sponsored education is generally welcomed by schools because of the opportunities it offers to supplement an overstretched budget. He notes, however, that "such assistance blurs social roles and raises serious moral concerns, especially those of moral agency" (Abbarno, 2001). Abbarno quotes critics of corporate sponsorship and states that "appropriating human choice under the guise of consumer need is excess control and a violation of autonomy." This is what, Abbarno states, the economist John Galbraith calls the "dependence effect" (Abbarno).

This issue is further complicated because on the surface at least it appears that the bank–school partnership, along with the training and resources provided, is certain to have a beneficial long-term effect. One of the concerns with corporate partnerships, however, has been that they all too often do not contribute to long-term systematic change. Recently, schools have changed their approach in working with community business to find ways that the school and business can create relationships that benefit all involved and create sustainable partnerships (Ghysels & Thibodeaux, 2006, p. 18). Results of a survey of 389 school staff members support the need for sustainable partnerships. The survey indicated that most school–business partnerships involved youth development organizations and mental health organizations but that communication and collaboration were limited in scope. The researchers suggest that partnerships might be more beneficial if "schools and local organizations would develop their relationships on the basis of some priority need area, thus creating a common purpose and shared vision for the partnership. This might in turn create the desire for stronger connections as a result of the buy-in and shared ownership created through a focused planning and action taking process" (Anderson-Butcher & Statler, 2006, p. 155). In the preceding case story, for example, a partnership plan was made hastily. After initial training, bank officials appear to have had limited communication with the school. Even the school principal didn't take an active role in seeing that the partnership work. He delegated all responsibilities to one of the teachers.

It is in this lack of planning, in fact, that the teacher in the case story and the school itself appear to have fallen short. Many of the poor outcomes related to the in-school banking project could have been avoided if the school had been proactive rather than reactive. Often school–business partnerships are formed without any preestablished guidelines for such relationships. This opens both the school and the business to questioning of motives. The business is suspected of using the school for tax write-offs and to ensure loyalty to their company. Schools are suspected of abandoning the school's agenda in exchange for receiving financial contributions. When considering any partnership activity, however, "local schools and community leaders should make decisions based on careful consideration of the needs and values of the students, schools, and local communities" (Englen, 2003, p. 37).

In an article related to forming win–win partnerships, two researchers suggest that schools and school districts should have a person designated as the "partnership executive." This individual would have to be someone with excellent communication skills and with knowledge of the business community and of school and district needs. Alan, the teacher in this story, was eager to participate in the project, but there is no indication that he had the skills to be the "partnership executive" for this project. Several suggestions are offered in the research for ways to ensure that funding is used wisely and ethically and that both the business and the school reap benefits as a result of the partnership.

a. School personnel must learn the best ways to work with businesses and other community organizations. This includes knowing similarities and differences between school culture and business culture.

b. Schools must have established guidelines for contacting potential partners and for communicating with potential business partners. A partnership executive with the necessary time, energy, and skills should be appointed to coordinate offers of assistance and see that they are implemented appropriately.

c. Schools (and the partnership executive) must determine whether or not the potential partner is a right match. All offers should be carefully considered and carefully researched before they are accepted.

d. Schools and districts should identify their needs. Schools can benefit by having a prepared "wish list" of ways in which business can assist. This not only makes decisions regarding the acceptance of funding easier, but it also demonstrates professionalism and leads to greater benefits.

e. It is not likely that the business will have the additional personnel or resources to manage plans that are made. There should be personnel available at the school level who can provide the necessary leadership to manage resources. Such a person should also have the authority to make decisions about how resources will be used (Johnson & Armistead, 2007, p. 43).

If such a plan had been in place at the school in this case story, the teacher would not be faced with the problems now before him, or at least the problems would not be of such magnitude. In these days of shrinking school budgets, an offer to provide needed resources is difficult to turn away. Critics of corporate sponsorship, on the other hand, state that "in each case, the school gets something—money, equipment, incentives for kids to learn, curricular material . . . and the companies also get something: access to a lucrative market" (Stark, 2001, p. 60). One of the problems with accepting funding from businesses is that the person supplying the funding necessarily has some control over the school's agenda from that point forward. The decision to accept or refuse to accept outside funding is never an easy one, but the INTASC standard related to school and community involvement makes it clear that decisions should be based on a commitment "to support students' learning and well-being." In this case story, a project was agreed upon before actual needs for learning were considered.

Summary of Research

School–business partnerships have been significant in making possible a number of projects and programs that would not exist without the extra funding provided. Very few schools, however, have preestablished policies in place outlining the conditions under which funding or resources will be accepted and spent. It is also wise for school districts or schools to appoint a "partnership executive" who is knowledgeable about the culture of companies and the differences and similarities between the culture of business and the culture of schools. Any decisions to accept or refuse funding and resources should be based on a commitment to support students' learning and well-being.

CASE 20: TOPICS FOR DISCUSSION

- Critics of corporate sponsorship state that "in each case, the school gets something—money, equipment, incentives for kids to learn, curricular material . . . and the companies also get something: access to a lucrative market" (Stark, 2001, p. 60). By using schools to advertise their products, companies build brand loyalty.

- One of the problems with accepting funding from businesses is that the person supplying the funding necessarily has some control over the school's agenda from that point forward.
- Often school–business partnerships are formed without any preestablished guidelines for such relationships. This opens both the school and the business to questioning of motives. The business is suspected of using the school for tax write-offs and to ensure loyalty to their company. Schools are suspected of abandoning the school's agenda in exchange for receiving financial contributions.
- School–business partnerships should be 50–50 arrangements. Each partner should contribute equally to the partnership.

CASE 20: EXPLORING THE ISSUES

1. Write school policies for receiving funding from outside sources. Include the position of a "partnership executive" in your policy.
2. Pretend that you a teacher in a pre-K through Grade 6 school. You are charged with managing a $200,000 donation. You are in a school with no written policies on receiving external funding, but you recognize that it is a very large sum to turn away. Write a memo to your school principal explaining your concerns and your suggestions for action.
3. You teach in a rural farm community and your school district has limited funds for extracurricular activity of any kind. As part of a school-based committee, you are part of a group of teachers and administrators who have invited to your school the director of the local Boys and Girls Club; the CEO of the main industry in the area, a printing plant; the community vice president of the local bank; and several business executives from the local shopping district. Write the agenda for what will happen when they arrive at your school. Write a memo to your principal describing your role in the day's agenda. Include what you hope to accomplish.
4. Open your Web browser to http://www.prenhall.com/teacherprep. This will take you to Merrill's Teacher Prep Web site. Once you are logged in, click on *Lesson Plan Builder* on the menu on the left side of the screen. When this window opens, click on *Lesson Plan Guidelines*. Use these guidelines to design a lesson that requires the participation of parents.
5. Once your lesson in item 4 is complete, write an assessment rubric that allows you to evaluate the outcomes of having parents actively participate in this lesson.

References

Abbarno. G. J. M. (2001). Corporate sponsored education: The limits of social responsibility. Retrieved December 24, 2008, from http://www.bu.edu/wcp/Papers/Educ/EducAbba.htm.

Anderson, K. J., & Minke, K. M. (2007, May). Parent involvement in education: Toward an understanding of parent's decision making. *Journal of Educational Research*, 100(5), 311–323.

Anderson-Butcher. D., & Statler, E. (2006, July). A case for expanded school-community partnerships in support of positive youth development. *Children & Schools*, 28(3), 155–163.

Brown, A. C., & McMurray-Schwarz, P. (2004, August). Preservice teachers' beliefs about family involvement: Implications for teacher education. *Early Childhood Education Journal*, 32(1), 57–61.

Englen, J. (2003, March). Guiding school/business partnerships. *Education Digest, 66*(7), 36–40.

Ferrara, M. M., & Ferrara, P. J. (2005, November/December). Parents as partners: Raising Awareness as a Teacher Preparation Program. *Clearing House, 79*(2), 77–81.

Ghysels, M., & Thibodeaux, K. (2006, November/December). A new approach to business partnerships. *Leadership, 36*(2), 18–21.

Grane, E. (2005, January). Theorizing and describing preservice teachers' images about working parents. *Teachers College Record, 107*(1), 157–185.

Johnson, J. H., & Armistead, L. (2007, April). Win-win partnerships: The two C's—climate and communication—are critical in creating positive relationships with businesses, corporations, and universities. *American School Board, 194*(4), 42–44.

Jones, A. D. (2007, April). Where have all the strong poets gone? *Phi Delta Kappan, 88*(8), 599–601.

Larocque, M. (2007, March). Closing the achievement gap: The experience of a middle school. *Clearing House, 80*(4), 157–162.

Raffaele, L. M., & Knoff, H. P. (1999). Improving home-school collaboration with disadvantaged families: Organizational principles. *School Psychology Review, 28*(3), 448–466.

Schecter, S. R., Ippoito, J., & Rashkovsky, K. (2007, March). Giving parents part of the PIE. *School Leadership, 64*(6), 69–71.

Stark, A. (2001, August/September). Pizza Hut, Domino's and the public schools. *Policy Review, 108*, 59–70.

Tichenor, M. S. (1997, December). Teacher education and parent involvement: Reflections from preservice. *Journal of Instructional Psychology, 24*(4), 233–239.

U.S. Department of Education. (2003). No Child Left Behind: A Parents Guide. Retrieved November 12, 2007, from http://www.ed.gov/parents/academic/involve/nclbguide/parentsguide.pdf.

Webster, K. (2004, Summer). No parent left behind: Evaluating programs and policies to include parental involvement. *Harvard Journal of African American Public Policy, 10*, 117–126.

Witmer, M. W. (2005, May/June). The fourth R in education: Relationships. *Clearing House, 78*(5), 224–228.

EXAMPLE OF A COMPLETED CASE ANALYSIS

In this case, a student teacher is completing the 10th week of his student teaching practicum. At his college, student teachers have two 7-week placements at two different grade levels. His first placement was in Grade 2, and the current placement is in Grade 4. The student teacher is popular with the children at both grade levels and gets along well with the cooperating teacher. He is frequently praised for his willingness to take on extra responsibilities. Already in this second placement he is teaching three subjects: English/language arts, math, and science. The cooperating teachers in both placements have remarked that this student teacher is very competent in content areas and that they also like it very much that he seems to be able to work independently without need of too much supervision from them. Both cooperating teachers are delighted to have a student teacher who loves teaching math and science. The student teacher majored in sociology and also completed a minor in biology, which required him to attend classes an extra semester (summer) to get in the needed classes. This student teacher was eager to be well prepared to teach not just humanities but also math and science.

On this day, the student teacher is being observed by the field supervisor. The student teacher just completed a lesson on equivalent fractions. While the cooperating teacher is conducting a follow-up assessment consisting of a written quiz, the student teacher is talking quietly with the supervisor. The supervisor notes that although the student teacher designs creative lessons and seems to truly engage students, the only form of assessment he has observed is written tests. The student teacher replies that he tries to use good questioning techniques and that the students' responses serve as material for formative assessment. The supervisor agrees that good questioning techniques can lead to an understanding of what students are grasping during instruction. "But," the supervisor states, "every grade you have given during your practicum has been because of a grade on a test and not from any other kind of assessment." The student teacher argues that the written test provides a summative assessment and clear evidence of whether or not his students understand what he has taught. The supervisor, however, states that the next time she visits the class she wants to see the student teacher using alternative forms of assessment. Before leaving, she adds that she also wants to take some time after the next lesson to discuss how alternative assessment can be a part of summative assessment.

DEEPS Method	Analyzing the Case
Determine the primary issue, problem, or concern in this case.	• ~~Student teacher's prep program didn't teach how to do alternative assessment as a summative eval.~~ • ~~Student teacher lacks confidence to take risks on learn on his own.~~ • ~~Some students may appear to be low performing but because of learning differences are not performing well on written tests.~~

(continued)

My notes: I'm not sure. I don't have enough information to know if the student teacher's program covered alternative assessment, but he just didn't learn it.

Enumerate the facts that support your belief regarding the primary issue, problem, or concern in the case.

My notes: Talk about NCLB: The Politics of Teacher Quality in the Kaplan and Owings article (p. 267 in Charting a professional course—talk about connecting certification to teacher quality).

Evaluate the case to find all the possible solutions for resolving the issue, problem, or concern.

- Cooperating teacher must not be modeling alternative assessment techniques.
- ~~Supervisor waited till 10ᵗʰ week of placement to criticize assessment measures.~~

- All the other areas above contribute to the concern in this case. The primary problem, however, is that the student teacher is not fully benefiting from his placement. Part of the job of the cooperating teacher is to help the student teacher to develop the skills he or she doesn't yet have.
- No mention of the cooperating teacher is given in this case. It is assumed nonetheless that the cooperating teacher didn't model good alternative assessment techniques. This assumption is made because the student teacher appears to not grasp fully the supervisor's explanations and expectations for the next visit.
- The student teacher is popular with students and well liked by the cooperating teachers. He also takes on additional responsibilities and is well prepared for teaching. The likability of this student teacher may be a factor in the cooperating teacher ignoring the lack of alternative assessment techniques. That is, the cooperating teacher may be enjoying the assistance provided by this student teacher and, because of this, he or she ignores areas where the student teacher is weak.

In regard to the primary problem:
- The student teacher on his own has to assume the responsibility of learning about alternative assessment techniques so he is able to apply them in the remaining weeks of his placement. It doesn't seem like anyone is going to teach him what he needs to know.
- The cooperating teacher has to assume responsibility for making sure the student teacher demonstrates competence in assessment and planning, including using a variety of formal and informal assessment strategies to improve learning.
- The student teacher could keep useful records of students' experiences, learning behaviors, and progress. This would allow the student teacher to know if results of written

tests correlate positively with results of alternative assessment strategies.

- Perhaps more staff development must be done with the cooperating teachers to make sure they know how to evaluate the student teacher's demonstrated competency in each area.

General Concerns:

- Why didn't the student teacher have these skills prior to student teaching? Is the teacher ed prep program deficient in this regard?
- Why did the supervisor wait 10 weeks to bring up this concern? Is more training needed for the field supervisors?

Problem solve by thinking critically about each possible solution and accepting or rejecting the solution based on its value in ensuring the professional growth of the teacher in relation to the INTASC Standard on which the case is centered.

Accept

Solution #1: The student teacher has to take on the responsibility of learning about alternative assessment techniques on his own in order to be able to apply them in the remaining weeks of his placement.

The student teacher has chosen the profession of teaching as his career. It is unfortunate that he lacks knowledge and skill in the area of formal and informal assessment strategies. The reality is, however, that in a few short weeks he will have his own classroom. It's his obligation to be fully prepared for teaching. This will require him to read related research and also to visit classrooms on his own to observe formal and informal assessment in practice. Once he is teaching, it would be wise to find a mentor who will help him develop skills in this area.

Reject

Each of the other possible solutions are rejected because they are all symptoms of a wider problem: basically, ensuring that the teacher education program has an assessment plan in place that measures student learning outcomes and, in this case, student achievement and effectiveness in areas related directly to teaching. A second related concern here is that the need for more training for the cooperating teacher and the supervisor also contributed to the primary issue. One of the responsibilities of the cooperating teacher is to provide guidance for the student teacher.

Summarize your conclusion/solutions and be prepared to present the best possible solution and your rationale to your professor and colleagues.

Basically, the student teacher in this case story should have had a better grasp of skills related to planning and assessment. For example, he

(continued)

My notes: Talk about formative assessment and use notes from September 18 class.

Use the research article on characteristics of an effective teacher.

should have been able to adjust plans to meet the needs of individual students, and he also should have been able to use assessment techniques (either traditional or alternative) that lead to improved learning. Because the student teacher does not have these skills at this time, it is his responsibility to master them before taking a full-time job.

The DEEPS method of case analysis should be used as a method to organize thoughts before class discussion. Notice that the student used the case analysis DEEPS form to keep track of thoughts, research, and points he or she wants to bring up in class. Ideas that were rejected were crossed out. The student also jotted down side notes about articles or ideas to bring into discussion to reinforce ideas. As class discussion develops, students may refine their thoughts. Some students may present stronger research articles as support for ideas, or they may have more experience from which to draw. At the end of discussion, however, a thorough discussion of the case should have occurred, and conclusions reached should be considered appropriate and beneficial by the majority of the class. A good litmus test of whether or not an in-depth and beneficial conclusion was reached is whether everyone in the class can agree that they would apply the same solution in similar circumstances. A major advantage of the DEEPS method of analysis is that, when there is no agreement among classmates, it is possible to go back and find where consensus broke down. For example, if many in the class do not agree on the primary problem in a case, then the class must go back and analyze the case again in order to **D**etermine the primary problem, issue, or concern. If a majority of the class cannot agree on which solutions to accept or reject, then there is a need to **P**roblem solve issues once again.